A Language for the Soul

"This book by Stuart Devenish is a retrieval of many key concepts of the spiritual life that have been developed over two millennia of prayer and reflection. It is especially valuable for Protestants, who have historically lacked a robust language of the soul. The love, devotion, and scholarship poured into this book is truly remarkable. A rare gem!"

—**Alan Hirsch**, founder, Movement Leaders Collective, founder, Forge Missional Training Network, author of *Reframation* and *Metanoia*

"Stuart Devenish draws on both his true life of faith and wide, deep reading, when he puts before us here a delicious meal: the experience of Christian spirituality. The adventure of faith is always transformative, touching the mind as much as the spirit, changing how we sense life and how we live, concretely and in many respects. We are blessed in this book with the ingredients that flavor Devenish himself: a farmer, a missionary, a pastor, an academic; a practical Christian; a reflecting believer. Always with a lively, attractive Australian tang of freshness. We are all nourished by this food for the soul."

—**Christo Lombaard**, head of department, faculty of theology, University of Pretoria

"Stuart Devenish is passionate about the spiritual quest in a post secular world, where language about spiritual experience is often lacking. Based on his pastoral and teaching experience, he offers a select dictionary (sixty entries) of terms relevant to a spiritual journey. Aimed at both Christian believers and committed spiritual seekers, this work offers concepts that help both pastors and practitioners name, understand and make meaning of their experience of the transcendent."

—**Diana L. Villegas**, research fellow, University of the Free State, author of *Growing in Love with Catherine of Siena*

"The literature of Christian spirituality is filled with countless word-concepts but suffers from a lack of a defining and integrating center. In this volume, Devenish has gathered selected word-concepts into a lexicon of language that enables us to communicate the substance of the faith we profess and experience as more real than real. He has given teachers of the Christian spiritual life an enormous gift by producing a shared and accessible language for the soul that enables us to make the unfamiliar familiar, and the sometimes opaque clear. This volume will be a key text for Christian spiritual education into the coming decades."

—GARY W. MOON, founding director, Martin Institute and Dallas Willard Research Center, director, Conversatio Divina, Westmont College California, author of *Becoming Dallas Willard*

"When platitudes, memes, and GIFs predominate communication, how do we learn to speak about the interior life and our relationship with God? Devenish's examination of Christian traditions from across the breadth of time provides a necessary resource to plumb the depths of the human soul that we might recover what it means to experience authentic spiritual conversation with God and one another."

—TAMMIE GRIMM, teaching faculty in spirituality and congregational formation, Wesley Seminary, Indiana Wesleyan University

"To grasp the spiritual wisdom of past saints is essential to personal growth as a disciple today. *A Language for the Soul* provides a tremendous service in bringing to our attention the depth and breadth of the Christian spiritual tradition. The interior life of grace and charity is where the personal encounter with Christ occurs. This book is a must read for anyone seeking the path of wisdom for greater intimacy with God in their own lives and for instructing others in the faith."

—MICHEL THERRIEN, founder and president, Preambula Group, author of *The Catholic Faith Explained* and *Wounded Witness: Reclaiming the Church's Unity in a Time of Crisis*

A Language
for the Soul

An Experiential Dictionary of the Christian Spiritual Life

Stuart C. Devenish

FOREWORD BY
Michael C. Voigts

☙PICKWICK *Publications* · Eugene, Oregon

A LANGUAGE FOR THE SOUL
An Experiential Dictionary of the Christian Spiritual Life

Copyright © 2024 Stuart C. Devenish. All rights reserved. Except for brief quotations in critical publications or reviews, no part of this book may be reproduced in any manner without prior written permission from the publisher. Write: Permissions, Wipf and Stock Publishers, 199 W. 8th Ave., Suite 3, Eugene, OR 97401.

Pickwick Publications
An Imprint of Wipf and Stock Publishers
199 W. 8th Ave., Suite 3
Eugene, OR 97401

www.wipfandstock.com

PAPERBACK ISBN: 978-1-6667-5457-5
HARDCOVER ISBN: 978-1-6667-5458-2
EBOOK ISBN: 978-1-6667-5459-9

Cataloguing-in-Publication data:

Names: Devenish, Stuart C., author. | Voigts, Michael C., foreword.

Title: A language for the soul : an experiential dictionary of the christian spiritual life / Stuart C. Devenish ; foreword by Michael C. Voigts.

Description: Eugene, OR : Pickwick Publications, 2024 | Includes bibliographical references and index.

Identifiers: ISBN 978-1-6667-5457-5 (paperback) | ISBN 978-1-6667-5458-2 (hardcover) | ISBN 978-1-6667-5459-9 (ebook)

Subjects: LCSH: Spirituality—Dictionaries. | Spiritual life—Dictionaries—English. | Spiritual life—Encyclopedias and dictionaries.

Classification: BV4488 .D48 2024 (paperback) | BV4488 .D48 (ebook)

VERSION NUMBER 10/17/24

Copyright permission has been obtained to republish material for the following authors from their publishers and/or literary agents:

Dietrich Bonhoeffer, *The Cost of Discipleship*, SCM Translation 1948, 1959 © SCM Press. Used by permission of Hymns Ancient & Modern Limited.

Christopher Fry, *A Sleep of Prisoners*, Oxford University Press 1951, © Oxford University Press. Used by permission.

Mary Oliver, "The Summer Day," House of Light, Beacon Press, 1990. Reprinted by the Permission of The Charlotte Sheedy Literary Agency as agent for the author. Copyright © 1990, 2006, 2008, 2017 by Mary Oliver with permission of Bill Reichblum.

This book is dedicated
to the memory of
Val Butler (1937–2016)
who served as a wise soul-guide and spiritual companion
to many people, myself included.

"How can I explain the riches and treasures and delights found . . . when the soul is united to God in prayer . . . ? . . . Since in some way we can enjoy heaven on earth, be brave in begging the Lord to give his grace in such a way that nothing will be lacking through our own fault; that he show us the way and strengthen the soul that it may dig until it finds this hidden treasure. The truth is that this treasure lies within our very selves. This is what I would like to know how to explain, if the Lord would enable me to do so."

—Teresa of Avila[1]

---

1. Teresa of Avila, *Interior Castle*, 85–86.

Contents

Foreword by Michael C. Voigts | xi
Acknowledgments | xv
Preface | xvii
Introduction | xix

Part One: Setting the Scene | 1

    Origins of the Project | 1

        Christianity: Outward Decay and Inward Renewal | 5
        The Arrival of the Post-Secular Age | 9
        Re-Learning the Language of the Soul | 14
        The Four Defining Frames that Give Shape to the Work | 18
        A Dictionary of Christianity's 'Lost' Words | 24
        Criteria for Selecting Word-Concepts | 26
        Audience, Outcomes, Limitations, Architecture | 28
        How to Use this Dictionary of Christian Words | 33
        How Well Do You Know Fire? | 36

Part Two: Foundational Word-Concepts | 39

    1. Homo Spiritualis | 39
    2. Spiritual Quest | 42
    3. The Believing Soul | 45
    4. Reception | 47
    5. Call and Response | 50
    6. Spiritual Education | 53

7. The Soul at White Heat | 55
8. Modern-Day Mystics | 59
9. The Felt Presence of God | 62
10. The Beloved | 64

Part Three: Alphabetical Word-Concepts | 68

11. Abandonment | 68
12. Acedia | 71
13. Agency | 74
14. Attachment | 77
15. Attunement | 80
16. Beauty | 83
17. Catechism | 86
18. Christian Knowing | 88
19. Concursus | 91
20. Contemplative Turn | 94
21. Dark Night of the Soul | 97
22. De Magestro | 100
23. Divine Embrace | 102
24. Desire in the Spiritual Life | 105
25. Eighth Day Theology | 108
26. Embodiment | 111
27. Epektasis | 113
28. Experience (the centrality of) | 116
29. Experts in Humanity | 119
30. Fullness | 122
31. God's Workshop | 125
32. Habitus | 129
33. [When] the Holy Spirit Meets the Human Spirit | 132
34. Imitation | 135
35. Imperfection (a spirituality of) | 137
36. Lex Orandi | 141
37. Logic of the Spirit | 144
38. Maladies of the Spiritual Life | 147
39. Martyr Moment | 150
40. Metanoia | 153
41. Mystagogy | 156
42. Ordo Amoris | 159
43. Paroikos | 161

44. Participation | 164
45. Recapitulation | 167
46. Sanctity: on being a Saint | 171
47. Second Naïveté | 174
48. Self-Implicating | 177
49. Self-Transcendence | 181
50. Shadow | 184
51. Sober Drunkenness | 187
52. Soliloquy | 190
53. The Soul | 193
54. Spiritual Intelligence | 197
55. (The) Spiritual Senses | 200
56. Supernatural Existential | 204
57. Theosis | 207
58. Tragic Spirituality | 210
59. Transformation | 213
60. True Self-False Self | 217

Bibliography | 221
Index | 237

Foreword

Michael C. Voigts

As a professor in a theological seminary, I have observed that the importance of language appears to be diminishing in influence. With AI-generated documents, video instructional manuals, audio books, and photographic journals, the prominence of written communication seems to be waning. We discuss in my classes the importance of explicating the whole of the Christian faith to those in local church communities and acknowledge the difficulty of such communication when parishioners are increasingly allowing social media to think and process information for them. The 'rapid-response' means of communication between individuals and on social media can result in less-thoughtful approaches to correspondence, leading to assumptions and speculations. This misunderstanding can even instigate unintended resentment and anger between individuals. What is needed is a comprehensive compendium of classic terms in Christian spirituality.

This brings us to the present, excellent work by Stuart Devenish. What makes this volume so valuable is the author's straightforward presentation of key terms in Christian spirituality with well-researched and historically faithful definitions. The resulting text is a clarification of clouded misunderstandings that can hinder spiritual development and a renewed connection with faithful Christians from our past. The encyclopedic presentation of this material is cited in ways that invites curious readers to explore more writings from these primary sources. While an exhaustive list of key concepts in Christian spirituality would be nearly impossible to compile, Devenish has prudently selected those historic terms which encompass other, more general terms.

Many people, when seeking to define a term (even a traditionally 'Christian' term), will often perform a simple internet search. The result is often a definition from a source outside the Christian tradition that provides a general, hypothesized understanding rather than a well-formed definition from an explicitly Christian source. This meshing of the secular and the sacred in formulating an understanding of a word can lead to problematic outcomes. For example, the word "contemplation" is a term used by followers of many different religious faiths, and even those from no faith tradition at all. Without a biblical and theological foundation for defining this important term, well-intentioned Christians can be led into an understanding of this term that looks more Hindu or Buddhist than Christian.

Today, Christian believers around the world find themselves adjusting to a post-Christian culture in which the language of faith is becoming meaningless. Words such as "justification," "sin," "grace," "holiness," and other terms increasingly have little substance or understanding. Even a foundational word such as "love" has so many meanings in just as many secular and religious traditions, that to use the term requires lengthy prerequisites. In fact, ministry leaders search for ways to describe major aspects of the faith without using what they call "churchy" language. The result is commonly a watering down of historic Christian teaching to accommodate the culture around them. In this compelling work, Devenish reminds us that the church is a community of language that gifts both words and their meanings to its members, which hold connections with those who have gone before us. Christian leaders do not need to re-invent the Christian faith or the language for "carrying" it for each generation, only to ensure that the faith is appropriately contextualized for the new season in which it finds itself. Such contextualization requires a foundation and faithful comprehension of key terms and phrases of the church.

After reading *A Language for the Soul*, I am deeply encouraged that Christian spirituality does in fact possess a language and does indeed have a voice. As a discipline which is reawakening in both the churches and the seminaries, it can now speak for itself. And in doing so, it is able to demonstrate to both its friends and its enemies, the considerable possibilities it has for producing a restored understanding of humanity that these difficult times so desperately need. What Devenish has *not* done is to restate the old doctrines of the Christian faith *de rigour*. Instead, what he *has* done is to show us how those doctrines and beliefs are interiorized, owned, and how they bear fruit in the life of the human soul. Perhaps due to the influx of technology, the *imago Dei* inherent in all of humanity is making people hunger for the affective, spiritual aspect of human nature. It therefore becomes imperative for Christian leaders of all vocations to understand how to explicate what represents not just spirituality in general, but *Christian* spirituality in particular. What makes us human? What is a soul? How do we communicate with God, and why should we do so? These questions have been addressed and answered by Christian writers for centuries, beginning with the Bible itself, and into the present day. Christian leaders need not search for new and fashionable answers to these questions, for definitions to these key terms in Christian spirituality are already in existence. Instead, our responsibility is to contextualize and apply these historic concepts in ways modern people can understand.

Today a list of ever-increasing problems confronts pastors and congregational leaders. Dwindling numbers, debilitating discouragement, and a loss of purpose are just a few of the realities facing church communities and their pastoral leaders. But renewal is the middle name of the Christian church. It comes from a reawakening of its spiritual life. Through the Holy Spirit, human connection with God and each other energizes and quickens the life of faith for both communities and individuals. Historically speaking, strengthened connections with the Holy Spirit have ignited ecclesiastical renewals which have extended into the surrounding cultures. Church-communities are reawakened when their prayer life and worship life is re-ignited. Seminaries and training institutions have the opportunity—and the obligation—to re-focus on the teaching of the Christian spiritual life, including offering pastors and congregational leaders a language for the soul.

What we have here in *A Language for the Soul* is a spiritual textbook that answers an important need for our times. The author brings to the project a broad and deep reading of the cultural, theological, psychological, and spiritual sources. Stuart Devenish has produced a book that is clearly conceptualized, appropriately ecumenical, and readily understood. I recommend it highly.

Dr. Michael C. Voigts
Professor of Christian Spirituality and Theology
Asbury Theological Seminary

Acknowledgments

THE WRITING OF A text such as this is the work not just of one person but many. I wish therefore to offer my thanks to the following people for their contributions to this volume.

In the early 2000s, three Christian psychologist-scholar friends, Maureen Miner-Bridges, Martin Dowson, Marie-Thérèse Proctor . . . and myself, formed the Psychology and Spirituality Society (PASS) in Sydney, Australia. The Society offered seminars, conferences, and publications at the points-of-connection between Christianity, psychology, and spirituality. At one of our regular Sunday afternoon meetings, we discussed the question of whether an accessible and usable language for the soul existed. For us at that time, the answer was clear. No accessible language for the soul was ready to hand. This realization represented a major obstacle to our desire to make a meaningful contribution to the field as we had hoped. In subsequent years, the Society disbanded as its members left to do other things. But that insight was a watershed moment for me, and this present volume—offered some twenty years afterwards—is my response to the question of an accessible and usable language for the soul. I can now say with confidence that such a thing does exist.

I want to acknowledge the encouragement that has flowed from the conversations I have shared with Alan Hirsch over the past several years. I consider Alan to be a friend and a fellow-traveller. He is an *aficionado* and an unacknowledged specialist in the thought and spiritual theology of Hans Urs von Balthasar. His enthusiasm for this project and his wealth of knowledge on the subject—among the many other specializations and projects to which he has put his hand—has been an important stimulus to my thinking and writing.

During the five years I served on the faculty of Tabor College in Adelaide, South Australia, I came to value Phil Daughtry not only as a colleague but as a soul friend. I have learned to trust his optimism about where we are in the present moment, and his deep insight into what it means to be a spiritual person in today's complex environment. Experiences of publishing and conferencing together (especially the international conference for the Society for the Study of Christian Spirituality in Adelaide in July 2023) will linger long in my memory.

I want to thank the following people who have offered support, feedback, and resources in response to the various outlines, excerpts, and iterations of the manuscript I shared with them over the months and years leading up to the publication of this volume: David McGregor, Glen Scorgie, Sally Jones, David Rensberger, Ivan Head, Andrew Staggs and Grattan Savage. The Kilmore Study Group led by Jon Newton, and whose members were André Du Plooy, Ruwan Palapathwala, Judy Newton, and Mark Woloszyn gave feedback and response. And Mandy Mayer, the Library Services Manager at Tabor College in Adelaide, took time to assist me to locate several hard-to-find journal articles. I also want to acknowledge those students who enrolled in my spirituality courses and who so often turned out to be my teachers. And I wish to thank my copy-editor James Cooper who has worked hard to strengthen my writing in preparation for publication.

And finally, I want to thank my wife Ros who generously released time for me to write, and who—as she often did in her life before her retirement as an awarded research librarian—found an endless number of 'lost' books in my library which in my haste I was unable to locate, and who also acted as proofreader in the final stages of editing.

To each of you I offer my thanks and appreciation. As always however, any faults and failings that persist in the text are my own.

Stuart C. Devenish
September 2024

Preface

IN THIS VOLUME, THE author addresses Christian spiritual instructors (variously labelled as priests, pastors, spiritual directors, mentors, chaplains and soul guides), offering them a language for the soul discovered from the ancient touchstones and storehouses of Christianity's 2000-year-long living spiritual tradition. That language describes the deep structures and soul movements that unfold in the human person in response to the Divine invitation. 60 word-concepts are offered in the form of an experiential dictionary that goes beyond standard collections, to name and explore the inward-human reactions to the whispering of God's Spirit within the soul. It is these reactions that result in the embrace of faith, the quest for consecration, and the journey of discipleship. The end-product is a dynamic resource that will be of immense benefit to Christian spiritual instructors working in churches, schools, colleges, mission agencies, inter-religious dialogue, as well as in youth work, aged-care, therapeutic settings and more. It offers something which has long been missing from their toolboxes . . . a workable, accessible, and up-to-date language for the soul generated from within the classical Christian spiritual tradition, for use in professional, educational, ministerial, and everyday life-situations. More than anything else available today, this experiential dictionary has the potential to inform, launch, and intensify the spiritual journeys of genuine seekers wherever and whoever they may be. The central argument put forward here is that, since the substance of any discipline lies in the language it employs to name the foundational elements of its teachings—if the Christian faith is to exert an influence on Western culture into the future, its adherents must relearn its spiritual language, and acquire the skills needed to teach it to those modern-day seekers who wish to make Christ the object of their highest desires and their deepest affections.

Introduction

MANY BELIEVERS TODAY SUSPECT that the emptying of our churches and the sidelining of the Christian faith in mainstream culture augurs the beginning of the end for Christianity in the West. But nothing could be further from the truth. While those of us in the churches check our pulse for signs of life and wonder why God has failed to show up . . . God *has* been showing up in all sorts of ways and unexpected places in the broader culture. The unanticipated result is an updraft of spiritual interest, energy and exploration in our world that would—if we Christians could see it for the opportunity it is—shake the very foundations of our faith. Instead of complaining about the re-paganization of our once 'Christian' culture, we should be finding ways to speak into the re-energized spiritual conversations happening around us as a strategic act of education, witness, and mission. It is time we Christians dared to re-imagine God at work in the world in ways we previously might never have thought possible.

God is "doing a new thing" in the new post-secular moment that is upon us, creating such a sense of spiritual hunger in our unbelieving friends and neighbors that they are being thrust out into spiritual quests they did not expect, driven by questions they cannot answer, longings they cannot articulate, and hopes they dare not whisper. Because of personal brokenness, a fractured culture, a fragile earth, and the collapse of the Western myth of progress . . . a growing number of "lonely mystics" in our culture are making it their priority to search for meaning and purpose in life. While many are undeniably searching in the wrong places and are coming to the wrong conclusions, one thing is clear—that science, consumer culture and the entertainment industry do not have the answers demanded by the re-activated spiritual questing going on in the present moment. Three questions come into view; the first is, "How can today's church leaders who hold responsibility for passing on the faith to new generations of believers, communicate genuine faith to hesitant young confessors who know more about doubt than they do about belief?" The second is, "What will it take for modern-day seekers to consider the possibility that the Christian spiritual life is a worthy pathway capable of addressing the aches and fevers that wrack their souls?" And the third is, "What language might Christianity use to describe and offer its ancient spiritual resources to people who want to know *how to be properly spiritual* in the post-secular age?"

These questions invite a decisive response from the churches and the Christian community. They also invite Christian spirituality which is a discipline that is currently reawakening, to consider what it would take to offer the deep truths of classical Christian teaching regarding the triune God, the crucified Son, the indwelling Spirit, the gospel of grace, and citizenship in the kingdom of God, to what is now a spiritually hungry society? Can Christianity get beyond its doctrinal dogfights to offer the core of Christian belief (the *what* of faith) to modern-day seekers who are desperate to re-connect to their inner soul-life (the *how* of believing) after more than a century of vacuous atheism? The classical Christian spiritual tradition contains within its treasure trove a remarkable language *of* and *for* the soul which, if properly recovered and brought into light for observation and use, could enable twenty-first century pilgrims—Christians and non-Christians alike—to link the journey of self-discovery to the journey of Christ-discovery. Now that Western culture is open to transcendence once again, this is a time—like no other time in the past 100 years—for Christianity to bear witness to the essential nature of our faith.

Part One

Setting the Scene

Origins of the Project

IN THE YEARS LEADING up to the publication of this book, I found myself engaged in writing and teaching a series of courses exploring Christian spirituality in Protestant Bible and Theological colleges in Australia and elsewhere. For the most part, my students were serving pastors who had chosen to return to studies for the purpose of enriching their personal faith and resourcing their ministries in churches, mission agencies and training colleges. The courses on offer were entitled, *Spiritual Formation in the Christian Faith-Community*, *The Dynamics of the Christian Spiritual Life*, *The Spiritual Life of the Minister-Leader-Missionary*, and *Discipleship in the Christian Spiritual Tradition*. While preparing lectures for those courses, I had cause to reach for a lexicon of words and concepts capable of describing, illustrating, and interpreting the heights and depths to which soul-work takes us. What I found was the rich language of biblical, historical, and systematic theology, with its varied descriptions of the person, words, works, will and ways of the Triune God in salvation history. Without God's gracious self-revelation of himself addressed to his human audience, we would have remained benighted, not knowing the light that exists through the gospel of Christ. This *God-ward* language (including such key concepts as trinity, election, mercy, covenant, reconciliation, righteousness, redemption, and kingdom) is available in any and every place one chooses to look in the canon of the Christian church. Its richness and profusion is astounding in its variety.

What is evidently missing, however, is any language belonging to spiritual theology that describes how these great truths of the Christian faith articulate with the inner lives of those who believe and how they are experienced by real human beings engaged in living their everyday lives. What difference does the Christian life make in the lives of believers—in seasons of great joy and delight, or in the midst of despair and deep distress? Here was an Old Mother Hubbard riddle: when I reached into the cupboard for *soul-type words* to describe the lived experience of God-at-work-in-the-human-heart—of Christ's call to "Come, follow me!" or of the Spirit's drawing near to call us to some great task or vocation—the cupboard was bare. There were rather too few *human-ward* words in circulation to adequately connect the great truths of Christian theology with the personal, spiritual needs of present-day seekers and believers. In a world that is otherwise filled with language, my sense was that spirituality with all its beauty, power and possibility for transformation was on mute.

This scarcity surprised me. If the point-of-contact between God and humanity—the sacred and the profane, spirit and flesh, mystery and the revealed, the soul and its love-object—is the first order of business for both theology and Christian education, I would have thought that developing a language for this life-giving connection would have been Christianity's first priority. Since spirituality is our point-of-connection with God, and since words and language are what enable us to grasp and communicate those whispers that come to us from the "other side," it astonished me that it was so difficult to locate a lexicon of word-concepts for discussing this unique conjunction of spirituality and life. Where was the language capable of expressing this crowning glory of the Christian spiritual life that describes our connection with Christ? If it was difficult for me as a specialist in the field of Christian spirituality, heaven knows how difficult it must be for novice insiders and rank outsiders who venture into this "space" to begin to explore and discuss their innermost spiritual intuitions and experiences.

The thought struck me that there must be a reasonable explanation for this apparent omission. Perhaps the problem arose because, as a Protestant Christian, I had not yet learned the full Christian experiential alphabet? Perhaps, our Catholic and Orthodox Christian colleagues might be better informed? Perhaps I had been looking in the wrong places to find the spiritual words and concepts I was trying to locate? Or perhaps the words I was looking for didn't exist? Maybe the Pentecostals had insights I hadn't yet discovered? As I pondered the matter over the following weeks and months, I began to realize that my suspicion was correct . . . *we do indeed have a problem with the language of the soul*. It has gone missing somewhere and needs to be recovered! If Jesus could tell a parable about the finding of the lost sheep, the lost coin, and the lost son (Luke 15), I wondered if it were possible for those of us working in what might be called the *classical Christian spiritual tradition*, to recover the lost language that once formed the center of its beautiful, beating heart. That season of questioning and wondering provoked me to venture on a journey of exploration in search of a language for the soul for the twenty-first century church, believers and seekers.

Since we will be saying a great deal about the classical Christian spiritual tradition, it seems both wise and necessary to describe what I intend by that phrase, since it is not a commonly used description. By "the classical Christian spiritual tradition" I mean the unifying 'core' of authentic Christianity, which contains the essence of Jesus' teaching concerning the kingdom of God, as exemplified through his person, life, teachings, death, and resurrection. It does not belong to any one of Christianity's four main families in the form of Eastern Orthodoxy, Roman Catholicism, Protestantism or Pentecostalism—instead, it is the wellspring and life-source that energizes and underwrites each of them. It is the genius of the Christian faith in so far as it offers a transformative journey towards union with God as a mystical pathway. It is that Way of life in the Spirit for which Christianity in its truest form is best known, as illustrated by the apostles, the saints, the martyrs, the mystics, the seers, the wise teachers, and those beautiful souls who are Christianity's most authentic witnesses and convincing exemplars. As such, the classical Christian spiritual tradition both indwells every true representation of the Christian faith *via* its movements and expressions . . . and transcends them all in so far as it represents the purest and highest form of spiritual wisdom and guidance available for believers seeking a profound connection with God.

What you will find in the pages that follow are 60 word-concepts, each offered in entries of approximately 1000 words, selected for their capacity to express in compressed form some essential aspect of the soul's journey towards God. The resulting dictionary represents an extended form of the lexicon I compiled for myself while teaching Christian spirituality in recent years. The importance of this task was further underscored by feedback given by my students during this time, which contained several repeated themes and observations on their part. In summary, my students observed that (1) they had not learned the language of the interior life in any spiritual theology classes during their theological education, and had spent their subsequent years in ministry trying to learn it for themselves—often without success; (2) what they had been hearing in our courses together was a series of word-concepts that provided them with the language for the interior dimension of the Christian spiritual life, and they wondered where it had been hiding all these years; and (3) now that they had mastered some of the word-concepts we were discovering together, they felt they could return to their ministries with a new confidence in using the language for the soul that would enable them to guide people towards growth and maturity in the areas of spiritual formation, discipleship, spiritual accompanying, sanctification, contemplative prayer, and soul-work of all kinds.

Of course, I am not the first to make this discovery regarding the paucity of a language for the life of the soul. Early in his ministry, Eugene Peterson—while trying to instruct his congregation in the sheer wonder, splendor, power and mystery of the spiritual life—began to look for expressions of the *holy*: holy lives, holy places, Holy Spirit. Observing the same lack of words and concepts I was later to encounter, Peterson wrote:

> I soon found that there were no adequate definitions . . . The dictionary didn't yield much, etymologies didn't get me very far, word-studies left me claustrophobic, and as I continued searching the Holy Scriptures and the faces and lives of holy men and women I discovered that there was no standard behavior dictated by the word. There are no instruction manuals written on the holy.[1]

But neither Peterson's discovery nor my own struggles meant that the Christian spiritual life has been wordless, voiceless, and map-less throughout its long and rich history. In Christianity's 2000-year-long history of responding to God's invitation to "draw near" to eat at his table, there are countless books written by thousands of authors using millions of words to describe—if human words can ever adequately describe the Divine mysteries—the soul's response to the advances of Divine love. What this conveys is first, that if we are to locate a lexicon for describing the spiritual experiences of ordinary people engaged in the love-encounter with God, we will first have to strive to uncover it from its secretive

---

1. Peterson, *Subversive Spirituality*, 66.

hiding places. Second, we will have to draw from the apostolic, patristic, monastic, creedal, confessional, sacramental, biblical, theological and renewal documents scattered across church history. And third, we will have to learn to speak the native language of the Kingdom of God all over again. Access to this language for the soul is both a spiritual necessity and a Christian right—regardless of what part of the human family we belong to, or the geographical location where God has placed us on his good earth.

And so, I set out on a journey to rediscover Christianity's "lost" words, to create a Christian lexicon that comprises a "language for the soul" suitable for twenty-first century teachers, believers, readers, and seekers. To this end, I employed four interconnected questions to guide my quest: (1) what words and concepts are available to describe the soul's response to God's advances; (2) with special application to the life of the human person engaged in the sacred encounter; (3) at a time when soul-spirit-faith perspectives are once again being given a "voice" in the culture; and (4) in light of what some are now calling the post-secular age, and others are calling the age of the Spirit?

Before we proceed, some additional context is needed to help make sense of the importance of Christian spirituality in our post-Christian, post-modern and now post-secular world.

Christianity: Outward Decay and Inward Renewal

In the early twenty-first century, anyone standing outside Christianity looking inwards is likely to observe a once-magnificent faith now suffering from clear signs of age and decay. The ravages of time, and the build-up of centuries of dust and detritus have taken their toll. By any measure, the Christian faith in the late modern West is in trouble. Evidence of the extent of the damage can be captured in a series of brief observations.

Sociologically, the Christian faith is suffering from a loss of numbers and momentum resulting from one of the largest people-movements in history—*out* of the Christian Church. This large-scale hemorrhaging of adherents has left a legacy of smaller, older, poorer, less dynamic congregations who struggle to retain their younger members, and which are less likely than they once were to attract new generations of followers. Their future is in no way assured.

Politically, whatever power the Church once wielded in the culture in the form of its moral authority, its call to unity around the centralizing themes of the family unit and its contribution to society has been eroded by its own internal divisions, clergy sexual abuse and the sheer force of the "push back" from its aggressive and increasingly bellicose opponents. Christianity has lost the vote of the majority populace in Western cultural settings.

Culturally, after fighting and losing key battles in the culture wars over the past decades, the Church's voice has diminished to a whisper. Factional in-fighting between liberals and conservatives together with the impact of the sexual revolution, which continues to reverberate throughout Western culture, has eroded whatever remains of the Church's ability to speak with any credibility. Christianity has become an inauthentic witness against itself and its designated role as a living witness to the gospel.

Intellectually, the Christian explanation of history as the work of a personal Deity who, on the basis of love, sent his hero Son to die in humanity's place for their disobedience, has been challenged by a growing array of alternative narratives, each of which has their own internal logic and claims to offer an alternative, and an appealing (to some) explanation for human existence.

Religiously, not only is there an observable resistance from Christianity's cultured despisers towards its teachings and moral imperatives (owing to what Martha Nussbaum has called the "new religious intolerance"),[2] there are also, ironically, a growing number of available religious options for people to buy into—should they be so inclined—including Buddhism, Islam, Hindu, Judaism, Indigenous, Neo-Pagan, and a range of other New Age alternatives. Christianity is now just one religious option among a surfeit of other available options, and who is to say which one is right?

And in terms of the *morale* of Christians generally, there are signs that Christianity as a social and religious movement has become deeply divided and demoralized. Its spokespersons are caught like deer in the proverbial headlights. Its leaders are unsure how best to move forward. Its members seem unprepared for the conflict at hand. And the identity and allegiance of its Sunday adherents grows weaker with each passing year. Put together, these observations suggest that the critical question for the Christian faith in the West in the twenty-first century is essentially

---

2. Nussbaum, *New Religious Intolerance*.

one of renewal: "Where can the Christian faith find the impetus, the resources and the energy to renew itself in the face of the significant challenges (and opportunities) that present themselves in this new historical moment?" The underlying concern of this book is to provide an answer to this fundamental question of how Christianity might renew itself. To address that question, this book offers a usable and accessible language for the soul that is capable of offering a pathway towards renewal.

In 2 Corinthians 4:16, the Apostle Paul wrote, "Though outwardly we are wasting away, yet inwardly we are being renewed day by day."[3] Paul's original audiences in Corinth and across the ancient Near East were blind to recognizing Christ as the fulfillment of humanity's ancient desire for God. He implored his believing readers not to lose heart but to fix their eyes on Jesus, who had reconciled a lost humanity to himself on the grounds that "God was reconciling the world to himself in Christ, not counting men's sins against them" (2 Cor 5:19). For Paul, the answer to the world's problems—their one great hope—was to turn to Christ and so begin to live a new kind of life based on a new order, a new truth, a new life-force, and a new form of existence . . . with Christ as its energizing center. Simply put, the spiritual life which forms the centerpiece of Paul's preaching and gospel possessed the power to radically re-orient and refound the unfulfilled lives of the people of first century Palestine. And that same spiritual life preached by Paul, which has Christ as its center, has the power, authority, and ability to enable Christian believers in the twenty-first century to rekindle the Church's ancient genius and life-force, now that it has become forgotten, marginalized and hidden under a bushel. Once again—and not for the first time in the church's long, meandering, and troubled history—God's way of renewing his church is set to involve a revival of the spiritual life in the form of re-digging the foundations, re-stitching the fabric of prayer, worship, commitment and the re-making of the human heart from the inside out. Such is God's way of renewing what has become old, tired, out-of-date, passé, and of making it new again.

What is this form of spirituality that holds such great possibilities? Spirituality is a form of lived belief and practice that seeks to bring mere mortals into contact with the transcendent in a way that is direct, real, and experienced as a kind of "felt presence" of the Divine. Christianity is an ancient spiritual pathway that claims to connect human persons to

---

3. Unless otherwise specified, all Scriptural citations are from the New International Version (NIV), 1973, 1978, 1984, International Bible Society, published by Zondervan, Grand Rapids, Michigan.

God in this way. Its storyline is based on the person, life, and teachings of Jesus Christ, who Christians believe to be the Son of God. It offers a way of life based on the invitation of a good and gracious God for we human creatures to become "members of his family" and to "eat at his table." The *broker* of the Christian spiritual life is not the human subject him or herself, but Christ, who by his Spirit invites human participants into relationship with the Trinitarian community of God himself (Father, Son and Holy Spirit), in a kind of dance which implies mutual cooperation and obligation, and which forms the core of the Christian spiritual life. Spirituality that is *properly* Christian is based on a trust-relationship between Jesus and his disciples, linking the Master, (who is the true "lover") with the follower (the "beloved") in a bond of mutual love and embrace. The possibility of such an intimate faith relationship is real; it has its origins in the biblical narratives, and it is experiential in nature, dealing with matters of both ultimate concern and practical everyday living. It exerts a powerful shaping influence on human life that is grounded in salvation-history, as well as worked out in the lives of disciples, moment-by-moment, through their lived experience in their earth-bound bodies.

Although ancient in its origins and practice, Christian spirituality is remarkably well-suited to the needs, desires, and longings of our twenty-first century, post-secular Western society. Yet, as Jacob Needleman has observed, "The problem of Christianity in the contemporary world [is] its inability to make itself known for what it really is."[4] In the push and shove of the culture wars, and in the transition from one axial age to the next in terms of how the general populace thinks about religion and how best to live one's life—the language of Christian spiritual experience has been lost in the rubble of cultural conflicts and in Christian forgetfulness. Recovering the essence of Christian spiritual life, finding words for it, and communicating it to a generation who can barely imagine its meaning and importance, underpins the project and intent of this book.

Needleman's observation that Christianity needs to find a language to make itself known for what it really is, provides an important starting point for this book and those who might use the resources it provides. Despite the existence of a substantial 2000-year-long living spiritual tradition that lies within and behind it, Christianity appears to have either mislaid or forgotten the language capable of expressing its truest and deepest inner meanings. Half the existence of a thing is found in

---

4. Needleman, *Lost Christianity*, 20.

the telling of it. To lose the language—in particular the language of the human soul—is to do collateral damage to Christianity in general and to Christian spirituality in particular. That is because spirituality forms the essence, the heartbeat, and the substance of the Christian faith itself. To negate the one is to destroy the other. It is therefore urgent that Christian believers find a way to re-discover the lost language of the soul if Christianity is to have any hope of continuing to make a meaningful contribution to Western society, most especially in terms of explaining the Christian gospel and what it means for human beings to live in the Divine Presence, and to what the Church brings to the table as a transformative and illuminative pathway of life.

In other words, the road to the recovery of the Christian faith in the late Modern Western world will not be achieved by more money, slicker marketing campaigns, better managerial techniques, higher profile leaders or more prestigious educational institutions. The only possibility for the recovery of the Christian faith will be a renewal of its heart towards God, based on Christians re-learning the language of the soul—the language of repentance, prayer, submission, and worship. From the earliest origins of the Church, this has been the way of renewal. And here we are once again, having to re-learn the lesson that the invisible link between the believer and his or her God is the strongest life-force there is. In response to this universal spiritual dynamic, otherwise ordinary human beings, young and old, the educated, the worldly, the hopeless, the losers and the dreamers alike, have left their homes, and wandered all over the world, in search of the Divine source. And having found him and been changed into his image and likeness, they have set about changing firstly themselves, then the world they live in by establishing God's kingdom on earth. The renewal of the Christian faith comes from inside its own citadel. It is Spirit-given. And it has a language at its beating heart. That language—I am arguing in this book—is the language of the soul.

The Arrival of the Post-Secular Age

To speak of the soul and soul-work in the twenty-first century is not an easy task. One is forced to navigate the cultural situation to see how it has conditioned the possibility of belief and spiritual practice in the season "after" religion. The secularization hypothesis that has dominated the Western intellectual landscape for the last 150 years, has imposed a series of limitations on what one can and cannot say, do and be with regards to matters of the spiritual life. The three great shaping "moments" that have conditioned our thinking about faith have been the *modern age* (the so-called age of reason), the *post-modern* age (the age of interpretation), and the *post-secular age* (which I am calling the age of renegotiation). Our task here is to provide a spiritual "reading" of the *post-secular* moment from a decidedly Christian perspective, while considering the background influences brought by the modern and the post-modern ages that have preceded it.

The thing to note about the way the post-secular manifests itself is that, like a chameleon, it changes appearance depending on the intellectual environment in which it is examined. The secular philosophers think of the post-secular as no more than a continuation of the secular age by other means. The sociologists tend to think of the post-secular as the social manifestation of the secular, as in the rise of the "nones" who profess no religious affiliation in census surveys. And the political theorists think of the post-secular as the no-man's-land between the secular State and a stubbornly persistent religious sub-majority in Western society who simply refuse to leave—however much their critics might want them to go away. But when considered from a religious perspective, when believers are allowed to speak for themselves, the post-secular looks and sounds like a promissory note, offering the possibility that—against the backdrop of the rise and demise of the secularization theory—there can be a continuing role for religious belief and practice in our twenty-first century Western liberal democracies. Three important questions arise from the so-called "return" of religion: (1) What exactly *is* the role of religion in twenty-first century Western society? (2) What is Christianity's place among the other religious options available in Western culture? And (3) Where does *spirituality in Christian mode* have its outworking in the public domain, the private domain, as well as in education, politics, and ethics?

We are concerned here with this third question, by providing a specifically *Christian* spiritual reading of the post-secular. Some commentary from the literature will assist to further broaden our understanding of the topic. One of the leading contributors to the post-secular debate is Jurgen Habermas. In an article titled "Notes on the Post-Secular Society,"[5] Habermas argues that religion is making a comeback in society

---

5. Habermas, "Secularism's Crisis of Faith," 17–29.

in a variety of ways, most noticeably *via* the mass of immigrants flooding into the West, bringing with them their religious identities, convictions, practices, and values. Today, your baker is a Buddhist, your storeowner is a Hindu, your taxi driver is a Muslim, your dentist is a Christian, your hairdresser is a Rastafarian, your neighbor is an atheist, and your children are more than likely becoming something you didn't expect them to become.

And as a result, we need a language for this continuing presence of religion in the world. That is why it is necessary for the language of the post-secular to be added to the lexicon of Western speech. The continued existence of communities of faith who hold strong religious commitments in the West—including Christian communities—demands that their interests and concerns be listened to and taken into account. It is unfortunate that (bad) religion has too often brought with it impulses towards terrorism, violence, the oppression of women, the marginalization of cultural minorities, and the abuse of children. These things are both an offense to God and all good people everywhere. But what has not been explored with any exactitude is what religion and spirituality might have to offer contemporary society in terms of its resources for peace-making, community-building, creating social-capital, and engendering life as a resource for human flourishing. As a result, the onus is on Christians to give an account of the hope within them. To this end it is imperative that Christians work to find a form of language that will enable them to offer an explanation capable of convincing themselves first of all, and then of convincing their unbelieving neighbors, that they have something useful to say in the spiritual conversations currently taking place in our society, and where we, as Christ-followers, "fit" within the cultural moment.

In his book *On Religion*, John Caputo writes, "The 'post-' in 'post-secular' should not be understood to mean 'over and done with' but rather *as having passed through modernity and come out the other end*, a little wiser for the experience."[6] With irony, Caputo observes, "A surprising thing happened on the way to the death of God."[7] Namely, that "Marx, Neitzsche and Freud are all dead, but God is doing just fine thank you very much."[8] Similarly, in his landmark book *A Secular Age*, Charles Taylor[9] discusses the cultural conditions that have shaped the

---

6. Caputo, *On Religion*, 65, italics in the original

7. Caputo, *On Religion*. 64.

8. Caputo, *On Religion*, 69.

9. Taylor, *Secular Age*.

(im)possibility of belief. While focussing on how secularism arose in the West, Taylor's work is quintessentially post-secular in character, insofar as he is keen not simply to hammer nails into the Christian coffin. Rather, as a convinced Christian himself, Taylor is concerned with the future of spirituality in general and Christian spirituality in particular. As such, he seeks to map the future of a Christian response to humanity's continued and indeed intensifying search for spiritual wholeness, or what Taylor refers to as the innate desire for "fullness," meaning:

> A place where life is fuller, richer, more worthwhile, more admirable, more what it should be. This is perhaps the place of power; we often experience this as deeply moving, as inspiring. Perhaps the sense of fullness is something we just catch glimpses of from afar off; we have the powerful intuition of what fullness would be . . . the moments of experienced fullness, joy and fulfillment, when we feel ourselves there.[10]

Summing up Taylor's overall argument, Andrew Lincoln writes, "Just as through the power of the Spirit, Jesus experienced fullness from God, so through the same Spirit believers experience the divine fullness that Jesus experienced in his humanity and are enabled in community to share in the communication of God's plenitude to others and to the world."[11]

A Christian spiritual reading of our post-secular *moment* reveals that these ideas accord well with the biblical expectation of a spiritual awakening that will mark the end of history—an anticipated age of the Spirit in preparation for the *eschaton*, the second coming of Christ at the end of all things to judge his enemies and to claim for eternity his Bride, the Church. In order to prepare for the arrival of that critical moment, therefore, Christians must rediscover their impulse to prayer. Here, too, while serious damage has been done throughout a long period of secularization, we are not without resources. Commenting on the plight of prayer in modern times, Roger Scruton has observed:

> Prayer and penitence have been interrupted, but not forgotten. To those who wish for it, the ethical life may still be retrieved. Ours is a catacomb culture, a flame kept alive by undaunted monks. And what the monks of Europe achieved in a former dark age, they (we) might achieve again.[12]

---

10. Taylor, *Secular Age*, 5.
11. Lincoln, "Spirituality in a Secular Age," 78.
12. Scruton, *Intelligent Person's Guide to Modern Culture*, 136.

So then, we might ask, is an authentic Christian spirituality actually possible in the post-secular age? Is it nothing . . . or is it everything? I think we can confidently claim that the question of spirituality is not off the table, as many pundits once predicted and still blithely assume. Instead, spirituality is very much *on the table*, as a growing number of thinkers, cultural trends, and an increasing number of spiritual seekers in Western culture seem to indicate. From a Christian point of view, we are living in the age of the Spirit—partly because every age is an age of the Spirit, but mostly because this age in particular marks a return of the sacred, a time of increased yearning for something more, a deep sense of need in peoples' lives, and a longing for something more deeply satisfying than one-dimensional consumerism, technology-driven ability and prosperity, or the bland optimism of pop-psychology.

Summarizing this strange set of circumstances, David Tacey writes:

> Sociologists have announced that we are living in a post-secular age, and are consulting leaders of religion about 'what is missing' in secular society. In a sense the ball is back in the religious court, but the religions don't know it. What is emerging does not tally with what they understand as 'religion', and they are not very interested. The religions are still in defensive mode, a stance consistently adopted in the modern era. They are temporarily inclined to view what is emerging from the secular domain as an antagonist or opponent. Their defensiveness is making them incapable of seeing what is before their eyes, a religious revival is at hand, and they could be part of it if they used their imagination and were prepared to experiment with existing forms.[13]

When he uses the phrase "the religions," Tacey is referring most directly to institutional Christianity, which is sitting on its hands and missing the opportunity to position itself as a leading contributor to the emerging spiritual conversation, and to sit at the table with those people and groups who will likely shape the spiritual landscape of humanity into the future.

Opportunities abound in the present moment, but few Christian influencers are taking them seriously. Yet this is a conversation we must have if Christianity is to bear witness to Christ in the future, especially in these next few decades that lie immediately ahead of us. Our conversation partners are no longer primarily the atheists and those doggedly committed to non-belief. Instead, our conversation partners are our

---

13. Tacey, *Postsecular Sacred*, 14.

fellow religionists who are open to religious exploration and spiritual practice and encounter. All we need do is to creatively set the table and to invite them to take a seat, and to invite Christ to demonstrate his active Presence among them/us. This was the essence of ministry in the early church. It must also be the essence of ministry for the church today. Rather than throwing out the Christian spiritual baby with the secular bathwater, now is the time for re-digging the old wells of classical Christian spiritual life to locate living water that will attract and sustain existing believers and new generations of spiritual seekers. The limits of the modern age's hyper rationalism have been reached. It is time to return to the deep wells of wisdom, insight and generativity that come from soul-work and connectedness to the reality of God, the author of all Creation, in whom "we live and move and have our being" (Acts 17:28).

Re-Learning the Language of the Soul

Western society, with its inherent belief in technological progress based on science and evidence-based logic, has developed significant expertise in the making of tools and systems suited to observing, measuring, and describing the physical world. Consequently, we have developed a language for engaging with the outer world based largely on categories proper to the natural sciences but which fall well short when considering human experience more broadly. For the most part, ours is a "surface" culture that has adopted a lesser language, comfortable with describing such things as cars, computers, movies, holidays, cultural "brands" and pop stars. But when it comes time to journey inward to transact the business of the soul, whatever evidence-based systems of thought, education, and language we have developed for making sense of the outer world suddenly proves inadequate for naming and evaluating the interior, intra-psychic phenomena of feelings, dreams, love, intuitions, hopes, fears, and anxieties that characterize the bulk of our inward human processes. Soul, spirit, and all that is most essential to human existence is left behind because fact-based language simply can't "reach" the heights or depths that human interiority and spirituality takes us. As a result, as Sue Monk-Kidd has observed, we in the West "have lost the ability to probe the soul, to know and refine its experiences."[14] Further emphasizing the importance of language for making sense of lived experience, Brené Brown writes:

14. Monk-Kidd, *Firstlight*, 17.

Language is a portal to meaning-making, connection, healing, learning and self-awareness. Having access to the right words can open up entire universes. When we don't have the language to talk about what we are experiencing, our ability to make sense of what's happening and share it with others is severely limited. Without accurate language, we struggle to get the help we need, we don't always regulate or manage our emotions and experiences in a way that allows us to move through them productively, and our self-awareness is diminished. Language shows us that naming an experience doesn't give the experience more power, it gives us the power of understanding and meaning.[15]

When it comes to the spiritual life, there are those who would argue that because of the mysterious nature of the Sacred, there are some things that simply cannot be said. The poet Rainer Maria Rilke once declared that some things are "unsayable," observing, in his *Letters to a Young Poet*:

> Things are not all as graspable or sayable as on the whole we are led to believe; most events are unsayable, occur in a space that no word has ever penetrated, and most unsayable of all are works of art, mysterious existences whose life endures alongside ours, which passes away.[16]

As a generalized principle, that may be true, but the naming of things is a part of our human creativity and necessity. Adam and Eve named the animals at creation, and the early disciples and apostles named the results of salvation in both the church and the world. Naming is what we do as human beings, with our God-given capacity to speak and to describe what is outside us in the everyday world, and also what is inside us in our interior existence. That means the task of naming the sacred is not simply one task among many other tasks. Instead, in the age of the post-secular, naming the sacred—including the inner operations of our own souls—is *the most important task* we can address ourselves to. As Mark Worthing has pointed out:

> Words are symbol-bearers. They convey and represent so much more than a collection of sounds or bits of information. Collectively, words are audible, and when written, the visible image of truths which transcend the individual sounds and meanings. There is something sacramental about words. They point to and participate in a reality greater than themselves. And when they

---

15. Brown, *Atlas of the Heart*, 20.
16. Rilke, *Letters to a Young Poet*, 18.

point to the loving grace of God and Jesus Christ, they fulfill their highest calling.[17]

This lively and sanctifying function of language is especially true when it comes to dealing with the interior dimension of the spiritual life. For the remainder of this section, we will discuss three distinct yet interrelated aspects of this interior "soul spectrum"; first, *when the soul speaks* in the first person; second, *when we speak to the soul* in the second person, and third, *when we speak about the soul* in the third person.

First then—when *the soul speaks* (first person). The true language of the soul is prayer. Prayer is what people who are aware they are living before the face of God (*corum Deo*) do when they wish to express themselves. For St. Teresa of Avila, "Prayer is nothing other than an intimate friendship. It is a frequent heart-to-heart conversation with him by whom we know ourselves to be loved."[18] Similarly, Eugene Peterson has described prayer this way: "Prayer is answering speech; it is not primarily 'address' but 'response.'"[19] In this sense, prayer is a form of communication, a 'going out' from the soul towards God in loving response. Prayer is capable of carrying and expressing every emotion and sensation of the human heart and soul and is—as a result—the highest form of communication.

Prayer enables us to speak to God, to confess our sins, to ask God for our daily bread, to offer ourselves in service to Christ, or to acknowledge when we have become immobilized by fear. To do any of these things is to pray. Our prayers reflect the true state of our souls, for they are our way of being absolutely, totally, completely honest with ourselves and with God. While there are times when set prayers can be enormously helpful, such as in times of deep grief and confusion when all we can do is cry out to God in pain, nevertheless prayers ought not to be empty incantations or dry formulas, but a deep outpouring of the self in a way that is utterly true, and which is connected to our authentic lives. To that extent, real prayer says something real to God about the true self. As Paul Evdokimov writes:

> It is not enough to *say* prayers: we must become, *be* prayer, prayer incarnate. It is not enough to have moments of praise. All of life, each act, every gesture, even the smile of the human face,

---

17. Worthing, *Sacred Life of Words*, 217.
18. Cited by Collins, *Intimacy and the Hungers of God*, 190.
19. Peterson, *Working the Angles*, 45.

must become a human act of adoration, an offering, prayer. One should not offer what one has, but what one *is*.[20]

Second, when one speaks *to* the soul (in the second person). People speak to the soul all the time, often without realizing it. When lovers say, "I love you," or when a parent says to their child, "You are special," or when a spiritual accompanist says to the one accompanied, "What has God been saying to you through this experience?"... this is soul-work of the highest order. This kind of language is always offered "at depth," is undertaken with the greatest care and is usually carried out on the margins of a person's ability to express what is intended. We utter small words in the hope that they will carry big meanings. There are times when images, metaphors, and symbols allow space for insight to arrive intuitively which are capable of carrying the freight of meanings that need to be conveyed. This is especially true in instances where grief, trauma, and utter despair are being discussed or grappled with. Some things, because of their weight and fragility, are both hard to speak out and equally difficult (if not impossible) to hear.

And third: when we talk *about* the soul (in the third person). Since the soul is immortal, infinitely precious and forms the substance of Christian spirituality, it must be capable of being spoken about. This is especially true when rehearsing what the classical Christian spiritual tradition has to say about the soul and its instantiations of spiritual response, reaction and embrace regarding God's invitation to "draw near." This mode of soul-speech is also a key aspect of theological reflection when, for example, we read Edith Humphrey's exploration of those moments "when the Holy Spirit meets the human spirit."[21]

This third aspect of soul-speech is especially important when it comes to spiritual education, soul-instruction, and the "living out" of the Christian spiritual life. When reading the writings of Evelyn Underhill[22]—that great authority on what transpires in the interior life—without her using these words exactly, one always has the sense that the essence of Christian ministry is to *speak to souls* directly. And that means to transfer the substance of the Christian spiritual life from one person to the other in a dynamic transfer of what is essentially the life-force of the Christian life itself. Notice that almost everything Underhill writes is

20. Evdokimov, *Sacrament of Love*, 62.
21. Humphrey, *Ecstasy and Intimacy*
22. Underhill, *Concerning the Inner Life*.

about the soul, its interior life, and its flourishing and enlargement. Her task is to bring the soul into the light of direct observation, drawing it out from its habitual hidden resting place.

In summary—if we are to re-learn the language of the soul in our late-modern context, in which we have progressed beyond the secular to the post-secular, all three aspects of soul speech . . . in the form of prayer (first person), nurture (second person), and descriptions of the soul (third person) . . . will become an essential feature of human speech going forward. Christopher Fry captures this thought memorably in his poem, "Affairs are Now Soul Size":

> Thank God our time is now when wrong
> Comes up to meet us everywhere
> Never to leave us till we take
> The longest stride of soul humanity ever took—
> Affairs are now soul size.
> The enterprise is exploration into God.[23]

Further, if, as Mary Frohlich has argued, spirituality is "the human spirit fully in act,"[24] we have no other choice but to relearn—or if we have not learned it previously, to learn it for the first time—the language of the soul. This is an essential component of what it means to be human, and in our newly authorized post-secular age—which is both the age of the Spirit, and coincidentally the age of the soul—this is the critical task that awaits us.

The Four Defining Frames that Give Shape to the Work

In a work such as this, a "frame" provides a reference point and an interpretive lens which invites the writer to stay "on message" in the construction of the book, and the reader to remain within the intended remit of the overall project. At its simplest, a frame tells those involved in creating and interpreting this shared text "where to look" and "how to think" about its foremost concerns. The four frames that scaffold this book are: (1) The *Cultural* Frame: the Rise of the Post-Secular Mystics; (2) The *Christian* Frame: the Emergence of the Old/New Discipline of Christian Spirituality; (3) The *Personal* Frame: the Human Person in the Divine

---

23. Fry, *Sleep of Prisoners*, 49. Used with permission.
24. Frohlich, "Spiritual Discipline, Discipline of Spirituality," 71.

Presence; and 4) The *Interpretive* Frame: Dorothee Söelle's Hermeneutic of Hunger.

Addressing the first cultural frame allows us to establish a baseline in the social environment at the outer-most perimeter of meaning. Second, we step closer to the center by reminding ourselves of both the intransigence and potential responsiveness of the Christian faith regarding moves to recover its spiritual life. Third, viewing the spiritual life through the lived-experience of the human respondent is a key value and priority for this text. And fourth, Söelle's hermeneutic offers a way of viewing spiritual experience that is both positive and true to the deepest impulses of the human soul.

For reasons of brevity, it is my intention to simply name each of the frames, and to do no more than to open the door to each of the four concepts and to hang up the sign, "please enter." Since the 60 word-concepts that follow this brief explanatory introduction form the bulk of the subject-material of this book, I do not wish to spend more time in this preparatory section than is necessary. But by the same token, I am strongly of the opinion that a series of guiding statements regarding "how to read" the 60 word-concepts that form the language of the soul discussed in this book, is of utmost importance.

1) *The* Cultural *Frame: the Rise of the Post-Secular Mystics.*

On the surface, judging by the mainstream media, the "woke" cultural agenda, and the opinion-driven debates about whether God is welcome in the late Modern cultural context, it would seem there is no place for faith, religious commitment, or spiritual questing in the current cultural environment. But beneath that crusted surface-impression lies something altogether more urgent and compelling. A growing chorus of credible writers and thought-leaders are now beginning to indicate that there is a deep-level spiritual awakening taking place in Western society. Driven by a sense of personal brokenness, a fractured culture, a fragile earth, and the collapse of the Western myth of progress, a rapidly growing number of people (referred to as "post-secular mystics" by Eric Pickerill,[25] as the "Remix generation" by Tara Isabella Burton,[26] and detailed by David Tac-

---

25. Pickerill, "Secular Mystique," 133.
26. Burton, *Strange Rites*.

ey in his extended discussion of the "post-secular sacred"[27]) now identify as self-declared "spiritual seekers," who as yet live, work, think and seek outside the walls of any church, but who are nevertheless genuinely engaged on a spiritual quest for both self-discovery and sacred encounter. Most of these "post-secular mystics" are not Christian by any means, but they are actively and self-consciously engaged in a quest for meaning and wholeness. It is entirely possible that there are now more spiritual seekers in the West than there have ever been before (numerically speaking). Further, despite their being unaware of what Christianity has to offer in terms of a genuine and authentic form of spirituality, they may well be open to discovering how to be spiritual people in the context of the classical Christian spiritual tradition *if* they were to receive a careful and appropriately crafted invitation from trustworthy Christian teachers and exemplars. God takes their spiritual seeking seriously, and so must we.

2) *The* Christian *Frame: the Emergence of the Old/New Discipline of Christian Spirituality.*

While many Christian activists and leaders are all-too-aware of the situation, the "institutional" Church appears either unaware of the implications of the post-secular age we have now entered, or are resistant (perhaps out of a well-meaning but misguided refusal to engage with people who have a different spiritual or religious approach to life than their own) to engage in the emerging conversation about the emergence of spirituality in Western culture. Dorothy Butler Bass has observed that whereas Christianity was front-and-center in the first three Religious or Great Awakenings that swept through England and America in the eighteenth century, today the Christian voice has grown strangely silent in what she calls the "fourth religious awakening," an awakening that is deeply spiritual in nature.[28] But there are also positive signs that Christianity is making a constructive response to the arrival of the post-secular era, through the emergence of the distinct academic and practical discipline of Christian spirituality.

Historians in the field of Christian spirituality such as Bernard McGinn, Philip Sheldrake and Sandra Schneiders, will tell you that spirituality has long been foundational to the life of the church even as it has

---

27. Tacey, *Postsecular Sacred*.
28. Bass, *Christianity After Religion*.

itself undergone a variety of identity-shifts throughout Christianity's 2000-year history. Having taken a backseat to the pronouncements of the theologians and the race for Christianity to stay relevant and connected to contemporary culture in these modern times, Christian spirituality is currently undergoing a clear and observable renaissance in the churches and their educational and mission agencies. What I will argue here, however, is that what is missing from these resurgent formulations of spirituality is a proper language for the soul, and hence any clear processes for addressing what it means to be a "spiritual person" in the context of the Christian life. It is my conviction that these modalities have yet to be properly thought out, expressed, resourced, and implemented in the churches to address the needs of the children and youth of Christian parents and families—as well as the new generations of spiritual seekers who may, if they are courageous enough, walk into our churches declaring, "We would see Jesus" (John 12:21).

3) The Personal Frame: the Human Person in the Divine Presence.

Often theology is thought of as a process for uncovering truth from the biblical and historical sources belonging to the Christian faith. But theology can equally be understood as biography. When we speak about God, it is his person, character, words and works that take center-stage to demand our attention. These are the building blocks of theology and can rightly be characterized as comprising a "biography" of the Divine. We may also think about theology as the work of a particular theologian who brings his or her own biographical story and sensibility to the task of theologizing. People undertake their theological reflections mostly because of discoveries, issues and situations they have encountered in their own lives. No theology is possible without the theologian's own unique life-story, which exerts a direct and unavoidable influence on their thinking. We may also adopt the view that theology can explore the life of God in the lives of other people—what we might call "soul-biographies." This is certainly what James McClendon does in his book *Biography as Theology*.[29]

Christian spirituality touches on all three biographical projects outlined above but is especially relevant to this third approach, which prioritizes understanding God not so much as-he-is-in-himself, but instead,

---

29. McClendon, *Biography as Theology*.

as-he-is-in-his-creatures—especially his redeemed creatures. And this has biblical warrant, as Bonnie Thurston has intimated:

> What the New Testament 'talks about' is the human experience of God mediated by the person of Jesus of Nazareth, and any study of New Testament spirituality must begin with the fact that the text is a record of the human experience... Christianity revolves around the distinctive experience of the person of Jesus Christ.[30]

Some more traditionally inclined thinkers in the field of Christian spirituality might want to focus solely on God and doctrine rather than his human creatures. But as Thomas Aquinas taught, grace works through nature, meaning that if we accept that the human heart and soul is God's preeminent workplace, then that is as good a place as any to make the focus of our theological and spiritual enquiries. Jesus did that, too, when he looked deeply into the recesses of the human hearts, minds and spirits of the people he was speaking to in the Gospels (Matt 9:4, John 2:24), and the apostle Paul did exactly the same in Romans, where the old sin-sick human in Romans chapter 7 was transposed into its new glorified and conquering form in Romans chapter 8. Theology uncovers ways in which God addressed himself to his human audience, making the impact of the gospel on his human listeners receive and interiorize its powerful implications.

A dogmatic, doctrine-led approach is too easily *abstracted* from real human existence. But a fully orbed incarnational theology makes room for the gospel embedded in human life and its reaction *via* the response of faith. Observing the human person in the Divine presence is one of the primary focal points of this volume, and readers are invited to read, think and re-experience the 60 word-concepts offered here, through this experiential lens of God indwelling the soul of the human respondent. In addition, one of the key principles I have adopted in the writing of this text has been the refusal to separate the two components of faith we might regard as (a) propositional content of belief, and (b) how faith is interiorized and experienced in the life of the believer. Instead, I have sought to retain the integrity of the *what* of belief, the *how* of believing, and the *who* of the believer. It is my conviction that in the post-secular environment in which we currently live, thoughtful explorations of the "how" of belief by both existing and new believers, will automatically lead

---

30. Thurston and Ryan, *Philippians and Philemon*, 55.

to a discussion of the "what" of belief, focussed on a specifically Christian understanding by way of the biblical accounts of the life and teachings of Christ.

Christian spirituality is concerned not only with the Divine Person—who is the subject of worship, adoration, prayer, and obeisance—but also the human person who is equally an actor in the "drama" of Divine-human interaction. After all, human beings are the ones doing the worshipping, the adoring, the praying, and the obeisance within God's "call and response" pattern of communicating with his human creatures. Jesus said to his disciples, "*You* give them something to eat" (Mark 6:37). Every person has an important part to play and, as such, is worthy of analysis and enquiry in his or her own right.

4) The Interpretive *Frame: Dorothee Söelle's Hermeneutic of Hunger.*

Against the backdrop of the damaging "hermeneutics of suspicion" (a phrase coined by Paul Ricœur) that has dominated Western intellectual history from the time of René Descartes (1596–1650) to the present—Dorothee Söelle has offered a more positive, constructive, and relationally-oriented model for interpreting human beliefs, convictions and experiences. She has defined this approach as the "hermeneutic of hunger." Söelle's construct of the "hermeneutics of hunger" is not dissimilar to where Paul Ricœur 'landed' in his threefold movement of doubt, rejection and then finally recovery of the dominant model of belief in the making of meaning, to arrive at a re-appropriation of previous models of positive meaning and hopeful valuation.[31]

In her book *The Silent Cry*,[32] Söelle adopts an appreciative mode of inquiry to explore three basic human hungers: first, physical hunger in an age when food insecurity is an emerging problem in the world; second, women's hunger for recognition, a voice, and a valued identity in what has up until now been a male-dominated world; and third, spiritual hunger in the form of the hunger for God and the upward movement of the soul. For the purposes of our discussion here, we take this third element as our primary point-of-reference. A hermeneutic of suspicion (whose common denominator is the interpretation of all datum through the lens of doubt) is diametrically opposed to the transcendental aspect of the

---

31. Discussed by Scott-Baumann in *Ricœur and the Hermeneutics of Suspicion*.
32. Söelle, *Silent Cry*.

Christian spiritual life which reinterprets the material world (i.e., history, persons, ethics) through the lens of a larger scripturally defined trans-material yet historically compelling redemptive narrative. A hermeneutic of hunger takes seriously the need to listen to the shy movements of the soul with its subtle and erotic reactions of passionate response to the movements of God within the soul and has much to offer our engagement with the Christian spiritual life.

In my judgment, a hermeneutic of hunger provides the ideal mode of inquiry for allowing the soul to speak for itself, providing the Christian spiritual "actor-cum-subject of inquiry" with a voice. It has the potential to offer an interpretive frame that has the capacity to enable the classical Christian spiritual tradition to advance its knowledge of itself, the inner lives of its adherents (who Paul Ricœur describes as "believing souls"), and a meaningful contribution to better understanding the "hungry" state of the human heart. After all, it is our hungers and our passions that drive we human beings, as much as if not more so than our logic and reason.

A Dictionary of Christianity's "Lost" Words

In 2020, the British-Australian writer Pip Williams published a novel entitled *The Dictionary of Lost Words*.[33] In that text, Williams depicts a fictionalized account of the lives of the people who contributed to the compilation of the first edition of the *Oxford English Dictionary* (published in 1884). A less fictitious and more historically accurate account of the 70-year period during which word-entries were submitted, collated and incorporated into the dictionary, was published by Simon Winchester in 1999—some 20 years prior to Williams's *Dictionary of Lost Words*—in his book *The Surgeon of Crowthorne*.[34] Williams's novel remains faithful to the remarkable story of the progress of the dictionary during the tempestuous years of the First World War and the social upheaval of the women's suffrage movement in the post-war period. But it diverges from the historical details to tell the (fictional) life-story of the central character Esme Nicoll, who spent much of her early life at the Scriptorium—the garden shed that served as the hub of activities for the team of editors and compilers who worked on the first dictionary—where her father

---

33. Williams, *Dictionary of Lost Words*.
34. Winchester, *Surgeon of Crowthorne*.

Henry worked as an assistant editor. In Williams's novel, Esme begins her lifelong fascination with words by collecting "lost" and discarded words while sitting on the floor under the table where the editors worked feverishly to sort, collate, and define the words that would later comprise the dictionary. Each word is recorded on a small envelope-sized paper "slip." As the slips are processed by the editors, a small number of discarded or duplicate words fall to the floor where Esme eagerly gathers and stores them in a box beneath her friend Lizzie's bed.

I want to draw the reader's attention to the relevance of this fictionalized account in the *Dictionary of Lost Words* to our present project of building a dictionary of the interior life and the language needed to construct it. There are three points of application. The first is that the Christian faith has managed—for reasons of forgetfulness, the long and extenuated nature of its history, and its adopting more modern terms which are less akin to its own faith-traditions—to mislay its deep and transformative spiritual life. And much of this is due to its loss of spiritual language. To that end, I want to remind readers of those words, language-forms and concepts which are particularly apt and applicable for describing the Christian spiritual life as a lived-reality and a satisfying way of life.

Second, language is not static; it changes and adapts over time. Sometimes this is due to the way language evolves naturally over time in response to common usage. On other occasions the change is more intentional, for example, when words and the concepts they denote are "taken captive" for ideological reasons in the cultural contest between competing interest groups. I am amazed at how often I hear media personalities and secular commentators using religious and spiritual language in ways that are clumsy and misleading. Sometimes their misuse of the language is a clear case of "dropsy" where the speaker has no understanding of the meanings of the words they are using. But on other occasions, one suspects a more sinister aim of intentionally trying to destroy the fragile but real things they are handling. They are using the language of faith with the intent of scuttling or dismantling it. If Christianity does not wish its spiritual language to fall into the hands of its cultured despisers, it had best make efforts to carefully re-claim and re-infuse it with the meanings and intentions that retain the substance of our central convictions and spiritual intuitions. Otherwise, these precious things are likely to be stolen and re-appropriated by New Age and other competing forms of spirituality. The results of such a development would be disastrous.

And third, if we learn anything from dictionaries, it is that dictionary-entries capture how a word is used in everyday speech and its intended meaning in common usage. This is what forms the dictionary definition. To lose, or to have words discredited or devalued (for whatever reason) means that our lives become impoverished. Beyond the practicalities of basic communication, language is important for the creation and sustenance of meaning and truthfulness, especially in those instances where *nuance* is required. From the discipline of anthropology, we know how Eskimos distinguish linguistically between multiple forms of *ice*—fresh ice, pack ice, thin ice and so forth. In many Asian countries, where rice is the staple diet of billions of people, different kinds of *rice* can be distinguished by vocal inflections—husked rice, black rice, cooked rice, sweet rice and more.

Similarly, a dictionary of the soul—effectively a lexicon for the interior life—must be able to describe, evoke, contain, and invite people to discovery by referencing the many facets of the intangible and ethereal world of the soul and the spiritual life for discussion and participation.

Criteria for Selecting Word-Concepts

There are likely hundreds if not thousands of possible words I could have incorporated into the language of the soul that comprises the central project of this book. But in the end, I have selected 60 word-concepts for inclusion here. In narrowing my selection, I was guided by the following criteria:

1. *Drawn from Historical Sources.*

I wanted the words and concepts selected for inclusion in the dictionary to have a direct connection with the classical Christian spiritual tradition. Many of the words incorporated here have a demonstrated presence in the literature generated by Christian thinkers, educators, and practitioners from earlier periods of church history. The 60 word-concepts were chosen variously from such sources as apostolic, patristic, monastic, confessional and mystical repositories.

2. Descriptions of Spiritual Experience.

The 60 word-concepts selected for inclusion in this dictionary were to be directly related to the lived-experience of disciples and believers who have found themselves wanting to live a life of allegiance to Christ. In the partnership between God and each of his human respondents, it is the human actor whose story is recounted in the biblical records, hagiographical accounts, and biographies of spiritual formation.

3. What I Found Most Helpful in my own Teaching.

I included those word-concepts I had been using in my own practice as a teacher of the Christian spiritual life. These were the word-concepts that helped me personally to understand more of the Christian spiritual life, and which helped me to explore, explain and offer guidance to others regarding the inward life of the soul. I believe that is why Christian educators of all kinds—pastors, chaplains, spiritual directors and counsellors—have responded positively and generously to these ideas in the course of my teaching.

4. Drawn from the Best Contemporary Literature.

In addition to the language contained in the older forms of biblical, creedal, confessional mystical and devotional literatures, more contemporary secular sources also offer a significant body of words for narrating the life of the soul. Such words are contained in the lexicons of philosophy, psychology, biography, poetry and literary sources. While not all are specifically Christian, the word-concepts chosen from these sources intersect with the spiritual life so forcefully, and their sensibilities are so sympathetic to Christian perspectives, that they demand to be included, and to discard them would be a terrible loss.

5. The Substance of Faith held Interiorly.

The word-concepts selected for inclusion were focused on the interior life of the believing soul, where love, touch, encounter, and sanctity mingle and interconnect with one another. The language of: awakening, illumination, discovery, being loved, forgiven and made whole, of being in the

Divine presence and receiving the delights and benefits of being with the Beloved, the One we love, is the primary concern. This is where convictional knowledge makes its presence felt and works its way out in the lived experience of the believer.

6. For the Purposes of Instruction.

A curriculum for the interior life that is person-centered, experience-based, instruction-focused and discovery-led needs a dictionary of the soul, filled with word-concepts which are wise, revelatory and tender. This is to enable spiritual educators to speak to the mind, the heart, the will, and the soul which is open to instruction and hungry for new insights, new experiences, and new understandings vis-à-vis the spiritual quest that forms the most compelling focal point of their lives.

7. Central to the Operations of the Soul.

Those words-concepts chosen for inclusion in the dictionary must have some direct relevance to the in-built operations of the soul of the "sacred self," whose inward movements, beliefs, allegiances, prayer, worship, sighs and repentance are to be discussed and analyzed. After all, it is the "believing soul" who comes to life and to light because of their relatedness to God—that is the focal point and subject-matter of our endeavors in the curriculum for the interior life, and which calls for and necessitates a dictionary of the soul.

Clearly not all the words used here are Christian in their provenance; however, I would argue, all the words included here (in those cases where they originated from outside the Christian faith) are sympathetic to spiritual forms and meanings that are in-keeping with classical Christian spiritual life experience. They have something to offer to a lexicon of the Christian spiritual life, and when sympathetically and creatively applied in that way, can be sanctified for Christian use.

Audience, Outcomes, Limitations, Architecture

Regarding my intended audience, I wish to address myself to three main groups of people: first, teachers of the Christian spiritual life; second, Christian believers who already confess the faith; and third, non-Christians who find themselves as spiritual seekers in a world where God is calling them to a deeper life. I especially want to prioritize the first group—teachers of the Christian spiritual life—as the intended audience for this text, with the other two groups "listening in."

1. *Teachers of the Christian spiritual life.*

It is vital that those people working in churches, schools, seminaries, and colleges know how to draw the substance of the Christian faith out from the interior life of lived experience so as to express it with clarity, purpose and conviction. The philosopher of language Ludwig Wittgenstein observed that, "The limits of my language is the limits of my world."[35] Simply put—if we don't have language, we don't have concept, and if we don't have concept, there is little chance of communicating the substance of faith to our students, trainees, disciples and novices. True, the substance of faith can be difficult to grasp and express, leading Lucy Shaw to describe spirituality as an "amphibious life," meaning that it is invisible, subterranean, and underground in nature. She wrote:

> The poet Christian, the visionary writer, must stand with the seer and the prophet, one foot in heaven and one on earth, likewise centered on both spheres at once, perpetually torn by this dual focus as divine dreams are channelled through eyes and ears to pen and vocal cords.[36]

Likewise, mystics have consistently argued that the full extent of the mystery of God lies beyond human language and complete expression. To that end, negative theology and non-being come into play, and with that the notion of the *apophatic* (negative, hidden, un-sayable) language, which is inexpressible. But in much of our discussions here, it is not God in his pure essence we are seeking to grasp; it is God as-he-is-in-his-creatures, with particular reference to his redeemed creatures. Language is available to allow us to discuss this lesser goal of the human person in the Divine life. That language exists in the *kataphatic* (positive, accessible, communicable) domain which sits within human reach. True, the spiritual life is often more "caught than taught," but the co-mingling of a winsome living exemplar of the faith along with convincing words which explain who they are and why they are spiritual people, is both

---

35. Wittgenstein, *Tractatus Logico-Philosophicus*, 68.
36. Shaw, "Living in the Gap," 48.

incredibly powerful and irresistible because their lives exegete (on the outside) the faith they profess (on the inside). Hence Christian teachers need a dictionary of Christianity's lost-but-now-found words to enable them to carry out their task of spiritual education and instruction.

2. *Christian believers who already profess faith.*

Christianity exists wherever there are believers ready, willing, and able to "bear witness" to the faith they carry within themselves. Such people include those who intentionally live out their faith in their homes, families, churches, workplaces, and social networks. Christianity often becomes "lost" for no other reason than our losing touch with the Christian story, and the language which "carries" it in everyday discourse. I'm reminded of a mid-week Bible Study I once visited, where a young man reported with tears in his eyes that he had recently shared a lunchbreak with a Muslim work colleague. What he discovered was that his Muslim co-worker was able to put his faith into words in a way that was full of conviction and commitment, and that seemed to encompass his entire life. The Muslim man's testimony was powerful, convincing and ready-to-hand to explain his faith, whereas this young Christian man struggled to blurt out two or three sentences with any real conviction. His attempted response came awkwardly and seemingly without conviction. His words were—by his own admission "formless and void," and he left that conversation feeling deeply dissatisfied with his performance. Realizing that he had grown used to not talking about his faith, he resolved to "find his words," as he might have said to his children when they were first learning to speak.

3. *Non-Christian spiritual seekers.*

Those persons who are looking for a higher form of life and have set their hearts on *godfaring* may also benefit from this book and the word-concepts it recommends. We have to take it on face value that these people are genuine, that their spiritual quests are authentic, and we must recognize that God is also the primary motivator—along with their human needs, hungers and appetites—in their seeking. Most contemporary seekers presuppose that Christianity is a dead religion, offering nothing of spiritual value. It is our task to convince them otherwise. Why is it that they (and sometimes by default we) are happy to associate deep mystery, truthfulness, and a bone-rattling form of inner life with Buddhism or Eastern mysticism but assign a milksop form of the spiritual life to Christianity? The language of awakening, of illumination, of enlightenment, of the power to change lives, of spiritual guidance, of transformation, of new beginnings, of cleansing, forgiveness, reconciliation, restoration, wholeness, and holiness—all this and more lies within our own inherited lexicon of Christian spiritual language and experience. We need to remember how to use it, to speak it, and to live it as if it were true in the here and now. True for us, true for them, true for the world.

Secondly, what are my intended outcomes for this text? I want to place in the hands of interested readers of every persuasion, a Christian language for the soul, which takes the interior life of the human respondent seriously, and which enables them to undertake their spiritual journeys with greater awareness, intensity, and conviction. And as a result of knowing *how* to be a spiritual person, I want for them to begin to think about God's invitation to follow Christ (the *who* and the *what* of a fully Christian spiritual faith-commitment). The human person made aware of the sacred (their own life, in the cosmos, in love, in sex, as spoken of by other religious and spiritual traditions) is in itself beautiful and valuable. But how much more valuable is the human person who is actually drawn up into the Divine life, living in the love of Christ, empowered by the Holy Spirit, committed to the adventure that is the redeemed life, and aware of the new creation that is the direct outcome of conversion, and the new beginnings that result from becoming a genuine disciple of Christ?

Third, what limitations accompany this text? The spiritual life that burns in the human heart determines every decision we ever make and lies at the root of every action we ever take. This makes the words, concepts and processes that enable us to know and participate in the Christian spiritual life something of great importance. Of course, I recognize that the 60 word-concepts I have selected for exploration in this book cannot do justice to the wonders of the Christian spiritual life in its entirety. And there is undoubtedly a very personal link to my own thought-life, my belief-system and my teaching. These are the words I have used in the courses I have taught on spirituality, and which have had a nurturing and formative impact on my own spiritual journey. Other writers, teachers and thinkers would likely adopt a slightly different approach, and a different set of words or key-concepts. As such, what I have offered in the pages that follow is not intended to be the "final word" on the topic or in any sense definitive, rigid or complete—as if it were the only possible curriculum or lexicon for opening up the interior life. Rather, what I have sought to do is to humbly suggest that in the age of the Spirit, a language for the soul needs to be the focus of ongoing enquiry, and therefore needs to be something generative and unfinished—a continuing task for the life of the church where thinkers, teachers, believers, and practitioners make the language of the faith and its unending renewal something of abiding interest and attention. I therefore offer the following 60 word-concepts as a provisional curriculum for the interior life, and as a project leading *towards* a more comprehensive lexicon of Christian spirituality. As a result, I invite others working in this space—in which we are all "eternal beginners"[37] in the school of the heart—to take what is of use here, and to use it in their own contexts, to see what works, adding new words, concepts, and ideas where they think necessary. In the future, I fully expect to see other writers making their own contributions to this dictionary—especially in multicultural, inter-faith and inter-generational contexts.

And fourthly, what is the "architecture" of this dictionary of Christianity's lost words as they are laid out in this book? For reasons of practicality, I felt it necessary to break the 60 word-concepts into two sections. The first section is comprised of ten word-concepts, where I have tried to lay a foundational understanding of the human soul engaged with the spiritual life. Trying to remain true to my overall goal of giving the reader a language for the soul and its operations, I have tried to build a conceptual bridge even as we are crossing it, so that word-concepts I have provided serve as steppingstones. So, for example, entry #1 *Homo Spiritualis* identifies the true nature of the human person as something innately spiritual. Entry #5 *Call and Response* describes God's normative pattern of speaking to humanity (i.e., the "call"), and of each person's response to that call within their own soul. And entry #7 *The Soul at White Heat* seeks to capture the very moment or instance when the soul is engaged in the "act" of responding to the Divine. Note that these entries are not presented in alphabetical order. Instead, they have been arranged to establish a foundational understanding of the human soul in the Divine presence, so that by the end of the tenth entry, readers (novices and advanced readers alike) will be well-equipped to progress to the body of word-concepts that remain.

The second section is comprised of 50 word-concepts, arranged in alphabetical order for convenience, whose intention is to provide a

---

37. To borrow the philosopher Edmund Husserl's phrase about our need to continually be open to discovering new aspects of any given phenomena.

more general overview of the Christian spiritual life from a variety of sources—historical, philosophical, psychological, theological, and literary. Concepts such as #20 *Concursus* demonstrate the way in which the human actor cooperates with the work of God's Spirit within them to achieve kingdom outcomes, while retaining their own essential freedom as human persons. Entry #31 *God's Workshop* identifies the human self as "the work"—that is, the place where spiritual growth and formation occurs. And entry #57 *Soliloquy* discusses the "self-talk" that goes on inside the "believing soul" whenever a decision is to be made regarding the cost of spiritual commitment, or the death of the ego.

Two things remain to be said here. First, the content of this book differs from standard dictionaries of Christian spirituality in that it does not seek to provide an all-inclusive summary of historical, biblical or theological concepts relating to standard representations of the spiritual life. Here, the focus is entirely on the human experience of the sacred, or as I have described it throughout the course of this introductory section, the human person in the Divine life. I have made no attempt to present everything in its full complexity. Other writers have begun that work, but—I would argue—there is more to be said.[38] Second, most if not all the word-concepts chosen for inclusion here already exists in the literature, and to that extent already have a life of their own, albeit a life which I have argued is inadequately developed and fragmentary. It awaits the moment when they can be brought together into a single repository of faith description and spiritual direction that has the human receptor and respondent fully in mind. This is that moment.

How to Use this Dictionary of Christian Words

Some of the key phrases I have used throughout the book are: "the human person in the Divine life"; "a language for speaking to, with and about the soul"; "the substance of the interior life which forms the essential core of our humanity"; and "that moment when the Holy Spirit meets with the

---

38. For example, in a non-Christian context, the book by Steven Nolan and Margaret Holloway, entitled *A-Z of Spirituality* (London: Bloomsbury, 2013); and in a specifically Christian context, the *New SCM Dictionary of Christian*, edited by Philip Sheldrake (London: SCM, 2005)—both list every possible category, doctrine and subject related to spirituality (Christian and otherwise). A particularly useful resource for understanding spiritual experience spread across a range of disciplines, religious affiliations and confessional contexts that is much broader than a specifically Christian application is Jeff Astley's book entitled *Religious and Spiritual Experience* (London: SCM, 2020).

human spirit." To explore each of these aspects of the human experience of God, I propose four ways this language can be put to good use by readers of this volume.

1. As a Navigational Tool.

Most if not all twenty-first century readers will be attuned to the three "turns" that have taken place during their lifetimes, in the form of the turn to the *self*, the turn to *subjectivity/interiority*, and the turn to *experience*. And with these turns comes an enormous hunger to know, to explore, to experience and to navigate towards something invisible yet real, within our grasp yet somehow strangely ungraspable. Since we all have a soul and are aware of its presence yet its strange non-availability, those people who function as spiritual guides need a language for the interior life. Sam Keen describes the Holy in this way:

> It is in plain sight, but cannot be seen. It is never silent, but cannot be heard. It is not lost, but cannot be found. God is unknowable, the soul unfathomable. But the Holy may appear at any moment.[39]

The same can be said of the spiritual and the sacred. When it appears, we must be ready to welcome it. And ironically, we do this by using language that is connected with the soul, that creates the conditions for the sacred to appear.

2. As a Resource for Teaching People How to Believe.

In the season we now call the *post-secular*, when faith and belief are returning to mainstream understandings and expectations, people are familiar with the inward sensations of their own spirit and oftentimes the Holy Spirit moving within them, but they have no words or language to describe the longings, the discoveries, the revelations and the awakenings that accompany their inward journeys. The Christian faith has long had a tradition of knowing *what* to believe in terms of the creeds, the doctrines, and the confessions that apply at the key moments such as birth, baptism, coming-of-age, marriage, childbearing and death. What is offered here is not intended to replace the doctrinal "core" of Christian confession.

---

39. Keen, *Hymns to an Unknown God*, 73.

Rather, it is intended to connect these things to the life of the soul in order for the human participant in the spiritual life to appropriate these realities for themselves. *Knowing how to believe* is a key component to knowing how to become a spiritual person at a time when such things are once again in vogue.

3. As a Means of Speaking to Souls.

The essence of Christian ministry is knowing how to speak to souls. Guiding people on their spiritual pathways through the use of Scripture and classical Christian teachings towards discipleship and commitment requires that ministry practitioners know how to address themselves to the souls of individuals, groups and entire faith-communities. This skill has declined to an all-time low in an age when the church has accommodated itself to the managerialisms and techniques of a materialist and acquisitive age. To speak to souls requires a language appropriate to the interior life. Learning these and other word-concepts that apply directly to the exertion of the self/human spirit in discipleship, sanctification and consecration is an essential feature of Christian ministry in present-day settings. To be true to Christ and his gospel requires that we learn or re-learn the language of faith.

4. As a Resource for Spiritual Education and the Nurture of Souls.

The life of any discipline is embedded in its literature, its language, and its models of education and instruction. This is especially true of Christian spirituality. Christian spirituality is blessed with a 2000-year-long tradition that has been in possession of abundant riches and resources. Tragically, however, many people are unaware of these resources. Too many of our people are baptized, life-long, card-carrying believers who know little or nothing about the faith, or its application to the souls they carry within themselves. If we are to offer an effective spiritual education program that properly nourishes and nurtures the souls of tomorrow's future-believers, there must not only be a language for expressing the faith and conveying its core substance, but also a language for educating (nurturing and forming) the lives, ethics, choices, characters and personal qualities towards Christlikeness into the future. Without the appropriate language for this task, no such shaping power and influence will be possible. In today's environment, to speak "Christianly" requires us—with a great deal of urgency—to learn to speak spiritually.

How Well Do You Know Fire?

Fire is a wonderful servant but a terrible master. As the hottest, driest continent on earth, Australia suffers from frequent bushfires and their disastrous consequences. But at a time when global temperatures are rising, Australia is not alone in this regard. Now, rather terrifyingly, parts of the United Kingdom, Europe, California, Türkeye, the Amazon and even the Arctic have either recently burned or are presently burning. With the increasingly hot summers that have impacted the east coast of Australia since the early 2000s, a series of destructive wildfires have visited themselves on virgin forests, agricultural land, rural farm-scapes, townships and even the outskirts of cities at the height of summer conditions that have been supercharged by heatwave conditions. Many hundreds of people, thousands of properties, and millions of wild and domestic animals have been destroyed, severely damaged, maimed or killed.

As a result, the Australian Federal government has aired a television campaign that poses the question, "How well do you know fire?" Its purpose is to educate urban populations who are increasingly disconnected from nature about the dangers presented by heatwaves and bushfires which are increasing in frequency and intensity. As a part of that awareness campaign, families and households are encouraged to develop evacuation plans in the event of a wildfire. When the conflagration comes to your street, there has to be a way of escape. But where does one go to when one's house is burning? It turns out that we don't know the dangers of fire very well and are ill-equipped to survive a wildfire.

In the *supernatural* dimension, fire is often understood as a cleansing and healing visitation brought by the Spirit to prepare a person, group or community to progress upwards in the journey towards God. In the biblical record, scenes of Moses's vision of the burning bush; Elijah's fiery defeat of the prophets of Baal; the coming of the Holy Spirit in the book of Acts accompanied by tongues of fire; and St. Paul's exhortation to the Roman Christians to "never be lacking in zeal, but keep your spiritual fervor/fire" (Rom 12:11), alert us to the potency of fire as an image for understanding the spiritual life. In the seventeenth-century, Blaise Pascal experienced a flaming encounter with God that utterly transformed his life. Following his death in 1662, a note was found sewn into the lining of his coat that read:

> In the year of Grace, 1654, on Monday, 23rd November, feast of St Clement, Pope and Martyr . . . From about 10:30 in the evening until 12:30, FIRE. God of Abraham, God of Isaac, God of Jacob, not of the philosophers and scholars. Certitude. Certitude. Feeling. Joy. Peace. God of Jesus Christ. My God and your God. Forget all the world and everything but God. He is to be found only in the ways taught in the Gospel. Greatness of the human soul . . . May I never be separated from him! . . . Renunciation total and sweet.[40]

The dazzling, ravishing, and revelatory event of the visitation of the Spirit is a normative feature in the spiritual life, as attested to by the saints, mystics, seers, and wise ones who have encountered it throughout Christian history. In the twenty-first century, however, in a season marked by a "return of Spirit," a distracted, risk-averse and ill-prepared society has lost touch with the spiritual life that once energized it. In the process, many have become strangers to their own souls and the inner dynamic of the Spirit within them. Long ago, Gregory of Nazianzus observed that although we are earthly creatures who feel ourselves to be weak and frail, nevertheless we are joined to God by means of an innate connection that reminds us of our spiritual dignity, "making us aware that we are both the greatest and the most lowly of creatures, earthly and heavenly, temporal and immortal, heirs of both light and *fire*."[41] This powerful spiritual insight remains true today, as Vladimir Lossky reminds us:

> Angels and spirits in the service of God participate in the brightness of this fire . . . This fire expels demons and destroys sin. It is the power of the resurrection, the reality of eternal life, the enlightenment of holy souls, the strengthening of the rational powers.[42]

The question "How well do you know fire?" opens the door to the possibility that citizens of the twenty-first century—both believing Christians who have become strangers to their spiritual selves, and the rapidly growing number of post-secular "mystics" who find themselves called upon to walk the path of the pilgrims—need to be reacquainted

---

40. Pascal, *Pensées*, 309–10.
41. Daley, *Gregory of Nazianzus*, 79.
42. Lossky, *Mystical Theology of the Eastern Church*, 219.

with the spiritual ecology within them, and to attend to the work of God in this new season of the *post-secular*.

It is my contention that we will not be able to move forward until we have gone beyond Sue Monk-Kidd's diagnosis that we have lost the ability to probe the soul, to know and refine its experiences, to locate a language that is big enough, and a lexicon of concepts sturdy enough for the task of knowing what we mean when we speak of *soul*, *spirit*, the *holy* and the *whole*. This book presents a dictionary of Christianity's language for the soul for consideration, which contains words and concepts that have been carefully mined from their historical repositories and literary resting places. The dictionary is needed because too many citizens of our twenty-first century Western society are not adequately acquainted with the experience of spiritual fire, having become strangers to the spiritual life within them, and disconnected from the power of *spirit* and the Holy Spirit whose role is to awaken and infuse them with new life.

Part Two

Foundational Word-Concepts

1. Homo Spiritualis

IT IS A DIFFICULT thing God has asked of we poor human creatures... to live out our three-score years and ten suspended between life and death, good and evil, heaven and hell, time and eternity. We hardly know how to measure the barometer of our interior life, let alone know how to respond to God's visitations there. And as for the possibility of describing these things to others... it's like catching water in a net.[1] So here we are—half-made human creatures who long to be re-connected to the God who made us, marooned somewhere in spiritual outer-space without a compass. We suspect that if we were to scratch our animal nature, underneath there is an angelic life, but we have no way of knowing whether the gleams of eternity that glisten in our eyes belong to us or are refracted light from elsewhere. We cannot seem to break through the chains of our mortal existence... we suspect but we cannot fully know that we possess within ourselves the seeds of eternity.

What is humanity's truest disposition? The psalmist posed the question, "What is man that you are mindful of him, the son of man that you care for him?" (Ps 8:4–5). St. Augustine inquired of himself, "What, then, am I, Oh my God? Of what nature am I?"[2] Alexander Pope described humanity as a creature suspended halfway between heaven and earth when

---

1. Webb, *Like Catching Water in a Net*.
2. Augustine, *Confessions*, 219.

he penned the lines, "Created half to rise, and half to fall; Great lord of all things, yet a prey to all; Sole judge of Truth, in endless Error hurl'd; The glory, jest and riddle of the world!"[3] Gregory of Nazianzus (329–90) described his own experience when he wrote, "In my earthly character, I am attached to the life I have down here, but being also a divine particle, I bear in my heart the desire for immortality."[4] If one looks beyond our enfleshed existence, we are able to see something deeper than the materiality of our mortal bodies. Spirit beckons us to look more deeply to see what is eternal.

As a species, are we *homo sapiens* (Latin for man [generic] the intelligent creature); *homo faber* (man the toolmaker); *homo viator* (man the curious creature who seeks answers); *homo ludens* (man the playful creature); *homo intellectus* (man the thinking creature); *homo religiousus* (man the worshipping creature); *homo politicus* (man the political creature); or *homo economicus* (man the economic creature)? There is good reason for suggesting that we are all of these . . . *and more*. But there is even better reason for believing that our primary nature is *homo spiritualis* (man the spiritual creature); on the basis that we were designed and created for a relationship with God, as suggested by St. Augustine who wrote, "You have made us for yourself and our hearts are restless until they find their rest in you";[5] and as stated by the Westminster Confession, "The chief end of man is to glorify God and to enjoy him forever."

The "sense of immortality" that we carry within us means we have the capacity to rise above the angels, but it is a capacity that must be developed through a lifelong process of spiritual formation and sanctification. The tension for us is to come to understand the "call to rise" and to know what to do with the spiritual and psychic tensions that wrestle within us for supremacy and superiority. If unresolved, these tensions threaten to destroy us (at worst), or (at best) to lead us on passionate but blind journeys into who-knows-where. If we are lucky (or graced!)— someone in the form of an angel, a wise instructor, our conscience, or the Spirit of God within us providing us with a "right mind," will come to us and we will awaken. "Wake up, O sleeper, rise from the dead, and Christ will shine on you" (Eph 5:14).

The spiritual nature of the human person encompasses a profound and integral aspect of our existence, transcending the boundaries of the

---

3. Pope, "Essay on Man," 516.
4. Cited by Clement, *On Human Being*, 34.
5. Augustine, *Confessions*, 1.

material world. Rooted in the quest for meaning and connection, spirituality delves into the essence of our being, and seeks a higher purpose beyond everyday conceptions. It is an exploration into the inner self, a journey that goes beyond standard materialist modes of existence, to embrace eternal mysteries and universal truths. Human spirituality, however, is not simply a journey inward. It is a journey towards God, to embrace transcendent realities which lie above and outside human existence.

According to John Wesley:

> The body is not the man; the man is not only a house of clay, but an immortal spirit; a spirit made in the image of God; an incorruptible picture of the God of glory; a spirit that is of infinitely more value than the whole earth; of more value than the sun, moon, and stars, put together; yea, than the whole material creation. Consider that the spirit of man is not only of a higher order, of a more excellent nature, than any other part of the visible world, but also more durable; not liable either to dissolution or decay.[6]

Frequently in books and sermons, flesh and spirit are placed in opposition to each other. This is understandable to the extent that flesh is thought to represent the fallen, sinful element of human mortality, whereas spirit is typically associated with that which bears the image of God (the *Imago Dei*). However, this un-biblical dualism misrepresents human nature, and does an injustice to the redeemed person—body and spirit together—in whom the divine image exists as a spark at creation and is perfected in redemption through sanctification and spiritual formation.

According to Vladimir Lossky, "In general, Christian anthropology has not received sufficient theological elaboration."[7] Although not all theology is explicitly anthropological—since God is the proper subject of worship, adoration, and reflection—nevertheless, anthropology forms a significant part of theology. Spirituality picks up on this anthropological directed-ness in theology, and provides a place for what Henry Scougal has called, "the life of God in the soul of man."[8] From the human standpoint and informed by biblical teaching regarding God's redemptive purposes under the auspices of the Spirit, half of theology is anthropology

---

6. Wesley, *"What is Man?"* 171.
7. Lossky, *In the Image and Likeness of God*, 185.
8. Scougal, *Life of God in the Soul of Man*.

(i.e., God's work in redeemed humanity), and half of anthropology is spirituality (i.e., the Spirit's revealing, teaching, guiding and forming work in the human spirit). The starting point for a Christian understanding of the spiritual life is that the nature of the human person who participates in that life is *homo spiritualis*.

2. Spiritual Quest

Alistair McGrath has offered a series of biblical images that represent key themes in the Christian spiritual life. They are: *the feast; the journey; exile; the struggle; purification; the internalization of faith; the desert; ascent; darkness and light;* and *silence*.[9] But there is one important image missing from McGrath's list . . . that of *spiritual quest*. The notion of quest is implicit in each of the themes he identifies—especially those of journey, desert, and ascent—but quest warrants consideration as a unique subject in its own right. The quest for God is *the* central motif in Christian spirituality, expressed through worship, pilgrimage, repentance, costly discipleship, the call to holy orders (from the priesthood, to monasticism, to mission, charitable works and Christian leadership), and the mystical journey inwards towards union with God.

In the church calendar, the season of Epiphany—which occurs immediately after Christmas—explores the quest of the Magi as they follow the star to find "the one who has been born King of the Jews. We have seen the star in the east and have come to worship him" (Matt 2:2). Epiphany is a biblical case study in questing after Christ. Since the definition of quest is to undertake a journey in search of something or someone of great value, the season of Epiphany invites all who seek after Christ to deepen their search. Jesus' promise is, "Ask and it will be given to you; seek and you will find; knock and the door will be opened to you" (Matt 7:7).

Recent decades have seen "quest religiousness" become an important topic of inquiry in the field of religious studies, informed by the psychology of religion. One leading contributor to this development has been Daniel Batson along with his associates.[10] In summary of Batson and associates' work, Klassen and McDonald write, "Batson defined quest as an approach to religion that embraces the complexity and ambiguity of

---

9. McGrath, *Christian Spirituality*, 88–108.

10. Batson, *Religious Experience*, 1982, and Batson et al., *Religion and the Individual*, 1993.

life while avoiding overly simplistic, trite answers. Furthermore, quest is seen as an open-ended approach to religion that may or may not include an affirmation of a transcendent reality."[11] In their work on integrating theology, spirituality and psychology, LeRon Shults and Steven Sandage shifted the focus from religion as a general category to spirituality as a distinct process, which assists our inquiry here. Shults and Sandage state:

> Spiritual questing is the movement of spiritual formation, the *becoming* that can result in second-order transformations of *being*. Questing is the epistemological search that potentially transforms developmental ontology, the willingness to not know in the hope of coming to know more deeply and intimately. In biblical terms, questing is asking, seeking and knocking.[12]

Richard Flory and Donald Miller have also explored the concept of "spiritual quest" in the American post-boomer youth generation.[13] They developed a typology of four emerging forms of the spiritual quest as undertaken by that generation. The first type are the "Innovators" such as emerging churches which exhibit a willingness to introduce diverse non-traditional practices to increase the sense of belonging and experience felt by adherents. The second type are the "Appropriators" who borrow trends and developments from the larger culture to give Christianity a contemporary look and feel, to increase their appeal to consumer-oriented attenders. The third type are the "Resistors" who prefer reason over the relevancy of contemporary cultural practices to defend the faith against heretical influences from outside. And the fourth type are the "Reclaimers" whose priority is to appeal to the perceived authority and practices of the early church and its historical tradition.[14]

Evan Howard places the category of quest within the larger schema of conversion, by making use of Lewis Rambo's stage-model of conversion in the form of: stage 1 = context; stage 2 = crisis; stage 3 = quest; stage 4 = encounter; stage 5 = interaction; stage 6 = commitment; and stage 7 = consequences.[15] While the category of quest fits well within this inventory, I would argue that it is an all-encompassing theme operating at every level of Rambo's stage-analysis.

---

11. Klassen and McDonald, "Quest and Identity Development," 190.
12. Shults and Sandage, *Transforming Spirituality*, 234.
13. Flory and Miller, *Finding Faith*.
14. Flory and Miller, *Finding Faith*, 13–15.
15. Howard, *Brazos Introduction to Christian Spirituality*, 241–45.

The Desert Fathers had a saying, "Having found him, yet we seek him still." Gregory of Nyssa stated in his *Life of Moses*:

> The knowledge of God is a mountain steep indeed and difficult to climb—the majority of people scarcely reach its base. If one were Moses, he would ascend higher and hear the sound of trumpets which . . . become louder as one advances . . . The vision of God . . . [is] never to be satisfied in the desire to see him. But one must always, by looking at what he can see, rekindle his desire to see more. Thus, no limit would interrupt growth in the ascent to God.[16]

In his book *Godfaring*,[17] Francis Clark describes the process of venturing after God as:

> Our pilgrim wayfaring . . . taking us towards God but (which) has its starting point in God . . . It is God himself who empowers us at every moment with strength to fare onwards to the goal; that the created universe, which is the terrain of our wayfaring, is translucent with the creative light of God, presaging his full revelation of himself; that all that we encounter in experience on the way, whether we fare well or ill, comes from God, tells us of God, and calls us to God; and beyond all our imagining, that God the Son has himself taken human form and stepped into time to join us on the way, where, his pilgrim staff a cross, he fares forth with us on the journey as our brother, guide, and saviour; and that he is not only with us in our Godward wayfaring but is himself the Way and our journey's end.[18]

According to Gregory of Nyssa, in a second attempt to grasp the concept of the vision of God and the believing soul's attempt to grasp it:

> This truly is the vision of God: never to be satisfied in the desire to see him. But one must always, by looking at what he can see, rekindle his desire to see more. Thus, no limit would interrupt growth in the ascent to God, since no limit to the Good can be found nor is the increasing of desire for the Good brought to an end because it is satisfied.[19]

---

16. Gregory, *Life of Moses*, 93.
17. Clark, *Godfaring*.
18. Clark, *Godfaring*, xiv–xv.
19. Gregory, *Life of Moses*, 116.

As with the claim of the Desert Fathers that, "Having found him, yet we seek him still"... all those who have encountered Christ for themselves as the one who is the "pearl of great price" (Matt 13:45–46) wish to continually enter his presence and to "be with him." Nothing will satisfy them or sustain them other than their desire to embrace the one who has first embraced them. Gerald May writes of the deep-seated nature of the spiritual quest, "The journey toward greater love is not something to be instilled in people; it is already there to be tended, nurtured and affirmed."[20] And as Henri de Lubac has observed, "Those who ascend never cease ascending."[21] It is what drives the seeker onwards on his/her spiritual quest is the hunger for a "Promised Land" which has only partly been sighted, and into which they long to enter in answer to the siren song of God's Spirit within the human soul.

3. The Believing Soul

The spiritual life does not disclose itself on the pages of a book, in a petrie dish, or through a piece of art or music. Instead, it unfolds in the lives of human persons, where it can sometimes lie dormant for long years; or when attended to and consciously developed at critical moments in a person's life, can erupt into a new form of life. It is human persons with eternal souls that play host to the life of the Spirit who takes up residence and lives out the larger Divine life in the smaller but no-less-important arena of enfleshed persons. With Paul Ricœur, we may refer to such persons as "believing souls."[22] They are the operating center where the "felt presence of God" makes itself real, and where the interior life we are concerned with in this volume takes place.

The notion of the "believing soul" derives from Paul Ricœur's book *The Symbolism of Evil*.[23] As a philosopher of sacred texts and an interpreter of the thought-worlds of readers who embrace the reality-structures they discover there as their own, Ricœur sought to "sympathetically re-imagine" the sacred meanings that inhabit the minds and hearts of believing souls as if they themselves were a kind of text. Thus the intuitions and feelings that unfold in their meaning-making processes were

20. May, *Awakened Heart*, 54.
21. de Lubac, *Discovery of God*, 164.
22. Ricœur, *Symbolism of Evil*.
23. Ricœur, *Symbolism of Evil*, 27.

his fundamental concern. Ricœur was at pains not to place the "believing soul" in an idealized world where everything was perfect. Instead, he placed the believing soul in a flawed world where sin, evil and fear threatens to blind one's mind and confuse one's spiritual perceptions. Within the tensions of the existential moment, Ricœur pictured a process of restoration of the human person to reclaim their originally created "wholeness" through redemption and sanctification.

Merold Westphal extended Ricœur's quest to understand the world from the point-of-view of the believer. He wrote, "the crucial concern . . . is [to think of] the sacred as a way of solving the problem of guilt and death."[24] For Westphal, it is necessary to "permit the believing soul to speak."[25] This openness to the voice of the "sacred self"[26] may seem strange to anyone who has grown up in the secular age, when the voice of the religious person is to be repressed on the grounds that their faith is an embarrassment to the principles of the Enlightenment and its associated ideals of human progress. There are those who promote the idea that the notion of guilt inherent in religious conviction is a sign of a "sick soul" that ought not to be tolerated in an age of human freedom and self-confidence. But Max Scheler has presented the possibility that the believer's sense of guilt and impulse to repentance *via* self-accusation can be seen in a positive light.[27] The remembering of one's sin before God may not actually be an act of self-harm on the part of the believing soul. Instead, it can be an act of "moral rejuvenation"[28] that leads to a "putting right" of one's past, and therefore a making *right/righteous* before God in the present time and into the future, because of Christ who "loved us and gave himself for us" (Eph 5:2).

In the Scriptures of the Judeo-Christian tradition, humanity is not excluded from God's table. Instead, the opposite is true. The covenants, laws, sacrifices, liturgies and teachings are what Mercia Eliade calls the "doors of the gods,"[29] meaning that they are points of connection between God and humankind. Ordinarily speaking, humanity—because we are sinful, profane and imperfect—might be seen as worthy only of exclusion from God's grace. But in the biblical record, God does the unexpected

24. Westphal, *God, Guilt and Death*, 16.
25. Westphal, *God, Guilt and Death*, 12.
26. Csordas, *Sacred Self*.
27. Scheler, *On the Eternal in Man*, 37.
28. Scheler, *On the Eternal in Man*, 42.
29. Eliade, *Sacred and the Profane*, 27.

and places humankind at the center of salvation history. God chooses to speak "through" his agents in the form of the prophets, priests, kings, servants, and saints. Their names, characters, words and actions fill-up the accounts of salvation history from the first word to the last. In the Divine economy, it is normal for Spirit to co-opt flesh to its purposes. And so it is right for Ricœur to want to listen attentively to the experiences of the believing soul, and for Westphal to want to make space for the believing soul to speak. After all, they are the "the human core of spirituality," as Daniel Helminiak has observed.[30]

God's normal pattern is to invite his human creatures to draw near to attend to his Word, his presence and power in order to consecrate themselves to the sacred form of life he calls them to embrace. And that form of life is *absolute*. "After consecration, there is no more 'life as usual.'"[31] Having undergone the transformations that taking up residence in the Divine presence implies, the believing soul begins to bear witness to what they have seen, heard, and experienced. This makes the believing soul a crucial part of the overall evidence for God in the world. If God gives believers a voice to be "witnesses of God,"[32] then we who observe, teach, and instruct them must also do the same. Their souls are—after all—ciphers of eternity and the thing in the spiritual life that most deserves to be nurtured, taught, drawn out, and instructed. Ricœur's concept of the faith of the "believing soul" and the response to the Divine invitation to "Draw near," enables us to examine the faith-response of the person who believes as a valid theological, philosophical, and spiritual enquiry. Our prioritizing of the "believing soul" and their internalizing of the sacred texts they have read, enables us to read them as if they were living "texts" themselves. The concept of "believing souls" enables soul-guides and spiritual instructors to account for the inner transformations produced in the inner life and to offer guidance, instruction and soul-care needed for the soul's continued journey towards God.

4. Reception

As a general concept, "reception" holds a special place in the diffusion of ideas, beliefs, language-uses, arts and practices that give shape to the

---

30. Helminiak, *Human Core of Spirituality*.
31. Panikkar, *Blessed Simplicity*, 91.
32. de Lubac, *Discovery of God*, 158.

building blocks of history and culture. Selected examples include the "reception" of French language by English-speaking intellectuals as a sign of *haute couture* (high culture); or the "reception" of ancient myths and fairy tales into childrens' bedtime stories such as Hansel and Gretel, Old Mother Hubbard or Rapunzel; or the "reception" of indigenous music, dance and art-forms into contemporary Western artistic expression.

In Christian theology and spirituality, the idea of reception designates the two-way movement between God's speaking and human listening. Since God is the communicator *par excellence*, his speaking is intended to evoke a definitive response from his human audience: "My word that goes out from my mouth . . . will not return to me empty but will accomplish . . . the purpose for which I sent it" (Isa 55:11). Before human creatures can receive, understand, and act on God's invitation into covenant-relationship, God must first speak to reveal himself through what is commonly called "revelation." In the process of God's self-revelation to humanity, a communication "goes out" from God in the form of an open invitation to participate in his Divine life. Conversely, the opposite mirror-image of God's self-disclosure *via* revelation is found in the human audience's *reception* of the "incoming" message. In this way, revelation and reception form an integral corresponding pair that can be described as a dynamic interplay between God's speaking and his human audience's listening. In the same way that God's speaking is free and open, so the human reception of God's speaking is also free and open, being received, understood, and interpreted as God's gracious and hospitable invitation to live in his kingdom, to eat at his table, to participate in his life, and to take part in his redemptive purposes. And human reception of God's self-revelation is itself an act of grace, which enables human persons to understand, accept, and enter into the "good life" God has offered to us in his kingdom.

Ormond Rush characterizes "spiritual reception" as being virtually equivalent to "faith" in the sense that it involves "a personal response and appropriation of God's salvific self-communication through Jesus Christ by the Spirit."[33] In Christian spirituality, this speaks further of two vital elements of reception. First, the church is a community of reception. According to Rush, "Reception marks the very nature and mission of the church, and reaches to all levels of its life." He quotes Joseph Komonchak when he says that apostolic teaching is accompanied by the power of the

---

33. Rush, *Eyes of Faith*, 8.

Spirit and is received by faith: "The whole ontology of the Church—the real 'objective' existence of the Church—consists in the reception by faith of the Gospel. Reception is constitutive of the Church."[34] And the second vital point about reception is that God's Divine will and word are received with the help of *sensus fidei* (the sense of faith in the individual believer) and the *sensus fidelium* (the sense of faith in the corporate church), both of which are arrived at through the reading of Scripture, and both of which depend on the right-functioning of the "ears and eyes of faith" in those who believe.[35]

In many ways, reception is foundational to redemption. God depends on human reception to make salvation work. He actively wills it. What if Abraham had rejected God's command to "Go to the land I will show you" (Gen 12:1)? What if Moses had rejected God's commission at the burning bush to "bring my people the Israelites out of Egypt" (Ex 3:10)? Or what if the disciples had rejected Jesus' invitation to "Come, follow me and I will make you fishers of men" (Mark 1:17)? In each case they would have been like those in Jesus' parable, who when invited to the Great Banquet responded in the negative: "I have bought a field". . . "I have bought oxen". . . "I have married a wife" (Luke 14:15–24).

In *The Call and the Response*,[36] Jean-Louis Chrétien suggests there is an "other voice" at large in the world which constantly invites human creatures to look beyond themselves, beyond evil, carnality and self-interest—to see what is truly beautiful, sacred, divine and real. This "other voice," Chrétien argues, is God's voice, constantly inviting us to make a loving response of commitment and obedience. God called Adam in the garden saying, "Where are you?" Jesus called the disciples in first century Palestine to, "Come, follow me." And he calls each "believing soul" today, inviting us to a make a response of love and whole-hearted surrender. What human soul—even the most irreligious, agnostic and uncommitted—has not felt a Presence, and not been addressed by that other voice saying, "Where are you?" For those who feel themselves summoned by such a voice, the important questions are "How ought we to respond?" and "What is it that is being asked of us?"

The role of the Christian spiritual director and educator is to provide the believing soul with some possible responses to God's call when

---

34. Rush, *Eyes of Faith*, 42.
35. Rush, *Eyes of Faith*, chapters 8 and 9.
36. Chrétien, *Call and the Response*.

it comes. "Called or not called, God is always present."[37] When the young prophet Samuel heard a voice calling him at night in the temple, he did not recognize the voice, and did not know how to respond. He was living at a time when "the word of the Lord was rare, and there were not many visions" (1 Sam. 3:1). And yet here was God's voice inviting a response. The priest Eli realized that the Lord was calling the boy and so instructed him, "If he calls you again, say, 'Speak, Lord for your servant is listening'" (v. 9). Eli provided proper guidance as to how Samuel should respond— even though he suspected God's message might count against him. God called the boy again. This time Samuel was listening attentively, and when the voice came a third time, he responded, "Speak, for your servant is listening." Samuel's careful listening—his hearing of God's voice and reception of God's word to him personally, and through him to the whole of Israel—was the basis of a new era under a new priestly order for Israel. Though Samuel could not have known it, his faithful reception was literally the means by which God would save Israel and, through Israel, the world. And by implication, a new openness to the Spirit of God on the part of "believing souls" in today's post-secular world, and a willingness to attend to our responsibility to receive God's self-revelation via "reception," will likely contribute to a renewal of the Christian spiritual life in twenty-first century church and society. And it will have consequences for humanity itself.

5. Call and Response

The spiritual life is primarily a life of "call and response." This is the argument put forward by Jean-Louis Chrétien in his book *The Call and the Response*.[38] It is first of all a call to *believe,* as in Christ's words, "Behold, I stand at the door and knock; if anyone hears my voice and opens the door, I will come into him [sic] and eat with him, and he with me" (Rev 3:20). And secondly, it is a call to participate in the *Missio Dei* ('the mission of God'). Thus, God called to Adam in the Garden of Eden, inquiring, "Where are you?" (Gen 3:9); God called Abraham to leave his country and his father's household so that he could become "a blessing and a great nation" (Gen 12:2); God called Moses to lead Israel out of Egypt to the

---

37. Tacey, "Spirituality, Religion and Youth in Secular Times," 11; a phrase central to the thinking of Carl Jung, and originally attributed to Erasmus.

38. Chrétien, *Call and the Response.*

land he had promised to give them, and encountered him at the burning bush, saying, "Take off your sandals, because you are standing on holy ground" (Ex 3:4–6). This is the pattern throughout God's dealings with his human creatures. The pattern continues in the New Testament, where Jesus says variously to the disciples, "Come, follow me" (Mark 1:17); to "be with him" (Mark 3:14), to "learn of me" (Matt 11:28–30), to "take up your cross daily" (Luke 9:23), and to "Go and do likewise" (Luke 10:37). Jesus' call to the disciples, and those among the crowds who had truly *heard* his words, was to become his disciples. It was a call to participate in his earthly mission, and to "stand in his place" as if they were his called, appointed, and anointed spokespersons and agents in the world. This continues as the default pattern throughout salvation history. As I wrote in *Ordinary Saints*:

> With the closure of the biblical record we might expect this remarkable history of experiential religion to come to a sudden end, never to be seen again. But it does not. In the subsequent 2000 years of Christian history, this remarkable narration of experiential religion continues unabated. In the earliest history of Christianity we see Perpetua being martyred, Justin defending the early Christian movement, Clement preaching, Antony teaching, Augustine writing his *Confessions*, Irenaeus ruling as a bishop, and Patrick evangelizing Ireland.[39]

In each case, these people were called by God to act in his name. Further, heeding the Divine call was rarely the "comfortable option," as Evelyn Underhill has described:

> St. Paul did not want to be an apostle to the Gentiles. He wanted to be a clever and appreciated young Jewish scholar, and kicked against the pricks. St. Ambrose and St. Augustine did not want to be overworked and worried bishops. Nothing was farther from their intention. St. Cuthbert wanted the solitude and freedom of his hermitage on the Farne; but he did not often get there. St. Francis Xavier's preference was for an ordered life close to his beloved master, St. Ignatius. At a few hours' notice he was sent out to be the Apostle of the Indies and never returned to Europe again. Henry Martyn, the fragile, exquisite scholar, was compelled to sacrifice the intellectual life to which he was so perfectly fitted for the missionary life to which he felt he was decisively called. In all these, a power beyond themselves decided

---

39. Devenish, *Ordinary Saints*, 86.

the direction of life. Yet in all we recognise not frustration, but the highest of all types of achievement.[40]

Note that the relevant question is not, "What is best for my soul?"; nor is it even, "What is most useful to humanity?" Instead, the vital question is, "What does God want me to do for his . . . great and secret economy?"[41] This is our task as children of God, to use our God-given freedom to obey the heavenly "promptings," to enjoy the Spirit's indwelling presence, and to use our bodies to bear witness to what God in Christ has done in our lives, and so to become "living proofs" that God is at work in the world. As Jean Pierre Caussade has written:

> We are in an age of faith; the Holy Spirit no longer writes Gospels, except in our hearts; saintly souls are the pages, suffering and action the ink. The Holy Spirit is writing a living gospel with the pen of action, which we will only be able to read on the day of glory when, fresh from the presses of life, it will be published. Oh what a beautiful story! What a beautiful book the Holy Spirit is now writing! It is in press; not a day passes when the type is not being set, the ink not applied, the page is not being printed.[42]

The consecrated life, with its total commitment to living in a God-saturated world, invites us to submission, gratefulness, and generosity. James McClendon has spoken of the spiritual life as a call to "radical" Christian discipleship. The sainthood to which we are called is neither a shallow nor a part-time endeavor. It asks everything of us in our totality . . . the whole of us without any reservation or exceptions. Christianity is not primarily a creed to be confessed, but a life to be lived.[43] The key to understanding Chretien's concept of "call and response" is the idea that God initiates the communication, calling his human respondents to wake up a purposeful existence and voluntary connectedness. And in response, his human respondents answer the call in a conscious, committed and ongoing engagement with the implications of God's and Christ's call to faith, discipleship and belief in an exchange of listening and answering prayer, worship and obedience.

---

40. Underhill, *Spiritual Life*, 7.
41. Underhill, *Spiritual Life*, 7.
42. De Caussade, *Sacrament of the Present Moment*, 101.
43. McClendon, *Biography as Theology*.

6. Spiritual Education

The phrase "spiritual education" is a neologism that has come into common usage in the United Kingdom as a response to the UK's *Educational Reform Act* of 1988, that obliged schools, colleges and other educational institutions to offer spiritual instruction to children and young people in the form of training in ethics, values, self-awareness and spiritual "connectedness." What the Act requires is difficult, because educational institutions must attempt to integrate atheist, secular, traditional religious as well as vibrantly spiritual (Christian and otherwise) approaches into a single offering, but without the capacity to differentiate between them. Understandably, certain commentators are opposed to this approach because it tries to force something intrinsic to human life, and therefore indescribably precious, into the rubric of a "secular institutional framework" that is neither friendly towards nor designed to deliver authentically spiritual instruction.[44]

Nevertheless, there is value in adopting the term "spiritual education" with respect to the classical Christian spiritual tradition for a number of reasons. The first is that, despite the need for care in defining what is meant, the phrase "spiritual education" avoids any unfortunate association with the pitfalls commonly associated with a "fading Christendom" which accompanies standard enterprises of "Religious" or "Christian" education. The second is that the term "spiritual education" provides a fresh opportunity to assess the possibility of a healthy linkage between education and spirituality in what many are now calling the "age of the Spirit." And the third is that the term "spiritual education" offers an opportunity to define what spiritual education is, from a Christian point-of-view, and what it is supposed to achieve.[45]

In the school-based educational context, spiritual education has been extensively discussed by David Carr in a series of articles published in the *Oxford Review of Education*, and further critiqued by Michael Hand.[46] Hand identifies four different ways Carr uses the phrase "spiritual education": (1) as education based on spiritual principles; (2) education of the human spirit; (3) education as a spiritual activity; and (4) education in a spiritual disposition. The two approaches I will develop

---

44. Blake, "Against Spiritual Education," 443–56.

45. As discussed by Fraser-Pearce, "Spiritual Education as a Subspecies of Relational Education?" 112–21.

46. Hand, "Meaning of 'Spiritual Education,'" 391–401.

here are: education of the human spirit (i.e., instructing the "believing soul"[47] in the act of responding to a transcendent reality—namely God), and education in a spiritual disposition (i.e., learning how to pray, to read the Scriptures, worship God, live by the Spirit, and understand how to respond when the "Holy Spirit meets the human spirit").[48]

As previously introduced, the emergence of the post-modern, post-Christian, and now a post-secular era has been marked by three significant "turns": (1) the turn to the subject; (2) the turn to interiority; and (3) the turn to experience. This inclination towards inwardness has shaped the values of our culture, including our educational institutions, in ways that are not without their challenges. Even so, I believe this represents an opportunity for those invested in Christian spiritual education to put to one side the limitations of our current educational systems, and for the first time since the birth of the Sunday School movement in the late eighteenth century, to think about how best to offer spiritual instruction to the children of Christian families (those inside the faith) as well as those "secular mystics" (those outside the faith) who have felt the call to a commence the spiritual quest and so have more than a casual interest in the nature of Christianity, both in terms of its theological claims and as a way of life.

This will require an un-learning of previous patterns of education, including our passive acceptance of a comfortable *status quo* imposed by models of secular Western education. Even in his own day, C. S. Lewis could observe, "Almost our whole education has been directed to silencing the shy, persistent, inner voice; almost all our modern philosophies have been devised to convince us that the good of man is to be found on this earth."[49] Redressing that oversight in the light of the arrival of the age of the Spirit will provide an opportunity to establish new modes of faith-based educational theory, curriculum and practice for instructing existing and new generations of Christ-followers. William MacLachlan has described five stages of historical change in the history of religion: (1) a crisis of legitimacy; (2) cultural distortion; (3) the articulation of a new vision; (4) the development of a new path; and (5) the institutional transformation that follows.[50] MacLachlan's third stage—the articulation of a new vision—is the right focus for our attention here. The present

---

47. Ricœur, *Symbolism of Evil*, 19.
48. Humphrey, *Ecstasy and Intimacy*.
49. Lewis, *Weight of Glory*, 31.
50. Discussed by Bass, *Christianity After Religion*, 33–34.

challenge is to lay the foundations for a new path of spiritual education that (if freed from the encumbrances of regulatory frameworks imposed by the secular State) could provide genuine spiritual formation consistent with the practices of the classical Christian spiritual tradition.

I would argue then, that the classical Christian spiritual tradition can make full and productive use of the phrase "spiritual education" for its own purposes. What is in-view here is not so much instruction in *what* to believe (in terms of the storied "shape" of Christian belief defined by Trinitarian theology and the classic creeds and confessions of the faith), but *how* to believe. I am speaking of the urgent need to re-learn (in order to teach) how to identify the inner movements of the human soul in response to the interior work of God, and so to cooperate with the Spirit in order to live a human life as a disciple of Christ. To that extent, it is decidedly not New Age spirituality that is in view here—what Paul Heelas describes as the "sacred inner-life spirituality" that belongs to the self-generated spiritual quest of non-theistic enquirers.[51] Rather, I am signalling a mode of spiritual instruction, and its confessional content, that Christians of every place and persuasion can recognize as belonging to the heart of Christian spirituality.

7. The Soul at White Heat

The provocative phrase "the soul at white heat," originates with the poet Emily Dickinson (1830–1886) in her poem, "Dare you See a Soul at the 'White Heat'?" It was written in 1862, and likely arose out of the emotional pains of Dickinson's complex sufferings brought about by the events of the American Civil War, her unrequited love for her friend and mentor Thomas Wentworth Higginson, her various illnesses, and her bearing the passions and tumults that routinely accompany world-class poets. Living—as she did—on the precipice of an acute intelligence and repressed religion, Dickinson was never able to throw off the doubts and tremors that beset her logical mind; but neither was she able to dispense with Christ and Christianity altogether. According to Roger Lundin, Dickinson's life was lived on the raw edge of nervous energy, hyper-intelligence and what he called the "evanescence of delight" that is evidenced in her extensive poetic *corpus*.[52] Citing Albert Gelpi's argument that

---

51. Heelas, "Spiritual Revolution of Northern Europe," 6, 12.
52. Lundin, *Emily Dickinson and the Art of Belief*, 34.

"Dickinson's peculiar burden was to be a romantic poet with a Calvinist's sense of things; to know transitory ecstasy in a world tragically fallen and doomed,"[53] Lundin observes that Dickinson "lived the most intensely focused inward life of any major figure in American history."[54]

Dickinson's unique talents for writing poetry were focused on the "inexhaustible inner domain" of the human heart, a domain that is the "only theatre recorded (which) the owner cannot shut."[55] The poem "Dare you See a Soul at the 'White Heat'?" imagines the soul as molten metal, super-heated in the flames of the blacksmith's forge, and beaten into shape by hammer blows on the hard face of the anvil. While Brenda Wineapple situates the action of the poem in the sexual tension between Dickinson and her friend Thomas Higginson,[56] Susan Kornfield limits the scope of the poem to the soul that is being "battered by God."[57] It is "white hot" because after all its impurities have been burned up, the color of the super-heated metal (Dickinson's metaphor for the soul) changes from red, to amber, to yellow, to white heat—the hottest of all the heat-phases. There, it "quivers," ready to be hammered into shape as molten metal that resists and "repudiates" the forge and the shape being imposed on it by the blows of its Divine adversary. The soul strains to retain its freedom, preferring "the light of her own fire" rather than any shape God might impose.

Dickinson's category of "the soul at white heat" offers the possibility of reflecting on the idea of the soul in the moment of *spiritual arousal* when it is alive to God and intensely awake to itself. Whereas Dickinson "dares" to resist God's advances, another perspective is possible. The self who is active within the Christian spiritual life, whose soul is set on fire by positive ecstasy, seeks creative ways in which it might submit to and conform to God's will and purposes. To unpack this moment as the essential movement in the Christian spiritual life, we might helpfully apply a phenomenological analysis in five steps:

1. Person: according to Nathan Kerr, the theologian Philip Blond—when discussing the essential experience of the Christian

---

53. Lundin, *Emily Dickinson and the Art of Belief*, 5 without source.
54. Lundin, *Emily Dickinson and the Art of Belief*, 5.
55. Lundin, *Emily Dickinson and the Art of Belief*, 96.
56. Wineapple, *White Heat*.
57. http://bloggingdickinson.blogspot.com/2013/01/dare-you-see-soul-at-white-heat-then.html

faith—might have pointed towards faith's proper object in the person of Jesus Christ and to rehearse the contents of the creeds in terms of Jesus' life, death and resurrection.[58] However, Kerr notes:

> ...this is manifestly what Blond does not do. He opts rather to explore the perceiving subject as the site of a universal, *a priori* 'perceptual faith'. Treating *la foi perceptive* (the one who has faith) as an intrinsic, essential dynamic of being human, Blond makes the believing human subject the focal point of his theological enquiry, and in turn introduces Christ into the discussion as a modifying feature or directional motif within the basic structure of perceptual faith.[59]

That to say, the person of faith who lives out of that faith represents a valid, necessary, and essential part of the expression of that faith. We are right to explore the person who is caught in the moment of encounter with the Divine.

2. Encounter: Authentic Christian spirituality dares to observe the believing soul in the moment of ecstasy, rapture and elevation where it is engaged in its embrace of God who is the "Divine lover." Its attention is not on the extraneous elements of religion whose purpose is to prepare us for what might lead towards any later encounter. Instead, it focuses on the encounter itself—the encounter for which everything else is merely preparation. There is no need now for any further priming of the pump . . . the moment of ecstasy, rapture, and awakening has arrived! This is the moment when the "Holy Spirit meets the human spirit," as Edith Humphrey so aptly describes it This is the moment that is worthy of analysis and celebration.[60]

3. Loved: The "doxological vision" that is imagined and discussed by Kerr describes the love of God for his created order; his election of Israel as his beloved people who are the "apple of his eye" (Ps 17:8); and his calling and commissioning of the disciples as the founding members of the church and the inheritors of the *Missio Dei* (the mission of God) at the birth of the Church at Pentecost. All of this is personalised in the love God has for the individual believer . . . for

---

58. Kerr, "From Description to Doxology," 174–200.
59. Kerr, "From Description to Doxology," 188.
60. Humphrey, *Ecstasy and Intimacy*.

me, for you. Individually and corporately, we are God's "beloved" children. He has carved us into the palm of his hands (Isa 49:16).

4. Vision: God in Christ gives to his People a vision of the love God has for the world—a love that is felt and experienced by him as burning with "white heat." It is not accidental, it is not incidental—it is intentional on his part, as something that *underwrites* the world itself. As Kerr writes, "To 'see' doxologically is to have our perceptions, our words, our lives, hallowed out by this cruciform manifestation of glory."[61] God is here, with us, *Emmanuel*. This awareness is the *telos*, the end-point, of Christian revelation and reception. We are not alone, and our experience of God is exhibited in moments of white heat experience.

5. Rapture: Enraptured souls suspend a mundane or worldly consciousness, and are transmuted to a higher order of consciousness in which the self is transcended, where the Divine presence dwells, where light is given, and where energy and rebirth are disclosed. According to John Wesley, an "inward impression of the soul as an experience not of the created grace in me, but of God's own love" is given as a convictional experience of divine rapture and ecstasy.[62] The spiritual arousal experienced by the soul at white heat has an important role to play in demonstrating the presence and power of God in the life of the believing soul. While experiences of rapture are often brief, nevertheless they are incredibly powerful, and those who have been to the "third heaven"—like the Apostle Paul (2 Cor 12:2–4)[63]—retain the impact of the experience for the rest of their lives.

Like St. Augustine's personalist anthropology in his *Confessions*, the approach taken in this volume seeks to draw out and enlarge the human person in the Divine life in the moment of its lived experience, in the actual consciousness of the person experiencing the God-sensation. And regarding the language of the soul, nothing in the retinue of superlative language we have available is sufficient to adequately describe the moment.

---

61. Kerr, "From Description to Doxology," 198.
62. Wesley, *Witness of the Spirit*, 124.
63. As discussed by St. Teresa of Avila, "In speaking of the prayer of union, this complete transformation of the soul in God lasts *only a short time*, but while it lasts no faculty is felt, nor does the soul know what is happening in this prayer." Teresa, *Collected Works*, 1/135.

Unprepared, when we find ourselves in the Presence of God, we remain silent in the face of the awe and wonderment we have encountered.

8. Modern-Day Mystics

The Greek word *musterion* (meaning "mystery," "secret," or "reserved teaching") is used extensively by the Apostle Paul in his epistles. Of the twenty occasions where Paul uses the word, three occur in Ephesians 3:

> Surely you have heard about the administration of God's grace that was given to me for you, that is, the *mystery* made known to me by revelation . . . You will be able to understand my insight into the *mystery* of Christ, which was not made known to men in other generations as it has now been revealed by the Spirit to God's holy apostles and prophets. This *mystery* is that through the gospel the Gentiles are heirs together with Israel, members together of one body, and sharers together in the promise of Christ Jesus. (Eph 3:3–6).

Simply put, from a New Testament perspective, we can say of mystery that: (a) it is something that was once hidden but which God has chosen to make known in the present historical moment; (b) its primary point-of-reference is the person of Christ Jesus; (c) it is revealed by the Holy Spirit: (d) when human persons handle the mysteries, they do so for the sake of others and not for themselves; (e) it is not so much a secret to be kept hidden, but a powerful message to be made known through the gospel; and (f) it is available to those with "eyes to see" and "ears to hear."[64]

According to Steven Fanning, "While Christianity is commonly regarded as a religion based on the acceptance of established theology or creeds and the performance of certain external acts, at the same time it is also a living religion based on a personal experience of God."[65] Mysticism has been defined in many different ways—all have to do with the direct and un-mediated experience of God.[66] Ironically, mystics have said more about what mysticism *is not* than what it *is*. This reticence to divulge the substance of mystical experience shows that by its nature it is hidden, closed, or reserved for those who have been inducted into the mysteries of Christ. In answer to the question "What is mysticism?" Evelyn Underhill

---

64. Humphrey, *Ecstasy and Intimacy*, 50.
65. Fanning, *Mystics of the Christian Tradition*, 220.
66. Cox, *Mysticism: The Direct Experience of God*.

suggests, "Mysticism is the art of union with Reality. The mystic is a person who has attained that union in greater or lesser degree; or who aims at and believes in such attainment."[67] Often the mystics themselves give hints or ciphers that equate to indirect and metaphoric communication. Underhill again:

> We are face-to-face with the 'wonder of wonders'—that most real, yet most mysterious of all experiences of religion, the union of human and divine, in a nameless something which is 'great enough to be God, small enough to be me.'[68]

Since there is a seemingly never-ending literature on the nature of Christian mysticism from the past, this entry will focus on modern-day mystics, offering a case study from the writings of Karl Rahner. In the years after the close of Vatican II (1962–65), Rahner reflected on how the changing social conditions of secular Western culture would impact the spiritual lives of Christian believers into the future. He foresaw that, "The devout Christian of the future will either be a 'mystic,' one who has 'experienced' something, or he [sic] will cease to be anything at all."[69] Rahner's use of the term "mystic" refers simply to the ordinary Christian believer who has experienced a genuine encounter with Christ and who has intentionally chosen to live their lives out of a lively faith instead of as a shallow portrayal of a false *cultural* Christianity. In other words, he was referring to a "true Christian," and not someone who confessed the Creeds without believing them. There would come a time, Rahner predicted, when the official church of the day would "no longer be in a position to do anything but leave many things . . . which involve particular concrete decisions, to the conscience of the individual [believer]."[70] To his initial readers (he was writing in the early 1970s), his prognostications must have sounded like the rantings of a madman. But in hindsight, his projections have proven to be astonishingly accurate. In today's world, the structural support given by the official Church to local congregations and individual believers is not what it was. In his own day Rahner observed:

> The young Christians of today must quietly develop a new way of Christian living and demand the right to practice it in the Church. If it leads to charity, joy, peace, patience, kindness,

---

67. Underhill, *Practical Mysticism*, 2.
68. Underhill, *Mysticism*, 100.
69. Rahner, *Theological Investigations*, 15.
70. Rahner, *Christian of the Future*, 98.

self-discipline and other manifestations of the presence of the Spirit one can only say with Paul (Galatians 5:23), 'against such there is no law.' Not even the law of the Church.[71]

Like Rahner, Louis Dupré has also predicted that the very future of Christianity will depend on the quality of the spiritual life of its followers. He warns that "Christianity has always started with a personal conversion of the heart," adding, "I am convinced that if Christianity isn't somehow everything, it will die altogether."[72] This makes mysticism and mystical experience a matter of life and death for the contemporary believer, and the contemporary church.

In *Mystify: Operating in the Mystery of God*, David Edwards, writes:

> The Mystic is one who desires to unveil the mystery—unwrap the gift. The book of Proverbs says, 'It's the glory of God to conceal the matter, but the glory of kings to search out a matter.' Mystics trek into the uncharted territories of the realms of God and become the architects who transform the cosmos. They are not content with knowing God outwardly; they must know why He thinks the way He does, what 'makes Him tick,' and the depths of love in his heart. He is their 'treasure island.'[73]

As Jean Danielou has observed:

> The extraordinary experience of the presence of God can and should be the normal atmosphere of our lives. During the times that it is, our relationships with our brothers and sisters reform themselves in the image of God; and we rediscover, through these relationships, the life of God that is their source.[74]

It was Thomas Merton who quipped somewhere that, "The only cure for the angst of modern man is mysticism." That is why Frank Tuoti writes in *Why Not Be a Mystic?*, that mystical faith:

> . . . is for those who are already "pray-ers" but who have an inexplicable hunger for something deeper and more experiential. It is for those who desire to "taste and see that the Lord is sweet" not by intellection, but by an ineffable experience of God as the living core-centre of their being. To experience God in this way, we must go beyond the juiceless formulas of dogma and

---

71. Rahner, *Christian of the Future*, 23–24.
72. Dupré, "Spiritual Life and the Survival of Christianity," 382–84.
73. Edwards, *Mystify*, front matter.
74. Danielou, *Prayer*, 21.

doctrine and existentially encounter the Spirit who enkindles them and makes them a luminous and vivifying reality.[75]

9. The Felt Presence of God

At the heart of the spiritual life is something John Bowker labelled the "sense of God."[76] That sense is sometimes referred to in the literature—often in connection with devotional practices such as spiritual direction—as the "felt presence" of God. Believing souls may experience the "felt presence" variously as a strange yet familiar lingering touch of the Divine in the *mind* (as a sacred way of knowing); as an awakening of *spirit* within the consciousness (as a form of intimate communion); and as sensations in the body (such as warmth, physical safety, or the sensation of being embraced). Charles Finney refers to the felt presence of God as "liquid love," while Bill Gaultiere refers to it as "the Jesus burn."[77]

The felt presence of God is a deeply personal encounter with the Divine that transcends our intellectual understanding of it, and our ability to convey it by means of human language. It is characterized by an overwhelming sensation of peace, presence, calm and reassurance that God is with us, for us, and in us. This subjective experience carries with it the sense that we have crossed over from everyday experience to the other side—to the sacred, to the mystical, to the wondrous, to a form of reality which we have seen in our mind's-eye, but which we have never before visited or been able to fully imagine.

In *The Spiritual Canticle*, St. John of the Cross—at the risk of his own destruction, since "No man can see God and live" (Ex 33:20)—nevertheless asked God to, "Reveal your presence."[78] God's presence has the power to both destroy and to heal. In a commentary on that passage, John Venard observes how St. John was making no effort to emotionalize the spiritual feeling, but rather made every attempt to unveil the actual experience of God's presence in the soul. In support of this approach, Venard recounts an experience from the life of St. Teresa of Avila:

> One day when I was at prayer . . . I saw Christ at my side—or, to put it better, I was conscious of Him, for I saw nothing with

75. Tuoti, *Why Not Be a Mystic?* 20.
76. Bowker, *Sense of God.*
77. Gaultiere, "Soul Shepherding."
78. John of the Cross, *Spiritual Canticle*, 80.

the eyes of the body or the eyes of the soul (the imagination). He seemed quite close to me ... Jesus Christ seemed to be at my side, but ... I could not see in what form. But I most clearly felt that He was all the time on my right side. . . . I could not but be aware that He was beside me ... The faculties are not suspended or the senses put to sleep.[79]

Mary Cutri describes St. John's request for Divine revelation as a desire for the "felt experience of God's presence."[80] Through prayer and worship, the believing soul experiences God's "touch," resulting in joy, peace, and love. However, it does not necessarily result in immediate fulfillment or consummation. Often, the promise of the heavenly vision which betokens union with God remains an unrealized possibility, awaiting its final fulfillment.

With reference to the felt presence of God, William James shared a self-report written by one of his subjects:

> I experienced a feeling of being raised above myself, I felt the presence of God—I tell of the thing just as I was conscious of it—as if his goodness and power were penetrating me altogether ... in this ecstasy of mine God had neither form, colour, odour, nor taste; moreover, that the feeling of his presence was accompanied with no determinate localisation. It was rather as if my personality had been transformed by the presence of a spiritual spirit. But the more I seek words to express this intimate intercourse, the more I feel the impossibility of describing the thing by any of our usual images. At bottom the expression most apt to render what I felt is this: God was present, though invisible; he fell under no one of my senses, yet my consciousness perceived him.[81]

In a similar fashion, Simone Weil, early on in her transformation from social revolutionary to spiritual mystic, experienced a mystical presence that surprised and beguiled her. She recalls:

> In a moment of intense physical suffering, when I was forcing myself to feel love, but without desiring to give a name to that love, I felt without being in any way prepared for it (for I had never read the mystical writers), a presence more personal, more certain, and more real than that of human being; though

---

79. John of the Cross, *Spiritual Canticle*, 81.
80. Cutri, *Sounding Solitude*, 38.
81. James, *Varieties of Religious Experience*, 68–69.

inaccessible to senses and to imagination, and it resembled the love that irradiates the tenderest smile of somebody who loves.[82]

In his book *The Shattered Lantern,* Ronald Rolheiser engages with Friedrich Nietzsche's notion of the "death of God" in terms of human awareness.[83] It is not so much that God has died, Rolheiser suggests, but that he has passed out of human awareness during the skeptical secular era. He explains, "Our present cultural currency, certainly in the Western world, is not equipped to help us imagine or feel God's existence. The air we breathe is agnostic, even atheistic."[84] For Rolheiser, the re-birth of the possibility of God in the twenty-first century comes as a result of the re-kindling of the felt-presence of God—something that is once again possible in the post-secular era when the reprise of spirituality and the turn toward interiority allows us to speak with confidence and conviction about God in the life of the soul.

The recovery of the spiritual life is a valid, necessary, and timely course of action that awaits elucidation beyond what it has thus far received from twenty-first century "explorers of the soul." Moments of convictional experience arising from prayer, worship, participation in the sacraments, Bible reading, and while seeking or awaiting confirmation of a call to vocational "holy orders"—all these are times when sacred selves most commonly experience the felt presence of God in a spirit of joy, welcome and eager connection.

10. The Beloved

The idea of being "God's beloved" is a theme that is foremost in the Old Testament, in God's election of Israel as his "beloved people" (Deut 10:15). It continues in the New Testament in God's sending his "beloved son," Jesus, into the world (Matt 3:17). He does this because the world itself is God's beloved creation, "For God so loved the world . . ." (John 3:16). The concepts of love and the beloved (Greek *agape* and *agapao*), intensify in John's Gospel to become one of its most celebrated themes. Written by the "beloved disciple," John's Gospel majors on love as its pre-eminent subject. As C. K. Barrett observes, "Love seems to be, for John, a reciprocal relation. The Father loves the Son . . . and the Son loves the

---

82. Weil, *Waiting for God,* 24.
83. Rolheiser, *Shattered Lantern,* 124.
84. Rolheiser, *Shattered Lantern,* 10.

Father . . . Jesus loves his own . . . and his own love, or should, [love] one another . . . They must also love him."[85] Dorothy Lee points out:

> Behind Peter's mission and commissioning lies a profound spirituality of love and friendship without which such (a) vocation is impossible. For John, not only Peter but also [the] disciples are called into the same love, the same filiation and friendship; called to be 'beloved disciples', to be the friends of Jesus and friends of one another even to the point of death.[86]

Henri Nouwen developed the concept of the beloved as one of the defining themes of his ministry. In *The Life of the Beloved*,[87] Nouwen tells the story of his friendship with a skeptical young New York intellectual who wanted to believe in Nouwen's God . . . but couldn't. He asked Nouwen to speak to him and his generation:

> . . . about the deepest yearning of our hearts, about our many wishes, about hope; not about the many strategies for survival, but about trust; not about new methods of satisfying our emotional needs, but about love. Speak to us about a vision larger than our changing perspectives and about a voice deep within the clamorings of the mass media. Yes, speak to us about something or someone greater than ourselves. Speak to us about . . . God.[88]

Nouwen's response was to examine his own life as a Catholic priest and a successful and highly respected theologian—but also as someone who continued to deal with his own sense of unworthiness as God's beloved. Standing before Christ to examine his heart, Nouwen was forced to confront his own self-rejection, his hidden motives, and his inadequate understanding of grace. On reading Mark's account of Jesus' baptism, when a voice from heaven was heard saying, "You are my Son, the beloved, on whom my favor rests" (Mark 1:11), Nouwen accepted that God could love Jesus, and that Jesus in turn could love other people. But he questioned whether God could love *him*. Am I worthy? Am I lovable? Am I truly God's beloved child?

In many families there is at least one child who feels unloved. They may sit at the table, but life doesn't "taste." They may feel their parents'

---

85. Barrett, *Gospel According to St John*, 215.
86. Lee, *Hallowed in Truth and Love*, 154–55.
87. Nouwen, *Life of the Beloved*.
88. Nouwen, *Life of the Beloved*, 15.

arms around them, but that love doesn't succeed in "connecting." They receive Christmas and birthday gifts just like their siblings, but somehow the other children seem more worthy of being loved than they are. They feel themselves to be "outsiders," having to earn love; but when it comes, they are strangely unable to receive it. And this is the source of a very great pain, a kind of *emotional estrangement* that causes a psychological disjunction. This can also be true of the spiritual life—there is always someone who reads about God's jealous, insane, and irrational love in Scripture as if it applied to others *but could never apply to themselves.* Somehow other people might be lovable, beautiful, worth dying for—but not themselves. This lonely, excluded child of God is more likely to feel that God hates them rather than that he loves them.

Following that experience, Nouwen made it the central goal of his ministry to help people to receive the love of God into their lives. But first he had to experience it for himself. During one of his annual retreats, Nouwen stared at length at a painting by Rembrandt entitled "The Return of the Prodigal Son." Suddenly the painting spoke to him at a very deep level, causing him to reflect on the question of where his ultimate value came from. Was it his role as a professor in several of America's most prestigious universities? Or was it simply because he was God's beloved? He came to see that he had developed the bad habit of living out of his ego, and at base, he was one of the loveless children just like his young skeptical New York friend and his social network.

In *The Life of the Beloved*, Nouwen then undertook a journey of self-discovery, having to learn and re-learn that he was God's beloved son. It was an arduous process, having to discover that God loved him deeply, strongly, and passionately—without qualification and without his having to earn God's love. Instead of listening to the voice of condemnation, he began to listen to God's affirming voice speaking within him:

> I have called you by name, from the very beginning. You are mine and I am yours. You are my beloved and on you my favor rests. I have molded you in the depths of the earth and knitted you together in your mother's womb. I carved you on the palm of my hands and have hidden you in the shadow of my embrace. I look at you with infinite tenderness.[89]

Eventually, Nouwen wrote to his young friend to say, "The greatest gift my friendship can give to you is the gift of your Belovedness. I can

---

89. Nouwen, *Life of the Beloved*, 24.

give that gift only in so far as I have claimed it for myself. Isn't that what friendship is all about: giving to each other the gift of our Belovedness?"[90] Nouwen learned that on the other side of guilt, of his own lack of self-forgiveness, on the other side of the negative script that always saw him accusing himself, was a love he could not earn and a status he did not deserve—but one which God was only too willing to bestow. He saw that if Christ was willing to die on the cross to reconcile him to God, and that God was eternally waiting for him—like the loving Father of the prodigal son—to "come home," then his first task as a Christian disciple was to surrender to that love, to receive his own belovedness, and to minister out of God's unreasonable, unfathomable, and irresistible love for his broken creatures who don't deserve it, but who desperately desire and desperately need it.

90. Nouwen, *Life of the Beloved*, 18.

Part Three

Alphabetical Word-Concepts

11. Abandonment

THE SENSE OF ABANDONMENT is a central feature of the spiritual life. It falls into three main types: (1) first, abandonment by God; (2) second, abandonment to God; and (3) self-abandonment. The first is the sense of being abandoned *by* God. This first sense—which is without doubt the most troubling but also thankfully the least frequent—was the experience of Jesus in his "cry of dereliction" in the garden of Gethsemane, "My God, my God, why have you forsaken me?" (Matt 27:46). In speaking these words from Psalm 22, it is clear Jesus was preparing himself to die on the cross for the sins of the world, bearing in his body God's judgment for all humanity. Jesus resolved to allow himself to be abandoned by God, determining to put his own self-interest to one side, as indicated by his words, "Not my will but your will be done." He placed the needs of others ahead of his own well-being. Jesus represents a "special case" because as God's eternal Son he was chosen to be "the Lamb slain from the creation of the world" (Rev 13:8). He alone was obligated to fulfill his calling of divine sonship and his office of eternal priesthood. God intended to save the world and to do so by means of the sufferings of Christ. The earth was not "God-forsaken"—as some have argued—as implied by the use of the Latin term *Deus absconditus* ("the God who absents himself"). It is against God's nature to abandon the very world he created, loved and redeemed. Rather, Jesus' actions demonstrate the continued love and presence God has for his human creatures and the cosmos he created.

The second kind of abandonment is abandonment *to* God. In that instance, the "believing soul" chooses to submit themselves fully and freely to God in a life of devotion and self-surrender. This requires us to hand over the reins of our lives, setting aside the demands of our own egos, and choosing to freely deny our God-given independence. One argument against this kind of abandonment is that some believe God "annihilates" the self, rendering it a non-entity. But as George Patterson has pointed out, what is "annihilated" is not the person or the self, but the *will* of the believer, who voluntarily and for the sake of love, adopts the position of disinterest in their own fate.[1] In the language of the ethics of self-sacrifice, the one who does the choosing is not God in the role of destroyer, but the sacred self in the role of lover. Often, it is only after a season of struggle and resistance that one is able to come to a place of realization that God can be trusted with our most treasured possession—our *souls*. The fundamental lesson to be learned is that, "The God of Christianity is friend, lover and fellow accused, not judge, patriarch and superego. He is counsel for the defence, not for the prosecution."[2] Having surrendered our will and submitted ourselves to the sovereignty of God and the Lordship of Christ, any sense of fear that once filled the soul's awareness is replaced by love. As Joan Puls has observed:

> Those in love have a secret . . . They speak a new language and walk with new grace. They learn the dance of life, listening and opening, the rhythms of intimacy and ecstasy . . . They wait with hope for love's direction. Freed by love's own dynamic to be sifted and to die, to be made whole and human. Love is creative and those who partake are enlarged and made fruitful. They give birth to new networks and have new visions.[3]

The Christian "beloved" is even willing to submit to being "wounded" by their Divine lover. There are instances in Scripture where God wounds his people, predominantly to prepare them to "return" to him (Jer 30:12; Hos 6 1; Job 5:18). The prophet Habakkuk described those things in his life that were desolate and hard to accept, responding, "Yet I will rejoice in the Lord" (Hab 3:18). Likewise, in the midst of soul-crushing tribulation, Job is able to declare of God, "Though he slay me, yet will I trust in him" (Job 13:15).

---

1. Pattison, *Phenomenology of the Devout Life*, 166.
2. Eagleton, *Culture and the Death of God*, 160.
3. Puls, *Every Bush is Burning*, 83.

The third kind of abandonment is self-abandonment for the purpose of *participating in Christ's ministry* to the world. The apostle Paul endured many hardships in his life of service for Christ. In the course of his ministry, he was abandoned, imprisoned, flogged, shipwrecked and stoned (2 Cor 11:232–35). He was even willing to lose his own salvation for the sake of the Jews, saying "For I could wish that I myself were cursed and cut off from Christ for the sake of my brothers, those of my own race, the people of Israel" (Rom 9:3–4). St. Therese of Lisieux was willing to share in Christ's ministry by taking the sorrows of the world into her own body as an act of vicarious suffering on behalf of others.[4] Although only Christ can suffer redemptively and vicariously for the world, the idea of co-mingling our suffering on behalf of others with the suffering of Christ as an act of penitential devotion does have some biblical warrant vis-à-vis, "For it has been granted to you on behalf of Christ not only to believe in him, but also to suffer for him" (Phil 1:29).

Abandonment, or "indifference" towards worldly concerns represents a key element of St. Ignatius of Loyola's *Spiritual Exercises*. There, "indifference" does not mean a disinterest or a refusal to decide, as if matters of daily life were unimportant. Rather, "it implies interior freedom from disordered inclinations. It is a key technical term of Ignatius's spirituality. His list of examples of indifference [includes] some which are fully under the control of our own free will . . . and some which fall outside our power to choose."[5] Ignatius described his concept of abandonment as "self-forgetfulness," which picks up on our second and third types of self-offering to God discussed above. At every level of Christian ministry—from lay members to paraprofessionals to the ordained—the call to Christian discipleship comes at a cost. In following Jesus the crucified Messiah, disciples recognize that self-abandonment leads not to the destruction of the soul, but to a form of increased wholeness through union with Christ—a totality of sacred freedom—which they could not achieve in any other way.

Gregory of Nyssa develops the theme of abandonment under the keyword of *apatheia* (Greek for dispassionate impartiality).[6] Three aspects of *apatheia* in particular come into view. The first is that *apatheia* has a direct relationship with the concept of *pathos*, meaning suffering or passion. *Apatheia* in Christian spirituality means to undergo sufferings,

---

4. Ermatinger, *St. Therese of Lisieux*.
5. Ignatius, *Spiritual Exercises*, 151.
6. Mateo-Seco, "Apatheia," 51–54.

but in a way that is dignified and worthy of Christ. The second is that Jesus himself is the perfect example of apatheia, in his incarnation, human limitations, being reviled by others, and ultimately his crucifixion serving as the christological template for his followers to replicate. "Gregory affirms that divine purity and apatheia here are in Christ, and that the soul receives them from Him as from their source."[7] And third, *apatheia* does not mean "coldness of heart". . . rather, "Gregory councils us to use the passions in the ascetic struggle, but reordering them, reorienting them, elevating them. Apatheia here is a triumph of purity, because it is a triumph of love."[8]

12. Acedia

Acedia (pronounced *a-chee-dia*) is the Greek word for the sapping of spiritual energy and strength that results in sloth, apathy, and weariness. In his *Rule* for monastics (chapter 72), St. Benedict makes reference to acedia as a dire spiritual affliction, while the entire monastic tradition of the fifth and sixth centuries described acedia as the dissipation and loss of spiritual motivation. It was described as a certain kind of "spiritual madness," like "going out in the noonday sun"—a kind of devil that beset monastics and sent them into a kind of "soul sleep." To give in to acedia was seen as a mortal sin, altogether different to the lower-level doubting of God's existence or the authenticity of one's faith. Evagrius of Pontus (d. 399) described it this way:

> The demon of acedia, also called the noonday demon, is the most oppressive of all the demons. It attacks the monk at about the fourth hour (10 am) encircling his soul until about the eighth hour (2 pm). First it makes the sun seem to be moving slowly or not at all, so the day appears to be 50 hours long. Then it compels the monk to keep looking out his window; it forces him to race out of his cell to watch the sun to see how much longer it will be until 3 PM, and it makes him look all around in case any of the brothers has come to visit him.[9]

---

7. Mateo-Seco, "Apatheia," 54.
8. Mateo-Seco, "Apatheia," 55.
9. Evagrius, *Prakticos and Chapters on Prayer*, 18.

But acedia as spiritual sloth and torpor is not limited to ancient souls. Geoffrey Chaucer made acedia the subject of his tenth and final Canterbury tales expressed through the voice of the Parson.

> For envy blinds the heart of a man [sic] and anger troubles a man; and acedia makes him heavy, thoughtful, and peevish. Envy and anger causes bitterness of heart; which bitterness is the mother of acedia and takes from a man the love of all goodness.[10]

Acedia is also a problem for citizens of the twenty-first century, where smart phones, televisions, online entertainment, and the speeding up of life distract us from reading our Bibles, setting aside time for prayer, and ensuring the centrality of our faith amid the many other demands that life presents us with. The Roman Catholic priest Paul Wilkes tells his own story of modern-day acedia. He writes:

> In my pursuit to be a true man of God . . . I had to go deeper and deeper into this desert of unknowing, with nothing familiar to grasp onto, no comforts, no rest. It was terrifying and bewildering, just as the great spiritual masters had told, but was required by anyone who wishes to enter into the mystery of being remade by God. As if this haze of unknowing were not bad enough, the "midday demon" often came to call. *Acedia* it is called, and the solitary know it well. It is the opposite of desire, and abandonment of faith, the absence of caring, a subtle but even worse agony . . . The print in the Bible before me, the texture of my table, the sound of the fluorescent light over the sink, the lining of the trousers on my numb knees—all unspeakable tortures. I wanted release. Anything. Anywhere . . . Acedia ruptures hope, courts despair.[11]

In a book entitled *Acedia and Me*,[12] author Kathleen Norris documents her own experience of living in a state of acedia. Having spent much of her life engaged in an informal spiritual search, she became associated with a community of monks who belonged to a Benedictine monastery, and subsequently became immersed in the literature of Catholic spirituality in general, and monasticism in particular. She first encountered the notion of acedia in an essay by Aldous Huxley entitled "Accidie." This led to her discovery that acedia was not simply an outdated religious

---

10. Chaucer, *Canterbury Tales*, 590.
11. Wilkes, *In Due Season*, 181.
12. Norris, *Acedia and Me*.

problem, but a universal human problem that afflicts a large proportion of the population. Norris writes:

> . . . standard dictionary definitions of acedia such as 'apathy,' 'boredom,' or 'torpor' do not begin to cover it, and while we may find it convenient to regard it as a more primitive word for what we now term depression, the truth is much more complex. Having experienced both conditions, I think it likely that much of the restless boredom, frantic escapism, commitment phobia, and enervating despair that plagues us today is the ancient demon of acedia in modern dress.[13]

Acedia is one of the many maladies of the soul that threaten to blight and wither the spiritual life, and it must be taken seriously. There are many defences against this disease, all of which amount to regaining a clear understanding that the healthy soul is one that is well-connected to Christ. It is by one's Christ-connection that the healthy soul remains deeply alive, wonderfully creative, and powerfully transformed. The soul that sees clearly, loves truly, and knows coherently has no fear of the noonday sun. It proceeds in the full knowledge that it is doing far more important things. As such, acedia is not normally a problem for converts at the early stage of their impassioned love for Christ. Nor is it a problem for those spiritual pilgrims who have found a way to keep their faith simmering at the boiling point of spiritual "white heat." The Apostle Paul exhorted the Christians in Rome to, "Never be lacking in zeal, but keep your spiritual fervor, serving the Lord" (Rom 12:11). The Greek word for fervor is *zeontos*, referring to a fire in full flame. This implies the need to sustain the temperature of the soul at "boiling point." But acedia is an insidious visitor to those whose faith has "gone off the boil"—those who become distracted by the detritus of life just long enough to forget the delights of worship, the discoveries found in prayer, the mysteries revealed in contemplative spiritual reading, and the wonders contained in the "felt" presence of God. Spiritual pilgrims who set out to travel to the City of God must be aware of both the reality and the dangers of acedia.

Historically, monastics have been encouraged, whenever they suffer from the *ennui* and boredom that arises from acedia, to return to their cells, to reconnect with their prayers, to re-discover the original "inspiration-point" that set them on their spiritual journeys in the first place, and so to start afresh on their spiritual pilgrimage. If the grace of God is big enough to forgive us for our many sins, then pilgrims—both ancient and

13. Norris, *Acedia and Me*, 3.

modern—must be wise enough to receive it, to apply to their own lives, and to allow themselves to "begin again."

Ironically, one of the symptoms of acedia is hyper-activity, which can be described as a frenzied yet disordered kind of commitment to and/or devotion to something. One of Blaise Pascal's most noteworthy statements on this matter is that, "I have often said that the sole cause of man's [sic] unhappiness is that he does not know how to stay quietly in his room."[14] For people living in the twenty-first century, the spiritual disciplines of prayer, worship, journal writing, the reading of spiritual literature, retreats, pilgrimage and putting aside invasive smart phones and personal technology is a must. A return to simplicity and slowness and therefore 'depth' are advised, as opposed to speed and over-engagement/over-achievement which leads to shallow hypertension which blocks one from participating in the genuine spiritual life.

13. Agency

Putting aside the big-ticket items of creation, redemption, and final judgement (in which God acts alone in sovereign singularity without the assistance of any other being), God's normative pattern of acting is to appoint a select group, a community, or an individual person to work with him under the inspiration of his Spirit. Despite God being the initiator of and key participant in what Hans von Balthasar calls the divine "Theo-drama" in which God works out his will and purposes in the world as a *singular* actor—God routinely chooses to make use of human agents as co-agents in his historical redemptive drama. Ironically, and graciously, the Spirit co-opts flesh to its purposes.

Throughout salvation history God has used any number of people and nations to achieve his purposes. The Protestant reformer Martin Luther determined that when it suited his purposes, God achieved good even through evil, observing that the devil is God's monkey. Pharaoh, King Darius, and Nebuchadnezzar are examples of God using his enemies to achieve his Divine purposes. But for the most part, God delights to use Israel and the church whom he gathers into covenant-relationship as a "people for himself." And it is these people whom he appoints as his agents in the world to bear witness to his sovereignty, to live according to his laws and covenants, and to represent him in the world as his substitute "real

---

14. Pascal, *Pensees*, 169.

presence," as living proofs that God remains at work in the world. Many such people are named in the Hebrew Bible, including: the naked Adam and Eve, the obedient Abraham, the beautiful Rebecca, the redneck Esau, the leader Moses, the prostitute Rahab, the kingly David, the suffering Job, the sensuous Solomon, the weeping Jeremiah, the fearless Daniel, and the questioning Habakkuk. From the Christian Bible, a representative sample might include: the diminutive Zacchaeus, the surprised Samaritan woman at the well, the candid Nathanial, the blind Bartimaeus, the laughing children who approached Jesus, the disloyal Judas, the doubting Thomas, the passionate Mary Magdalene, the thunderbolt Paul, the believing merchant Lydia, the intellectual Apollos and the mostly unfamiliar (to us) Epenetus, who was one of the earliest converts to Christ.

The apostle Paul employs such phrases as "God's fellow workers" and "ambassadors" to highlight the fact that redeemed believers have a role to play in the outworking of the Kingdom of God on the earth. John Barclay and Simon Gathercole further extend this thought:

> [Redeemed] human agency is bound up with that of God, because the two are essentially identical when properly aligned . . . Humanity is most itself not when it is 'self-sufficient' vis-à-vis God, but when it acts in dependence on God and wills what God has willed. For human beings participate in the nature of God, and might even be described as 'fragments' of God: what makes them most effective as human agents is what they share with God.[15]

So when Jesus says to his disciples, "*You* give them something to eat" (Mark 6:37), "[You] Go into all the world and make disciples" (Matt 28:20), and "*You* will be my witnesses" (Acts 1:8) . . . he shows he is serious about the concept of agency. Perhaps this comes into focus most clearly in Jesus' calling and appointing of the twelve disciples who would become his apostles. Despite this group of probable teenagers being an unlikely, unready, and untested group, Jesus nevertheless placed the fate of his earthly mission in their hands—a pattern we see repeated throughout the history of the Church. In his address to the 2013 World Youth Day in Rio De Janeiro, Brazil, Pope Francis told his 3-million strong audience, "Jesus is calling you to be a disciple with a mission . . . Jesus Christ is counting on you! The Church is counting on you! . . . 'Go and make disciples of all nations.'"[16]

15. Barclay and Gathercole, *Divine and Human Agency in Paul*, 6–7.
16. Francis, "World Youth Day Address," 2013.

Despite the partnership being fundamentally unequal in nature, God is clearly interested in partnering with human beings to achieve his divine purposes on earth. Thus, mission and evangelism, pastoral care and charitable works, Biblical and theological teaching, spiritual formation and Christian education, Christian parenting and the raising of the next generation of those who believe—are all placed in the hands of faithful people who understand and enact the principle of agency. The reality is that the life of the church (including both saints-departed and today's very-much-alive "activated disciples") depends on the quality of the lives of those who confess Christ in the world. They are the message, the messenger, and the working model of the gospel in 3D form. Their lives are revelatory in the same sense as Scripture and the testimony of the Church as a whole, since they are the living exemplars by means of which God's grace and providence are revealed in every moment, and in every place throughout the earth.

Michael Gorman, in his book *Becoming the Gospel*,[17] further explores this idea of agency or partnership, arguing that the lives of believers are "[a] living exegesis of the gospel of God" before their unbelieving neighbors.[18] Thus, the life of the missionary, evangelist, priest, pastor, or saint is to become a living *impresario* of the good news, providing a form of living commentary and interpretive hermeneutic of their own message concerning what it means to believe, accept and participate in the new reality of the kingdom of God.[19] In her careful explication of Hans Urs von Balthasar's work, Victoria Harrison also recognizes the centrality of human agency in the Spirit-driven dynamic of evangelism, writing:

> [von Balthasar's] core claim is that in observing holy people, one becomes attracted to what they do, and then one begins to imitate them. Hence the living a holy lifestyle is . . . What performs the essential role in moving others into a Christian faith-stance. And here, imitation is crucial—for it is by imitating what holy people do . . . That one is able to come to live the holy life for oneself, and this then enables one to see God's reality in all its fullness.[20]

If Jesus gave authority to the disciples to "cast out demons and to heal diseases" (Luke 9:1), and if St. Paul could look forward to the end of

---

17. Gorman, *Becoming the Gospel*.
18. Gorman, *Becoming the Gospel*, 43.
19. Devenish, "Human Agency in the Divine Mission," 5.
20. Harrison, *Apologetic Value of Human Holiness*, 189.

history to foresee a time when the "saints will judge the world," including the angels (1 Cor 6:2–3); and if Blaise Pascal could ask the question "Why has God instituted prayer?"—answering, "to impart to his creatures the dignity of causality"[21] . . . then we can say that God entrusts more to his redeemed human creatures than we might ever have dreamt.

14. Attachment

The concept of *attachment* is central to the psychological model known as "Attachment Theory" developed by British psychologist John Bowlby (1907–1990). Bowlby's pioneering model has become a key construct for a range of psychological and therapeutic disciplines. Interestingly, Bowlby's theory of attachment arose out of his own life-experience. He grew up in a well-to-do English family where he was cared for by his nanny; he saw his mother for only an hour a day during the evening meal; soon after his seventh birthday, his nanny found other employment, resulting in the young Bowlby experiencing a very deep grief that left an enduring mark on his person. Later in life, as a trained psychologist, he pioneered attachment theory, based on object-relations, with reference to the relationship between a mother and the breastfeeding infant. Bowlby explains:

> To say of a child (or older person) that he [sic] is attached to, or has an attachment to someone, means that he is strongly disposed to see proximity to and contact with that individual and to do so especially in certain specified conditions. The disposition to behave in this way is an attribute of the attached person, a persisting attribute which changes only slowly over time and which is unaffected by the situations of the moment.[22]

When growing up, the child needs its mother to affirm its own existence. The bond of attachment between the mother and the infant—especially during breastfeeding—effectively "programs" the emotional and relational well-being of the child for the remainder of its life. Categories of attachment are well known in psychological clinical practice, where positive attachment is affirmed, and negative attachment becomes the focus for therapeutic intervention.

In the opening lines to the *Handbook of Attachment*, the editors Jude Cassidy and Philip Shaver make the observation that attachment

---

21. Pascal, *Pensees*, 159.
22. Bowlby, *Secure Base*, 120–21.

theory has become "one of the broadest, most profound and most creative lines of research in twentieth-century psychology."[23] This is because attachment theory is able to get to the heart of people's most fundamental pre-commitments in life, held in the deepest levels of their psyche. The notions of positive and negative attachment set the "internal working models" for a person's lifelong state-of-mind, and emotional state of wellbeing, further determining their relative happiness or satisfaction/dissatisfaction in life. Much of the clinical and therapeutic concern of psychology has to do with correcting or repairing a person's distressed, neurotic, or misguided sense of self and its fundamental securities/insecurities in a broken world.

Because of the fruitfulness of the attachment concept, Christian psychologists and philosophers have applied attachment theory to the Christian believers' relationship to God, giving rise to the "attachment to God" (ATG) construct. Bowlby spoke of those resources that create a "harbour of safety" in a person's life. Beginning with a child's sense of security at being held in the unconditional loving embrace of its mother, Christian psychologists have extrapolated from this and applied it to the human-to-God relationship. In the divine case, the love of God knows no bounds, it is offered unconditionally and is given to the "child" of God as an act of gratuitous and unqualified grace and affection. Since God is described in the biblical texts as Father, his role in a person's life in bringing them to salvation and working within them by his Spirit in sanctification is that of a kind and gracious parent. As the Divine parent who provides for a child's physical and spiritual needs, God guides them in the making of right decisions about what pleases God and what is best for the human participant in the divine-human drama. It is for this reason that Pehr Granqvist has argued that religion is a form of attachment, with God seen as the transcendent parent and the spiritual life of the believer seen as encompassing a range of religious "coping" strategies.[24]

A large literature has arisen around the concept of "attachment to God," focusing on its clinical applications in counselling and psychotherapy. Since our concern in this volume is primarily with Christian spirituality, it is important to note that the concept of "attachment to God" has significant implications for the theory and practice of Christian spirituality. In their article "Exploring Christians' Explicit Attachment to

---

23. Cassidy and Shaver, *Handbook of Attachment*, xi.
24. Granqvist, "Religion as Attachment."

God Representations," Proctor, Miner and McLean et al., identified the two major operations implicit in a Christian "attachment to God" bond. This bond involves:

> i. God psychologically functions to provide: (a) protection and comfort in times of threat (*haven of safety function of attachment*); and (b) a psycho-spiritual base from which Christians move forward to explore and engage life (*secure base function of attachment*); and ii. the Christian believer who ideally: (a) relies upon God's protection, support and comfort when faced with threat (external and internal), and (b) confidently moves forward and embraces life, strengthened by his/her knowledge of God's future willingness to respond in future times of new threat.[25]

Likewise, Brian Rosner in his book *Known by God: a Biblical Theology of Personal Identity*,[26] explores the foundations of Christian identity as one that is rooted in the experience of being loved by God, leading to an unwavering stability, confidence, identity and conviction that we matter to God to an extent that is beyond reckoning. Despite our circumstances, we are loved unconditionally, and our names and faces are known by him. Spiritual attachment lies at the heart of Christian spirituality, according to which God loves us unconditionally, and we love him back without limit or pre-condition.

Believers are able to leverage the concept of attachment to God in numerous ways. Four suggested possibilities follow: firstly, the possibility of thinking of God as our primary attachment figure and "haven of comfort and safety," especially in times of challenge, disruption, illness or disturbance. The idea of going to God first rather than to prescribed medication for anxiety or to other destructive behaviors such as addictions as coping mechanisms must be a real option for people whose "home" is God. Second, the idea of accepting that we are God's "beloved" and that we are not excluded from God's heart, home, table or thoughts. This means believers need to have a well-defined understanding of grace, in that God gives us the good things we do not deserve, but that he gives them nevertheless. Third, while God's grace is freely given and does not need to be earned, nevertheless believers are invited to contribute sustained effort not in qualifying for God's love, but of demonstrating its presence in their lives. Dallas Willard states, "Grace is not opposed to

---

25. Proctor et al., "Exploring Christians' Explicit Attachment to God Representations," 246.

26. Rosner, *Known by God*.

effort, it is opposed to earning. Earning is an attitude. Effort is an action."[27] And fourth, spiritual directors and soul guides will benefit from having an understanding of attachment to God in both its weak and strong forms, and needing to be made the central operating system of the "believing soul's" inner condition. Further work on how such transformations are facilitated in spiritual direction and accompanying is required.

15. Attunement

The concept of attunement finds a comfortable "fit" within the discipline of music, which requires having an "ear" for rhythm, melody, and harmony—of being "in tune" and "on song," musically speaking. Analogously, the concept has been applied in a range of other disciplines, such as psychology, where theorists speak of being "attuned" perceptually, intellectually, and emotionally to the self, others, and the world around us. In a similar way, attunement has proved to be a pivotal theoretical concept when it comes to explaining certain connections between Christian spirituality and how it unfolds in the life of the human who is—knowingly or unknowingly—a spiritual person in their everyday lives. Two examples may act as "bridges" that will help illustrate this concept of attunement. First, Paul Fiddes, in *Seeing the World and Knowing God*,[28] has explored the concept of attunement with special reference to wisdom. Wisdom is not something automatically given but which must be sought out, prepared for, and put into practice in one's life. Wisdom calls for attunement between head, heart, and mind based on a certain "openness" to the world. And second, without him using the word "attunement" in his exploration of John Owen's theological anthropology,[29] Kelly Kapic employs a concept very much like attunement. Kapic describes Owen not as a "rationalist, nor a theologian simply interested in abstract speculations . . . Instead, we will [label] Owen as an *anthroposensitive* theologian." Kapic defines *anthroposensitivity* as "refusing to divorce theological considerations from practical human application, since theological reflections are always interwoven with anthropological concerns."[30] Owen's *anthroposensitivity* could be called a spirituality of attunement, to the

---

27. Willard, *Great Omission*.
28. Fiddes, *Seeing the World and Knowing God*.
29. Kapic, *Communion with God*, 33.
30. Kapic, *Communion with God*, 33

extent that it "consistently moves between divine action and human response." In that movement, human responsiveness represents a clear example of attunement to Divine prompting. It is concerned with understanding humanity "in its relationship with God."[31] *Anthroposensitivity*, then, is human attunement to God. Such attunement involves openness, attentiveness, and sensitivity on the part of the human subject that goes beyond normal everyday patterns and practices, to apply to the role of the sacred and the Divine, including the presence, leadings, and whisperings of the Spirit in the inner life.

To explore the human person in the divine presence more fully, we turn to the work of Hans Urs von Balthasar. Numerous books from the secondary literature summarize von Balthasar's writings, such as *The Cambridge Companion to Hans Urs von Balthasar*,[32] and Aidan Nichols's *A Key to Balthasar*.[33] These generally offer a synthesis of von Balthasar's extensive *oeuvre* and discuss the key themes that comprise his thought. One especially helpful commentary is Steven Wigley's *Balthasar's Trilogy*,[34] in which the central chapters correspond to von Balthasar's three main bodies of writing: (1) The Glory of the Lord: a Theological Aesthetics on beauty; (2) Theo-Drama: Theological Dramatic Theory on goodness; and (3) Theo-Logic on truth. Each section explores the leitmotifs, influences, and points of application that comprise von Balthasar's unique theological contribution. But few offer an extensive investigation of the theme of attunement for which von Balthasar has become well-known. And for that purpose, we must turn to von Balthasar himself on this important theme.[35]

For the sake of brevity, I will restrict our discussion to three key points. The first is that God, by means of election which is his free act of divine love for his human creatures, is attuned to his world and his Church. Without this founding "fact," whatever might be said about attunement (spiritually speaking) would be a nonsense. Unsurprisingly, this is where von Balthasar begins—in grace, in the giving of the Spirit, and in the *connaturality* (making the unnatural natural by repetitive action to make it second nature) of the soul with divine things. He writes, "The inspiration, therefore, descends upon believing man [sic] from the

---

31. Kapic, *Communion with God*, 33–34.
32. Oakes and Moss, *Cambridge Companion to Hans Urs von Balthasar*.
33. Nichols, *Key to Balthasar*.
34. Wigley, *Balthasar's Trilogy*.
35. Especially Hans Urs von Balthasar's *Seeing the Form*, 241–57.

heights of the absolute is the absolute genius which is essentially superior to man in every respect."[36]

Second, the possibility of attunement is placed in the human soul by God himself, but in a way that it has not yet achieved full flowering—it is dependent on humankind acquiring the kinds of skills needed to advance in the art of God-relatedness:

> The concept of attunement (*Stimmung*) embraces both the aesthetics and the theological elements. An existence is envisaged which is like an instrument tuned by the Spirit; at the breath of the spirit, the instrument like the Aeolian harp rings out in tune. This is attunement (*Gestimmtsein*) which is a concordance (*Uberinstimmung*) with the rhythm of God himself, and therefore an ascent (*Zustimmung*) not only of God's Being, but to his free act of willing which is always being breathed by God upon man. And finally in virtue of this pliancy it is also the order (*das Stimmen*) within man himself—his Augustinian *rectitudo*— which makes him to be himself the work of the Divine Artist.[37]

And third, von Balthasar situates Christian attunement to God in its proper christological center—in Christ. In just the same way that Christ attuned himself completely to the Father—and out of that flowed the possibility of redemption for both the world and the church—so Christian discipleship attends to this point-of-connection between the Christ-worshipper and Christ who is his/her love object. According to von Balthasar, "We speak of a sensorium for Christ's 'instinct of obedience' which forms the essence of the spiritual life that becomes the Christian's normal disposition and 'pitch.'"[38] Von Balthasar also speaks about "dogma" (by which he means simply the Christian "teaching") being incorporated into the human person, "down to the very foundation of the self and in every fibre and vibration of his [sic] sensibility: to be sure, it is 'he' who still lives, but he is no longer an autonomous ego since Christ has begun to live in him . . . (including) his acts of knowing and willing."[39] Matthew Moser summarizes von Balthasar's position this way:

> Knowledge, as Balthasar insisted in his theological aesthetics, is a form of attunement. It is being 'attuned' intellectually, yes, but also ontologically, existentially, and *spiritually* with that which

---

36. von Balthasar, *Seeing the Form*, 250
37. von Balthasar, *Seeing the Form*, 251
38. von Balthasar, *Seeing the Form*, 253
39. von Balthasar, *Seeing the Form*, 254

is known. It is the Spirit who attunes through his illumination; he is the one who makes us *knowers* insofar as we are *lovers*.[40]

"Crucial to the act of faith," writes Aidan Nichols, "is a power of a perception experienced as a gift from a source beyond oneself . . . [with which] we have to cooperate."[41] And that cooperation requires something which Michael Fishbane said of Jewish theology, that it is a "living practice . . . not life itself; it is rather a preparation for it; an attunement for attunement . . . This is the double-faced nature of attunement: it involves both perception and performance."[42] Christian theology takes this "attunement to attunement" to the next level, whereby it is the indwelling Spirit who ushers us into the presence of the divine, in order to teach us and show us the very heart of God himself (John 14:26).

16. Beauty

The maxim, "beauty is in the eye of the beholder" rightly has a place in our everyday language. That is because beauty catches the eye as something irresistible. As both observers of the world and participants in that same world, we see beauty all around us in scenes such as a mountain vista, a horse at full gallop, a storm at sea, a newborn baby, a face that takes one's breath away. In scenes such as these, beauty is present, but it must be "taken in" by the attentive observer. It is always "there," but not everyone can see it or is conscious of it. The fact that there are many people who find it difficult to receive beauty into themselves—such as the clinically depressed, those who are imprisoned (judicially or psychologically), or those who are preoccupied with looking elsewhere—only serves to highlight the importance of attending to beauty and its centrality to the human experience.

From a Christian point of view, beauty is more than something which merely resides in the sub-structures of the cosmos, as is the case with Plato's identification of beauty as a trans-historical "Idea" or "Form." The biblical depiction, by contrast, suggests beauty has its origins in the Being of God himself. As Gerard Manley Hopkins wrote in his poem, 'Pied Beauty':

---

40. Moser, "Love Itself is Understanding," 193.
41. Nichols, *Key to Balthasar*, 29.
42. Fishbane, *Sacred Attunement,* xii–xiii

> All things counter, original, spare, strange;
> Whatever is fickle, freckled (who knows how?)
> With swift, slow; sweet, sour; a dazzle, dim;
> He fathers-forth whose beauty is past change;
> Praise him.[43]

Everything that is good, beautiful, and perfect originates from and resides in the person of God. The God who "makes all things beautiful" (Eccl 3:11) is himself beautiful, and the source of everything that is good, true, and lovely. When he created the world, including his human subjects, God saw that "it was very good" (Gen 1:31). According to Gerhard Nebel, "something of God's own splendor passes over into his creatures."[44] In this way, we learn that "there is an intrinsic relationship between beauty and the divine."[45] In Plato's parable of the cave, the inhabitants of the cave know only darkness and tried without success to make sense of the shadows cast by the fire on the walls of the cave; but only those who are able to escape the cave discover what is truly "real" in the full light of day. Similarly, in the context of Christian spirituality, in order to "see truly," one must have undergone an awakening, a conversion, in order to see things from a God's-eye point-of-view. And this necessitates tying everything that is good, beautiful, and ideal back to God. The requirement to "give thanks in all things" (Greek, *eucharisteo*, "I give thanks") is predicated on the Christian "eye" being attuned to the divine aesthetic.

Hans von Balthasar is well-known for placing beauty at the center of his theological framework. Here we will explore just four features of his aesthetic theology. First, von Balthasar situates everything that is good and beautiful in the person of God himself. That is why his theology is variously called *doxological, glorious,* and *enraptured*. There comes a point when theology must cease speculation and proceed to its logical endpoint, which is the worship of God. "A moment of grace lies in all beauty: it shows itself to me far beyond what I have a right to expect, which is why we feel astonishment and admiration ... What is demanded of us now, as we stand before this pure grace, which no longer reveals beauty but rather glory, is not to admire and be enraptured. Now we must worship."[46]

Second, God's beauty is demonstrated most fully and clearly in the person of Jesus Christ. According to W. T. Dickens, for von Balthasar,

---

43. Hopkins, "Pied Beauty." 30
44. Cited by von Balthasar, *Seeing the Form*, 64.
45. Garcia-Rivera, "Aesthetics," 245.
46. von Balthasar, *Epilogue*, 66.

> The incarnation of Jesus Christ . . . is 'the appearance of an infinitely determined super-form' . . . As such, he is 'the very apex and archetype of beauty in the world,' 'the form of all forms and the measure of all measures' . . . God's beauty is beheld in all its fullness on earth in the cross of Christ.[47]

Third, for the believing soul who worships God as Father, and knows Christ as Savior and God's true Son, a perceptual change has occurred in their thinking, allowing them to see the world *Christianly*. The awakening they have experienced is more than an escape from Plato's cave—it is, rather, to have seen in Christ one who is ultimate beauty, who has overcome the ugliness of evil and sin and despair. As John O'Donnell informs us, "I can only know Christ in the form of divine beauty insofar as I surrender myself to the evidence, but in that surrender I really do know."[48] And fourth, the new angle-of-vision that has Christ as its interpretive "lens," enables the believing soul to perceive all beauty, all arts, all colour, all of human life in a spiritual way. "In order to understand, he [sic] (the observer) must recreate the truth in himself in a living manner. This is how he becomes a 'disciple.'"[49]

Fyodor Dostoevsky placed the words, "Beauty will save the world" in the mouth of Prince Myshkin, a key figure in his novel *The Idiot*.[50] Dostoevsky is implying we need more beauty, not less, and beauty in the sense of something more than mere aesthetics . . . beauty as in deep knowledge of the reality and goodness of the world. The Christian faith places Christ at the heart of its theological and aesthetic vision. It is Christ and his self-giving love for the world that becomes the thing of ultimate beauty that mystifies and enraptures his disciples. As Roger Scruton suggests:

> What is revealed to me in the experience of beauty is a fundamental truth about being—the truth that being is a gift, and receiving it is a task. This is the truth of theology that demands exposition as such. Hence our exploration of the face of the earth guides us to the real topic of my argument, which is the face of God.[51]

---

47. Dickens, von Balthasar's *Theological Aesthetics*, 44–45.
48. O'Donnell, "Logic of Divine Glory," 163.
49. von Balthasar, *Seeing the Form*, 183.
50. Dostoyevsky, *Idiot*, 701.
51. Scruton, *Face of God*, 151–52.

Any approach to spiritual formation and education must take pains to develop a sense of (or sensitivity towards) beauty in the believing community and its individual members, through proper teaching from the biblical narratives, focusing on concepts such as the inherent goodness of creation, an appropriate wonder and worship towards God, and in particular a reverence for Christ who makes all things beautiful. The last word here goes to C. S. Lewis, who wrote, "We do not merely want to see beauty, though, God knows, even that is bounty enough. We want something else which can hardly be put into words—to be united with the beauty we see, to pass into it, to remove it into ourselves, to bathe in it, to become part of it."[52]

17. Catechism

The practice of catechism (from the Greek *katechesis*, meaning "instruction") has played a pivotal role in Christian history from the earliest days of the faith. Catechism was employed by the early bishops in the second and third centuries when the Christian faith was increasing in popularity and influence. Many pagans (un-believers) wished to enter the Christian faith at a time when becoming a Christian was becoming progressively more popular, perhaps as a result of transitioning into the new faith with other members of their family in a 'group mind' culture, or to take advantage of new business opportunities within the Christian community as it grew in numbers and influence. As such, the bishops faced a dilemma: they needed a mechanism for instructing large numbers of people into the nascent faith in a way that produced deep and not "surface-level" believers, and which safeguarded the church's teachings against distortion. In the second century, most citizens of the extensive Roman Empire, from present-day Turkey in the east, right across to Portugal and Ireland in the west, were polytheists, who as a matter of course assumed that the worship of multiple gods (e.g., the deities of Caesar, tribe, territory, family and household) was perfectly normal. They would simply have assumed they could "add" Jesus—the Christian God—to the existing Greek and Roman pantheons and to the many other gods they already worshipped.

But Christianity is a monotheism, requiring the worship of Jesus exclusively. Becoming a Christian required newcomers to abandon all previous religious affiliations and allegiances, and to worship Jesus *only*.

---

52. Lewis, *Weight of Glory*, 42.

What was needed by the early church, therefore, was a mechanism with the capacity to induct large numbers of people who had no prior understanding of the Christian faith or teaching, into the "way" of Jesus, through a process that was deeply transformative and life changing. It was also important to "weed out" any corrupting "root" of pagan religion, beliefs or practices that might infiltrate the church during this early and vulnerable stage of its life. The process they chose was instruction by way of catechism (or catechesis). According to historian Alan Kreider:

> Catechism was designed to . . . re-form pagan people, to re-socialise them, to deconstruct the old world, and reconstruct a new one, so that they would emerge as Christian people who will be at home in communities of freedom. And to help the catechumens (those under instruction) progress on this journey, the catechists (teachers) needed especially to instruct them into areas essential to the life of the community, history and folkways.[53]

The process of early catechism was based on a three-year cycle, with transition points focusing on Easter and the admission into the life of the church at the moment when the new adherents were baptized. The process of catechism achieved its culmination in the public rite of baptism. At baptism—which included a rite of exorcism (a public renunciation of all lesser gods) and the confession of Christ as Lord—neophyte believers were inducted into the new faith and so effectively became "Christians." Prior to baptism, however, catechumens underwent a process of intensive spiritual formation and mentoring under the guidance of the catechist. During their first year, the catechumen copied the life, practices, and beliefs of the catechist whose life served as the model for faithful living. Like the apostle Paul, who said, "Follow my example, as I follow Christ's example" (1 Cor 11:1), the life of the catechist became the living example of what it meant to believe in Christ, and a working model of what it meant to become a Christian. During this early stage, catechumens could only attend carefully selected parts of Christian worship. They could hear scripture read and participate in limited aspects of the liturgy. But they were not yet able to participate in the culmination of worship in the form of the sacraments. One of the roles of the deacons was to ensure that the catechumens were excluded from the central "mysteries" of the Christian faith, located in the Eucharist. In the second year, catechumens continued in their process of ongoing spiritual instruction and moral reformation,

---

53. Kreider, *Worship and Evangelism in Pre-Christendom*, 23.

and at the same time were allowed to remain in worship services to listen to preaching, to confess the creeds, and make their confession of faith.

In their third year—following an interview with the bishop and after satisfying him through their life, morals and intention to live a Christian life—catechumens could be baptized just prior to participating in the Eucharist, receiving the body and blood of Christ, and so becoming full members of the Christian community. In the weeks leading up to Easter—and prior to their baptism—catechumens were subjected to intense instruction in the course of salvation history, the Old Testament prophecies concerning Christ, the significance of the Apostles' Creed, and the relevance of the Christian sacraments. They were required to keep night vigils and to learn by heart the truths of the gospel, repentance, baptism, and the new life. They were instructed in the Christian world-and-life-view in such a way that they came to internalize its essence as their new way of life, with Christ at the center. They were now in possession of all the "secret mysteries" of the Christian faith and its central teachings concerning Christ, the extent of redemption, the freedom to live a new life in Christ, the requirement for sanctification, and the hope of heaven. The focus for instruction was on Romans 6, where immersion into the water and emergence from the water depicted new life. As they arose out of the baptism pool into the arms of their sponsor, they were now truly a new creature in Christ, and were welcomed as such by their church community.

Most if not all churches in the twenty-first century West retain some form of catechism, but relatively few make use of them. Eastern Orthodox churches together with the Roman Catholic Church are some of the few bodies that make use of a modern-day catechism. Today, churches have few if any ways of teaching their followers the substance of the faith they profess, of inducting them into the life of the church, and preparing them for baptism and the reception of the sacraments. As a result, Christianity in the modern world has few "nurseries" capable of rearing new generations of believers in times of foment and change. The need for a new catechism relevant to our times is more urgent than almost any other area of Christian activity. The future of the faith depends upon it.

18. Christian Knowing

Contemporary book titles such as *Inside the Criminal Mind, Inside the Atheist Mind, Inside Muslim Minds,* and *Inside the Mind of Unchurched*

Harry and Mary offer insight into the mindset and outlook of selected groups of people. This entry takes as its primary concern an exploration of what governs the inner contents and workings of "the Christian mind." The goal is not to map the Christian worldview in its entirety. Instead, it aims to explore the radical nature of the Christian "vision" of the world, how it gets inside people's heads, and the significance of such a Christian mode of perception to the way people actually live. This epistemological "lens" is important because it is what sets Christians apart from other people. And it has special significance because it constitutes the *telos* or "endpoint" that Christian spiritual educators, catechists and faith-formators try to establish in believers, since it is foundational to all Christian belief, ethics, behavior, identity, and spiritual practice.

The four topics discussed in this entry are: (1) the scripting nature of scripture; (2) convictional experience; (3) embedded knowing; and (4) reasoning from faith.

First, "the scripting nature of scripture." Serious readers of the Bible find themselves coming to see the world from a God's-eye point of view. As I've suggested elsewhere:

> Having read the Bible, heard the stories, sung the psalms, prayed the prayers, and encountered Christ in its pages, something happens that shapes the way believers look at the world. The faith community that truly listens to the stories of Scripture comes to confess it, to re-enact it, and to interpose their own lives into the text of Scripture and in turn, to read their own existence out of the Scripture.[54]

Through reading the scriptures, we acquire what Richard Hays calls the "syntax of salvation."[55] Every worldview and every kind of spirituality is rooted in a story that constitutes what is real for those who live within it. To inhabit that world requires the believing soul to learn the story (and stories) of their newfound faith-community in order to enter that world as an active participant. As George Lindbeck has argued, "To become a Christian involves learning the story of Israel and of Jesus well enough to interpret and experience oneself and one's world in its terms."[56]

---

54. Devenish, *Seeing and Believing*, 30–31.
55. Hays, *Moral Vision of the New Testament*, 138.
56. Lindbeck, *Nature of Doctrine*, 34.

Second, "convictional experience." In his book *The Transforming Moment*,[57] James Loder unpacks the nature of convictional experience, suggesting it requires a "figure-ground shift" whereby a complex of meanings (concerning life-and-death, the sacraments, Christian teaching, and one's personal existence) come no longer to reside outside oneself, as some kind of distant truth, but are instead taken into the deep-self, so as to form the defining principle by which one lives one's life. Loder writes:

> At the heart of convictional knowing is a radical figure-ground shift that is not merely perceptual but existential, in which the truth of Christ's revelation transforms the subject from a knower into one who was fully known and comprehended by what he or she first knew. Convictional knowing describes the structural and dynamic link between knowing about Christianity and becoming Christian.[58]

The Christian spiritual life is fundamentally a life of transformation; for, "If anyone is in Christ, he is a new creation; the old has gone, the new has come" (2 Cor 6:17). At the center of Christian knowing is a new interpretive framework that identifies Christ as the teacher, the lesson, the interpreter and the wisdom-principle at the heart of all knowledge. For those who have become his disciples, Christ is now the energizing center of their "controlling stories" (Wright, 1992), their "control beliefs" (Wolterstorff, 1976), their "master stories" (Fowler, 1981), and the "tacit dimensions" of their personal beliefs (Polanyi, 1974).

Third, "embedded knowing." Esther Meek, in her book *Loving to Know: Covenant Epistemology*, describes human knowing as based in "covenantal epistemology."[59] It is covenantal in the sense that it is based on relationship, reciprocity and intimacy. It is epistemological (or knowledge-based) in the sense that it creates the "grounds" upon which not only one's own life but also the world as a whole ultimately rests. This "participatory" knowing is what establishes one's ability to "see" (which is to know) as a Christian. Meek writes:

> I believe that seeing, as a human activity, actually can be and must be redeemed, recast so that it is thought of as a sort of visual touch, one that evokes mutuality and reciprocity. For there is a kind of seeing that distances us from the object; there is a

---

57. Loder, *Transforming Moment*.
58. Loder, *Transforming Moment*, 121–22.
59. Meek, *Loving to Know*, 395.

kind of seeing that moves beyond objective and allows us to see from the inside out . . . There is also a kind of seeing in which we sense possibilities and significances hitherto overlooked.[60]

And fourth, "reasoning from faith." Here, I borrow from the title of Justin Sands's book *Reasoning from Faith*[61] as it neatly serves the purposes of this entry, even if the complexity of Sands's argument (comprising a discussion of Richard Kearney's and Merold Westphal's respective treatments of onto-theology) is a step too far for our purposes here. After conversion—i.e., after experiencing the kind of transformation that dislodges everything one previously knew, or thought one knew—a rewriting of the structures of reality takes place. And with that comes a new mode of knowing, of being, and of seeing. According to James Hart:

> Spiritual knowing is not primarily a matter of religious beliefs or systems of doctrine. . . Spiritual knowing or knowing spiritually is more authentically approached as knowing focused in hope and trust. Knowing what direction to take in a universe surrounded by mystery, knowing which guides to accept in the face of life's existential boundary conditions, is not a matter of faith rather than knowledge, but a matter of fiduciary rather than rational knowing, even though a rational dimension is not absent.[62]

Thus, because scripture "scripts," because convictional experience "convinces," and because one undergoes a change in the way one sees the world through the "embedded" or participatory knowledge of the faith community, the "sacred self" now reasons from faith. To that end, the reason supplied by faith trumps (or subsumes) all other modes of perception and practice held by the general populace in the host culture. This is what constitutes the radical vision of Christian knowing, which is always a "knowing otherwise."

19. Concursus

Concursus is a largely underdeveloped doctrine of the Christian faith which is "a corollary of the doctrines of God as *premum movens* [the Prime Mover] and of providence as *continuata creatio* [a continuation of creation] that defines the continuing divine support of the operation for

---

60. Meek, *Loving to Know*, 26.
61. Sands, *Reasoning from Faith*.
62. Hart, *Person in the Common Life*, 44.

all secondary causes (whether free, contingent, or necessary)."[63] As such, concursus deals not so much with the occurrence of random events, but with how free agents (both human and Divine) may work together to generate divinely ordained outcomes which serve God's Kingdom, without compromising the fundamental free will of the individual human actor. In that sense, causation is not merely accidental but truly intentional. The concept of *concursus* originates from the Latin root *concursum* or *concursia*, meaning a convergence or conjunction. At its root, *concursus* is a doctrine that arises out of God's creative activity, and overflows as a "secondary cause" into human activity. *Concursus* is a correlate of God's omnipresence in the world.[64] God's generative activity in the world incorporates human agency for the purposes of strategic ministry-actions to impact the world with his gospel. This can properly be called a "shared agency" under the *aegis* of his Holy Spirit.

Karl Barth draws attention to the way in which God, as loving Creator, allows his human creatures to go about their ordinary earthly business freely and without any kind of manipulation. But as they do so, under grace, those same creatures may choose of their own free will to live, work and act in such a way as to providentially bring about God's purposes in the world. Barth writes:

> The free God is always a step in advance of the free creature. The free creature does go of itself, but it can and does only go the same way as the free God. It goes its own way, but in fact it always finds itself in a very definite sense on God's way . . . At this point there is actualised in its original form the fact that the activity of the creature along the way in which God accompanies it and it can accompany God is simply a confirming of the divine activity . . . At this point, where we do not see any law but under grace, the fact of God's accompanying can and must be understood as the law of the whole divine co-existence with the creature, and as the law of the activity of the divine providence.[65]

In the unfolding of such actions, God can be said to be the originator of the action, and the human actor to be a secondary co-agent, because they have cooperated with God to achieve outcomes that are beneficial to both human and divine ends. Approaching the same idea from a Pentecostal point of view, Joshua Reichard suggests:

63. Kapic, *Communion with God*, 33
64. Muller, "Concursus," 76–77.
65. Barth, *Doctrine of Creation*, 93–94.

The concept of the Spirit as the presence of God working in cooperation with human beings is characteristic of Pentecostal notions of [a] sequenced *concursus*. While this type of *concursus* is more difficult to directly identify, it is evident that within the Pentecostal movement, human actions are often understood as directed by the Spirit, willed not independently by human agents, but oriented to will certain actions in cooperation with the Spirit.[66]

Elsewhere, Reichard draws together several lines of thought about God's agency and ours:

> Wright similarly concluded, 'God acts, creatures act, but sometimes these two lines of activity inter-twine, with God's line allowing the creaturely line to share its base.' As Peters noted, 'Primary causation is not absent when secondary is in effect; rather, they constitute two dimensions of a single reality.' As such, the act can be said to originate from both God and the human being.[67]

A striking biblical example of concursus can be found in Joseph's experience of imprisonment in Egypt. Addressing his brothers, who sold him into slavery in Egypt, Joseph declares, "God sent me before you to preserve life" (Gen 45:5). This leads Todd Billings to question:

> Who really sent Joseph into Egypt? The doctrine of concursus is a way of saying that both God and Joseph's brothers were actors in the event. God is sovereign, and human beings perform responsible, contingent acts. Divine and human agency do not compete with one another—as if God's action could undermine human agency.[68]

From the viewpoint of the ordinary Christian, Tanya Luhrmann describes the average believer as having an experience of God that is both personal and intimate. They are aware that God is at work in them in ways they cannot account for, and so on reflection they perceive there is a higher power and purpose at work. Luhrmann describes this revelation as like coming to see God as "a supernatural buddy with a thunderbolt."[69]

---

66. Reichard, "Toward a Pentecostal Theology of *Concursus*," 100.

67. Reichard, "Beyond Causation," 121.

68. Billings, Reformation21. https://www.reformation21.org/articles/divine-providence-occupying-the-mysterious-middle.php.

69. Luhrmann, *When God Talks Back*, 50.

Discussing those who exercise their ministry under the authority, guidance and inspiration of the Holy Spirit, Luhrmann describes three main ways concursus works in the world. First, through the unmediated action of the Spirit who works in sovereign singularity; second, through the immediate action of the Spirit through human beings; and third, by the action of human beings themselves. Variously, these categories are expressed through miracles, spiritual gifts, and the broad range of spiritual giftings. Whereas the miraculous or the supernatural are totally dependent upon the Spirit for its outworking in the world, spiritual gifts cannot function without human cooperation and agency, In between those two is the "mediate" space where the human person cooperates with the Holy Spirit in obedience, sanctification and the "flow" of blessing that nurtures all concerned. And finally, the concept of concursus provides a clear explanation of how human agents in God's redemptive drama, can write texts which are clearly derived from the process of human thought, writing and generational transmission. And yet, they remain at the same time Divinely inspired and Christians have historically come to believe that the origins of the Scriptures are from a Divine source in the form of the mind, heart and hand of God. Both are true, both are needed. And both are spiritually authoritative. Such is the necessity of our human-Divine partnership.

20. Contemplative Turn

In 1986, Carlo Petrini set up a public protest against the opening of a McDonald's fast-food restaurant in the famous Piazza di Spagna in Rome. The "slow food" movement was birthed from that protest, producing a subculture of "slow cities," "slow work," and "slow living" aimed at better facilitating the savoring of life.[70] In a similar way, Christian spirituality has always been grounded in the work of "the God who walks slowly."[71] Prayer, worship, Bible reading, deep faith, pilgrimage and spiritual growth are all limited in speed because of their unfolding at the speed of the soul.

John Mark Cromer, in *The Ruthless Elimination of Hurry*,[72] recounts the moment he realized he was addicted to the fast-paced lifestyle of twenty-first century consumer culture. Cromer was serving as a pastor

---

70. See Honoré, *In Praise of Slow*.
71. Discussed by Aldous, *God Who Walks Slowly*.
72. Cromer, *Ruthless Elimination of Hurry*.

of a mega-church in the US when he was forced to admit that his chronic busyness had made him "so emotionally unhealthy he was . . . leaking chemical waste all over his staff."[73] Noting the epidemic of haste today, Cromer cites philosopher Byung-Chul Han's haunting observation that most people in the Western world "are too alive to die, and too dead to live."[74] Cromer writes, "We all have our own story of trying to stay sane in the day and age of iPhones and Wi-Fi and the twenty-four-hour news cycle and urbanization and ten-lane freeways with soul-crushing traffic and nonstop noise and a frenetic ninety-miles-per-hour life of go, go, go . . ."[75] Cromer tells the story of how he came to realize that speed, hurry and haste are the polar opposites of the healthy spiritual life. He makes reference to Jesus' habit of "slow walking" as an essential way of staying attuned to God. Eugene Peterson's 'take' on this text in Matthew's Gospel brings a forceful challenge:

> Are you tired, worn out? Burned out on religion? Come to me. Get away with me and you'll recover your life. I'll show you how to take a real rest. Walk with me and work with me—watch how I do it. Learn the unforced rhythms of grace. I won't lay anything heavy or ill-fitting on you. Keep company with me and you will learn to live freely and lightly (Matt 11:28–30, *The Message*).

Cromer's discovery arose from Dallas Willard's advice on how to remain spiritually whole. As Willard advises, "You must ruthlessly eliminate hurry from your life . . . Hurry is the great enemy of the spiritual life in our day."[76]

Today, many people have become soul-sick, unable to find meaning, value, joy and purpose in their lives. The implications of such speed-sickness for the declining mental health of citizens (particularly children and young people) of Western society have yet to be fully demonstrated. Churches have yet to discover the art of slowing down their worship offerings to meet the need of the moment and to offer a "quiet revolution" of encounter with God in the place of sacred meaning-making. Entertainment-based worship delivered through loud, fast-paced music, accompanied by flashing lights and the projection of cinematic images, may grab people's attention, but it does absolutely nothing for the soul.

73. Cromer, *Ruthless Elimination of Hurry*, 17.
74. Han, *Burnout Society*, 51.
75. Cromer, *Ruthless Elimination of Hurry*, 21.
76. Willard, in Ortberg's *Soul Keeping*, 20.

The soul is a snail, slow, reclusive in its shell. It lives in the under-story of our human emotions and travels at the pace of insight which is often painfully slow. The soul—after all—is doing the work of eternity even as it is curled within its nautilus time-machine which is the human body. It spends most of its time looking downwards at its terrestrial, earth-bound existence, but there are moments when it looks upwards to reach for the stars. In the meantime, the soul needs time, space and quiet to think, reflect and discover what it truly means to be alive in the presence of God our Maker. Alan Jones, in his book *Soul Making*, suggests:

> It takes time to make a human being, and conversion is a continual process of being made and re-made. In one sense, it is never complete. To be human, from the believer's point of view, is to be in a continual process of (ongoing) conversion.[77]

What is needed in the soul-department, therefore, is not a speeding up but a slowing down, a deepening of intent to increase our connection with God and our coming-of-age in a spiritual sense.

No wonder many Christians have taken a "contemplative turn" as a sort of 12 step program for recovery from life in the twenty-first century. The soul can only be slowed down by frequently pausing to withdraw from the world, and discarding the small things that will not endure beyond the present age to focus on what endures into eternity.

Ronald Rolheiser, in *Domestic Monastery*, offers the distracted and heart-weary spiritual seeker a panacea for what he calls our "pathological busyness."[78] He recommends a form of "inbuilt monasticism" that does not require one to take up holy orders, adopt an ascetic lifestyle, or to become celibate. Rolheiser suggests there are many kinds of monasteries: "A monastery is not so much a place set apart for monks and nuns, as it is a place set apart, period."[79] Anyone can adopt an ordered lifestyle which may contribute to a contemplative form of the spiritual life. There in that place—in the midst of family life, professional life, economic life, political life—it is possible for lay-monastics to "center" themselves via a balanced pattern of prayer, worship, reading, journal writing, personal growth, and spiritual formation that together enable them to grow into the image and likeness of Christ, which is the soul's true calling. Work itself—as Brother Lawrence discovered—can be a domestic monastery,

---

77. Jones, *Soul Making*, 161–62.
78. Rolheiser, *Domestic Monastery*, 77.
79. Rolheiser, *Domestic Monastery*, 23.

where "practising the presence of God" is not only possible, but a place where Christ can be invited to add the dimensions of joy, creativity, and purpose to the work of our hands. This is one of the sanctifying graces of the domestic monastic lifestyle.

One of the most beneficial features of this domestic monasticism idea is the intentional adoption of a pattern of prayer, and a clear process for ongoing spiritual formation in the everyday life of the believing soul. Thomas à Kempis says it simply and powerfully when he says, "Progress means a programme."[80] Rolheiser repeats à Kempis's teaching when he says to his audience of monks and nuns, "Go to your cell. Your cell will teach you everything." Reinterpreting this idea for modern-day disciples, he writes: "Go inside your commitments, be faithful, your place of work is a seminary, your work is a sacrament, your family is a Monastery, your home is a sanctuary."[81] This routine of prayer and the reading of scripture, together with work, worship, service, justice, and truth telling, are the marks of true Christian discipleship. But this requires what Joan Chittester calls a "monastery of the heart,"[82] which reflects and augments Rolheiser's pattern of the monastic domestic. Ultimately, this is the place where Cromer arrived at: he got into the slow lane; he ditched his smart phone for a dumb phone; he turned off his TV; he submitted himself to the simplicity of single-tasking; he walked slower; he took regular days off for silence and solitude; he took up journaling and experimented with mindfulness and meditation; he took up cooking and eating food with the family; and—where possible—he now recommends long vacations to himself and to others. And what did he discover? He was surprised at how close God feels now that his new life has adopted a contemplative turn.

21. Dark Night of the Soul

"Dark Night of the Soul" is a famous poem written by St. John of the Cross (1542–1591), a Spanish Carmelite monk. It reads:

1. On a dark night, kindled in love with yearnings—oh, happy chance! I went forth without being observed, My house being now at rest.

2. In darkness and secure, By the secret ladder, disguised—oh, happy chance!

---

80. à Kempis, *Imitation of Christ*, 45.
81. Rolheiser *Domestic Monastery*, 37.
82. Chittester, *Monastery of the Heart.*

In darkness and in concealment, My house being now at rest.

3. In the happy night, In secret, when none saw me,

Nor I beheld aught, Without light or guide, save that which burned in my heart.

4. This light guided me More surely than the light of noonday, To the place where he (well I knew who!) Was awaiting me—A place where none appeared.

5. Oh, night that guided me, oh, night more lovely than the dawn,

Oh, night that joined Beloved with lover, Lover transformed in the Beloved!

6. Upon my flowery breast, Kept wholly for himself alone, There he stayed sleeping, and I caressed him, And the fanning of cedars made a breeze.

7. The breeze blew from the turret, As I parted his locks;

With his gentle hand he wounded my neck And caused all my senses to be suspended.

8. I remained, lost in oblivion; My face I reclined on the Beloved.

All ceased and I abandoned myself, Leaving my cares forgotten among the lilies.[83]

These eight stanzas have become renowned in the literature of Christian mysticism for their poetic representation of the soul's seeking God, its true love, while suffering the pangs of love, loss, wounded ego and abandonment. The darkness of the poem foreshadows and unveils the process of spiritual purgation that unfolds in a season of lostness and wandering in search of God. As to who St. John was, and the historical circumstances in which the Dark Night poem and related commentary came into being, this much we know:

St. John of the Cross was born to a poor family in Fontiveros, Spain. To obtain an education, John studied with the Jesuits, then entered a Carmelite monastic order. Ordained at the age of twenty-five, he moved to a discalced (barefoot, more ascetical) Carmelite monastery as its confessor, then to a farmhouse where he established the first monastery for male monastics within the Order. However, a group of traditional (shoed, meaning less ascetical) Carmelite monks banned the discalced dissidents, and took John as a prisoner to Toledo, attempting to force him to reform his ways. When he refused to recant, he was imprisoned in a windowless cell. He was given bread and water only three times a

---

83. John of the Cross, *Dark Night of the Soul*, 33–34.

week. He was beaten for his refusal to return to traditional Carmelite teachings. He wrote some extraordinarily noteworthy poetry during that time, before escaping and finding refuge with some nuns in a nearby monastery. He and Teresa of Ávila went on to become the co-founders of the discalced Carmelite order. John became Rector of Carmelite colleges in Baeza and Segovia.

John's writings include several significant poems and essays, including the Dark Night of the Soul, the Spiritual Canticle, and the Living Flame of Love. During his middle years, John became familiar with mysticism and wrote of the elevation of the soul toward union with God. Like Teresa of Ávila, he learned much through his experience of suffering and marginalization, including how to rely on the powerful resources he found in God and in the interior life. Sadly, John was distrusted by his superiors and was eventually removed from the Friary at la Paneula to Úbeda, where he died after a series of beatings at the hands of his shoed Carmelite brothers. He was canonized as a saint by the Roman Catholic Church in 1726 and made a Doctor of the Church in 1926. John's spirituality is characterized by a deep mystical discernment, one that pays particular attention to the journey of the soul towards its completion in Christ.

Often, the experience of the dark night of the soul is thought of as exhibiting abandonment by God, leading to despair and unspeakable anguish. But that is not how John understood it. Using the accepted (at that time) spiritual formula of the soul's natural ascent towards God, John voiced his stanzas from the point of view of a mature contemplative, reflecting on his experience of "the Beloved." Mature contemplatives speak from a "state of perfection," which is essentially a form of union with Christ in God. As such, they have already passed through the early stages of the spiritual novitiate, with its many struggles to remain focused on God. Instead, the mature contemplative has gone on to better things by learning to focus on God specifically by means of spiritual exercises designed to bring them more fully into the presence of God. If, in the process, God wishes to abandon them for a season, then so be it. Job's declaration, "Though he slay me, yet will I hope in him," (Job 13:15), is replicated in St. John of the Cross, where the contemplative stalwartly rests his or her faith on God who is their *Beloved*, the one who loves unconditionally and is loved in return—in spite of the prevailing circumstances. Thus, in a state of passive yet impassioned waiting, all worldly strivings cease (Ps 131), and the soul "abandons itself" to God who alone is free to either wound, reward, or induce ecstasy as he wills. As such, the dark night is not ultimately an experience of darkness, torment, humiliation, or being abandoned by God. Instead, it is often a vital period of spiritual preparation, of "waiting" for delight, culminating in rest, awakening, and spiritual ecstasy arising precisely because of the soul's newfound and hard-won proximity to God.

The dark night of the soul has continuing relevance for modern-day disciples and mystics. Its use as a manual for spiritual instruction for the upward movement of the soul towards union with God remains as relevant today as it ever was.

22. De Magestro

The phrase *de Magestro* (along with its parallel phrase *Magister internus*—both meaning "Inner Teacher"), originates in the writings of St. Augustine (354–430) and represents an important contribution to our understanding of first-person spiritual experience, that forms the central concern of this book. In his early career, Augustine was a teacher of grammar and rhetoric, and in his later work as preacher, philosopher and theologian, his skills in the use of language, rhetoric and argumentation were carried over to produce and give shape to his extensive body of writing. The phrase *De Magistro*[84] is the title of a dialogue between Augustine and his son, Adeodatus (who was 17 at the time), published in ca. 389 in his hometown of Thagaste in North Africa. The dialogue was contained in the expected form of how a language instructor might have presented a lesson to students in the third century, exemplifying the skills of rhetoric (spoken language and argumentation) and grammar (written language and expression), which were the hallmarks of "true" learning among scholars of the day.

The dialogue begins by exploring the nature of words which act as signs and symbols of the reality being communicated. However, it soon becomes clear that what Augustine has in mind is how communication works in the teaching of truth to the "inner man" [sic] (Eph 3:17). Augustine writes, "Our words are signs merely of things. It is the sign and not the thing signified which comes out of the mouth of the speaker."[85] In his previous role as teacher of rhetoric and language, Augustine was paid to deliver lessons on language as if in a marketplace of ideas: i.e., he "sold" words and

---

84. Augustine, "Teacher (De Magistro)," 69–101.
85. Augustine, "Teacher (De Magistro)," 86.

symbols, knowledge and techniques without any particular investment in their meaning on his part. But now as a bishop and a preacher of the Word of God, his purpose and deep wish was to communicate the substance of Christian faith in a form that might help unwrap the reality of Christ to his audience. To achieve this, Augustine recognized his dependence upon Christ, who is the "real Teacher." He writes:

> Our real Teacher is he who is so listened to, who is said to dwell in the inner man, namely Christ, that is, the unchangeable power and eternal wisdom of God. To this wisdom every rational soul gives heed, but to each is given only so much as he is able to receive, according to his own good or evil will.[86]

Augustine does not presume that the simple speaking of words by the preacher will suffice. Only the hearing of God's Word by means of the "inner ear" results in the hearing of God's truth. But it is not Christ alone who does the teaching; there is another "agent" involved in the learning process. It is the listener, the "audience member" who must not only hear, but also respond, and believe. It is the mind and consciousness of the one being taught that also has a role to play.

> If anyone is ever deceived it is not the fault of Truth, any more than it is the fault of the common light of day that the bodily eyes are often deceived. Confessedly, we must pay heed to the light that it may let us discern visible things so far as we are able.[87]

A simple statement of truth by the preacher or teacher is not enough. It must be held in the mind of the learner and rehearsed; as Augustine says, "with the intelligence and with reason, we speak of things which we look upon directly in the inner light of truth which illumines the inner man [sic] and is inwardly enjoyed."[88]

Theresa Fuhrer[89] offers insight into the communication of truth between (a) the teacher, using words, symbols and actions addressed towards the interior life of the learner; (b) God who by his Spirit is the "inner teacher," the *Magister internus*, who opens the eye of the soul to grasp truth in the "inner man"; and (c) the human receptor, who has the responsibility to receive, process, own and interiorize the message

---

86. Augustine, "Teacher (De Magistro)," 95.
87. Augustine, "Teacher (De Magistro)," 95.
88. Augustine, "Teacher (De Magistro)," 96.
89. Fuhrer, "On Augustine's Didactic Concept of Interiority", 129–46.

that is spoken and received in the inward life. Fuhrer observes in Augustine's teaching practice a "theory of inner language" that comes into full flower in his later work *De Trinitate* (ca. 417). Following Augustine, Fuhrer contends that the truth that is conveyed about God's Being is not solely communicated in hard-to-understand theological language; there also needs to be a vital "personification of truth" which is communicated to the "inner ear" and received by the human receptor in ecstatic experiences which are auditory, visual, and haptic (via divine "touch").[90]

The concept of *De Magistro* (or "the inner teacher") is especially important for spiritual education. Augustine's theory of inner language—grounded in the dialogue between God as the inner witness, the Holy Spirit whom Jesus sent to "teach you all things" (John 14:26), the human teacher of spiritual truths, and the human receptor whose own curious mind and inward needs and longings—discloses a "partnership" in the process of spiritual discovery and learning where each participant has a role to play in unveiling and perceiving the mystery of the love of God lived out in the spiritual and sensory organ that is the human soul. Augustine's concept of the inner teacher has profound implications for Christian spiritual education in the contemporary context. It calls for a shift in the mere dissemination of religious knowledge, to a more holistic approach that nurtures the inner life of the disciple/learner. Employing this approach, the concept of "the inner teacher" prompts Christian educators to prioritize the role of the student/receptor in their teachability and openness to the inner voice of the Spirit to learn the things of Christ above all else.

23. Divine Embrace

If spirituality is about anything, it is about connection. The spiritual life is about finding oneself in the presence of God—a place that leaves us feeling variously challenged, restored, reconciled, convinced, awestruck, transformed, and elevated. The idea of the "Divine embrace" is a recurring theme in the spiritual literature, as Robert Webber highlights in his book *The Divine Embrace: Recovering the Passionate Spiritual Life*.[91] For Webber, the Christian spiritual life is a life of proximity to God and participation in the life of God, echoing the words of the Apostle Paul, "It is no longer I who live, but Christ who lives in me" (Gal 2:20). In

---

90. Fuhrer, "On Augustine's Didactic Concept of Interiority," 139.
91. Webber, *Divine Embrace*.

characterizing this closeness to God as an embrace, Webber borrows explicitly from *The Book of Common Prayer*:

> Lord Jesus Christ, you stretched out your arms of love on the hard wood of the cross that everyone might come within the reach of your saving embrace; So clothe us in your Spirit that we, reaching forth our hands in love, may bring those who do not know you to the knowledge and love of you; for the honour of your Name. Amen.[92]

Throughout the remainder of his book, Webber extrapolates the historical development of the idea of a Divine embrace. Webber grounds the story of God's Divine embrace in the incarnation, death and resurrection of Jesus as defined and defended by the ancient creeds and debates of the early Church. In addition to story, Webber ties the divine "embrace" to the power of experience, when God embraces his human child/children, there is an enveloping presence, which produces a profound and transformative encounter that transcends intellectual assent. The believer is held, and in that "holding" there is the healing Power of love, and a deep sense of security and belonging. And thirdly, the idea of the embrace as an empowering of the human respondent is on the basis of the strength of Divine love which overcomes any anxiety and uncertainty, replacing them with a profound sense of God's sustaining, healing, reassuring and unrelenting love.

Webber observes how the Reformers returned spirituality to the Divine embrace by re-routing it through grace, faith and a genuine encounter with God. Reformation spirituality in its early years was preoccupied with forensic justification, and only later turned inwards to employ a sanctification model guided by gratitude. It is possible to see the experience of conversion in Reformation spirituality as a flight from the world, but it is better understood as a flight towards God in Christ.

Webber goes on to document how twentieth-century Evangelical spirituality inherited these modifications from the past and further developed a privatized spirituality of legalism, intellectualism, and experientialism. In the present day, Evangelical spirituality has become separated from the Divine embrace, and is inadequate to the challenge of countering the growing popularity of New Age and Eastern spiritualities grounded in an impersonal, pantheistic conception of God and the

---

92. Webber, *Divine Embrace*, 22.

world. The challenge before us, Webber contends, is to recover a spiritual life and a form of spirituality which is rooted in the Divine embrace.[93]

A primary concern for Webber is to ensure that Christian spirituality is properly grounded in God's story in the world. It is a story of God's making and creating, of Christ's incarnation and redeeming, and of the Spirit's in-filling and sanctifying power. In the Divine embrace, God was united to humanity so that we might be united to God. And Christ, by the Spirit, recapitulates the world (by re-making it again through redemption) and returns it to the Father. He writes: "God has come to us in Jesus so that we may come to God through Jesus. That is Christian spirituality. And living in that union, the Divine embrace, that is the spiritual life."[94]

For Webber, baptism into union with Jesus is the most potent sign of our new spiritual identity with the Triune God and with each other in the Church. In baptism, Christians embrace the new life that is the gift of God's grace through Jesus Christ by the Spirit.

The spiritual life can be understood as living into our baptism—i.e., dying to all that is sin and death, rising through new birth into the new life that has been modelled to us by Jesus, the one who images humanity completely united to God's original purpose for creation. For Webber, the spiritual life moves us to contemplate the mystery of God revealed in Jesus Christ and so to participate in the purposes of God for all humanity. At its heart, the Christian spiritual life is disciplined by the rule of steadfastness, fidelity, and obedience, tending to prayer, study and work; it seeks to meet God in daily life, in material things, and in other people. Webber concludes by noting how the spiritual life of the believer is nourished by the church, which is the continued presence of our human encounter with Jesus in and to the world. Specifically, the spiritual life is nurtured by worship, song, prayer, preaching, and the church's corporate celebration of holy seasons and festivals following the Christian calendar (the liturgy).[95]

Outsiders to the Christian spiritual life who have no knowledge or understanding of God, may suspect that God's embrace of human subject is intended to crush the life out of them as an act of judgment and condemnation. But nothing could be further from the truth. According to Brian Rosner, in his book *Known by God: a Biblical Theology of Personal Identity*,[96] human persons are special to God because he made us in his

---

93. Webber, *Divine Embrace*, 30.
94. Webber, *Divine Embrace*, 23
95. Webber, *Divine Embrace*, 218.
96. Rosner, *Known by God*.

likeness, creating us for a relationship with himself, electing us into his family, declaring us the "apple of his eye" (Ps 17:8), remembering us in our sufferings, and engraving us on the palms of his hands (Isa 49:16).[97]

The only appropriate response on the part of the believing soul is to welcome God's Divine embrace as a sign of God's love towards them, and not to resist or resent it in the manner of a recalcitrant child. As James K. A. Smith indicates, "Spirituality is not a self-generated achievement but a gift given to us by God. This gift sets us free to see life in a new way and to live life as God intended, in union with the purposes of the Creator and Redeemer of the world."[98]

24. Desire in the Spiritual Life

Ronald Rolheiser has described desire as the energizing center of human life. He says:

> There is within us a fundamental dis-ease, an unquenchable fire that renders us incapable, in this life, of ever coming to full peace. This desire lies at the centre of our lives in the marrow of our bones, and in the deep recesses of the soul . . . Desire is the straw that stirs the drink.[99]

Speaking subsequently of the spiritual life, Rolheiser notes:

> Spirituality is, ultimately, about what we do with our desire. What we do with our longings, both in terms of handling the pain and the hope they bring us, that is our spirituality. Thus, when Plato says that we are on fire because our souls come from beyond and that beyond us is, through the longing and hope that its fire creates in us, trying to draw us back towards itself—he is laying out the broad outlines for a spirituality. Likewise, Augustine, when he says: 'You have made us for yourself Lord, and our hearts are restless until they find their rest in you.' Spirituality is about what we do with our unrest . . . Spirituality, essentially defined, is how we handle that eros.[100]

And according to Huston Smith:

---

97. Rosner, *Known by God*, 93–112.
98. Smith, *How (Not) to Be Secular*, 18.
99. Rolheiser, *Holy Longing*, 3.
100. Rolheiser, *Holy Longing*, 5 & 23.

> All great literature, poetry, the arts, philosophy, and religion tries to name and analyse this [unquenchable fire]. We are seldom in direct touch with it, and indeed the modern world seems set on preventing us from getting in touch with it by covering it with an un-ending *phantasmagoria* of entertainments, obsessions and distractions of every sort. But the longing is there, built into us like a jack-in-the-box that presses for release.[101]

With reference to the biblical foundations of desire vis-à-vis spirituality, Philip Sheldrake has observed that God is filled with desire for his people: "The Lord is compassionate and gracious, slow to anger and abounding in love . . . As a father has compassion on his children, so the Lord has compassion on those who fear him" (Ps 103:8, 13). Hans von Balthasar even speaks about the "Divine eros" that energizes God's love for his creatures and his creation.[102] Further, this longing is mirrored by the people of God in their desire for him: "As the deer pants for streams of water, so my soul pants (longs) for you, O God. My soul thirsts for God for the living God, when can I go and meet with God?" (Ps 42:1–2).

Sheldrake goes on to affirm that, "Desire is at the heart of all spirituality."[103] Desire expresses itself in multiple forms of passionate engagement, whole-of-self surrender, and spiritual arousal. The language of spirituality is rife with the language of desire, including such terms as "enthusiasm" (meaning the God within), "devotion," "passion," "ecstasy," and "intimacy." Sheldrake observes:

> The fourteenth century Italian mystic Katherine of Siena recognised this positive and extraordinary power of our desires when she wrote that it makes it one of the few ways of touching God: 'You have nothing infinite except your soul's love and desire' (*Dialogue*, 270). The German Dominican mystic of the same period, Meister Eckhart, suggested that the reason we are not able to see God is the faintness of our desire.[104]

St. Augustine could say:

> Give me one who loves, and he [sic] feels what I am saying. Give me one who desires, give me one who hungers, give me one travelling and thirsting in this solitude and sighing for the

---

101. Smith, *Soul of Christianity*, xii-iii.
102. von Balthasar, *Glory of the Lord*, 121–22.
103. Sheldrake, "Desire," 231.
104. Sheldrake, *Befriending our Desires*, 14.

fountain of an eternal homeland, give me such a one, and he knows what I'm saying. But if I speak to someone coldly unresponsive, He knows not what I speak.[105]

So where does this leave us? Are we forever condemned to wage war with ourselves because of our "bent" towards wrong desires expressed in the form of sin and avarice, as Thomas à Kempis suggests? "I, poor piece of humanity, am the theatre of a civil war, a burden to myself, with the spirit trying to soar aloft, and the body endeavouring to stay below."[106] Not necessarily. Anders Nygren has suggested that "Desire is the mark of the creature."[107] This means that desire is a normal part of human life. Further, desire for God *via* the inward spiritual life is not just a curious feature of human experience, but is indeed central to our human nature. God—knowing his creatures better than the creature knows itself—uses the in-built desire he placed there by his own hand to draw us inexorably to himself. So it was that Thomas Traherne (1636–1674) thanked God, "For giving me desire, and eager thirst, a burning ardent fire, a virgin infant flame, love with which into the world I came . . . a Paradise . . . be thy name forever praised by me."[108]

Timothy Gorringe has suggested that since "the physical appetites are instruments of grace,"[109] the purpose of spiritual formation is not to get rid of our human desires, but to "educate them." Since God placed our physical and spiritual desires within us, the way forward is not to seek to destroy, expunge or eradicate those desires, but to learn how to direct and to use them appropriately. We are to "befriend" them through the process of spiritual formation. As Dairmuid O'Murchu argues:

> The restlessness of the human heart is a divine endorsement. Born from mystery, we are programmed for mystery . . . The mystery, therefore, for which we are programmed is our co-creative responsibility for birthing the new. This is the primordial base for all our desires.[110]

Desire can be described as the wind that blows through the house of God. It begins with God's passionate desire to call to himself a people for

---

105. Cited by Hans Geybels, "Experience Searching for Theology," 33.
106. à Kempis, *Imitation of Christ*, 177.
107. Cited by Meilaender, *Way That Leads There*, 16.
108. Traherne, "Desire," cited by Sheldrake, *Befriending Our Desires*, 26.
109. Gorringe, *Education of Desire*, 12.
110. O'Murchu, *Transformation of Desire*, 180.

his own pleasure and possession—first Israel, and then the church. That desire worked its way out in the ministry of Christ in the passion of the cross, for no other reason than that "he loved us and gave himself for us" (Eph 5:2). That desire is demonstrated in the worship life of the church and the sending of unending prayers of worship, love and desire for God that ascends upwards. And finally, that desire is borne out in the hearts of "believing souls" for whom a passionate love for God is their predominating quality and characteristic as *homo spiritualis*. They are spiritual persons for whom, by comparison, every other need, desire, passion and hunger is less than a gnat's breath.

25. Eighth Day Theology

The idea of an "eighth day" theology lies in Christian antiquity. It brings together the three themes of creation, redemption and the future eschatological "present." The creation story itself is foundational to the Judeo-Christian faith. From our reading of Genesis, we know that on the first day of creation, God called forth light out of darkness. On the second day of creation, he separated the earth from the sky. On the third day of creation, he brought forth all kinds of plants and fruit-bearing trees. On the fourth day of creation, the great lights of the sun and the moon came into being. On the fifth day of creation God created the living creatures—the birds of the air, the animals of the land, and the fish of the sea. On the sixth day of creation, God created man and woman in his own image and likeness, commanding them to be fruitful and to increase. It was then that, "God saw all that he had made and it was very good" (Gen 1:31). And on the seventh day, God rested. God's rest became a mandated rest for all creation in the enduring principle of the Sabbath.

Next comes redemption. Redemption is both a process and an event. As a process in the Hebrew Bible, we see Adam's disobedience, pitching humankind into sin. And thereafter the whole of the human family finds itself cast out of the garden of Eden, strangers both to themselves and to God who is their creator. If the fall is creation disrupted, then redemption is creation restored and "put right." As an event, redemption is grounded in Christ's work on the cross, enacted in the shedding of his blood, resulting in his defeat of sin and death. The completion of the work is signposted by Christ's resurrection, ascension and exultation. Humankind's reconciliation back to God (2 Cor 5:19) is the result. Adam and Eve's offspring can now re-enter the garden and can once again "commune" with God. Finally, the "eighth day" refers to the fulfillment of both creation and redemption, leading to the "new age" of the *eschatos* in which redeemed humanity joins God in celebrating his eternal rest in a state of what might be called a *super sabbath*. This is the state of eternal communion that God had imagined long-ago as his ongoing relationship with humanity. On the eighth day, heaven and earth are brought together, ending the church's state of exile by ushering in a new state of harmonious coexistence between God, Christ, humanity, and creation. In anticipation of that future coexistence in the future "eighth day," humanity can—in the present historical moment—experience now what heaven will be like then. It is a foretaste of glory that will arrive when Christ returns at his second coming.

The notion of an eighth day has been present in Christian theological reflection since the time of St. Augustine (354–430) in the fourth century and has been a recurring theme in the writings of patristic writers such as St. Basil the Great and St. Gregory of Nyssa. Later Orthodox Christian writers such as Alexander Schmemann and Jean Danielou locate the eighth day at the close of salvation-history, as its crescendo and fulfillment. Schmemann's book *The Mystery of the Eighth Day*[111] and Steven Underdown's *Living in the Eighth Day*[112] both highlight the role played by the eighth day in Christianity's long liturgical tradition. Within a liturgical frame of reference, Jesus' resurrection from the dead corresponds to the Sabbath, and the Christian eucharist represents the eighth day in which the Messiah is not only recognized as the creator (Col 1:15) but also as redeemer (Col 1:19–20), one who is to be worshipped as the "Lord of time" and the "King of the universe." Christian liturgical expression has matched the so-called "days" of creation with the "days" of redemption, and built the liturgy (i.e., the cycle of Christian worship) around these days. The eighth day looms large in the worship life of the liturgical churches—even if the so-called "low" or Protestant Evangelical non-liturgical churches do not habitually incorporate this into their pattern of worship.

In Eastern Orthodox Christianity, the idea of an eighth-day theology has retained its place as one of the key themes in its theology and liturgy. And this has special relevance to the Christian spiritual life in three

---

111. Schmemann, *Mystery of the Eighth Day*.
112. Underdown, *Living in the Eighth Day*.

ways. First, in this time between Christ's annunciation of the Kingdom of God in the first century, and the arrival of the *eschatos* at some unnamed time in the future when Christ will return in glory, the people of God find themselves in a "season of waiting." The promise of heaven has been given, but it has not yet arrived. The people of God are invited to live in the anticipatory space of the "eighth day," during which the resources of heaven are available to those on the earth, even as the sovereignty of Christ operates in the lives of those who must live—temporarily—under the rule of sin, evil, and various "powers and principalities" (Eph 6:12). Second, while living in this "in-between state"—without any proof or evidence as to the certainty of the fulfilment of Christ's promises, other than those of faith and the liturgical clock—Christians must wrestle with the question of sanctification. How does one remain a sanctified believer in the face of temptations to abandon one's faith, or to adopt the soft option of a convenient and recreational faith when it happens to suit? How can one be a happy, holy, and whole Christian given such the provisional state of affairs we live with vis-à-vis war, injustice, violence, addiction and repression? The answer? . . . by drawing ever closer to Christ in our spiritual lives, by deepening our prayers and energizing our worship lives. Having "found the pearl of great price" (Matt 13:4–6), now is not the time to throw it away.

The early spiritual masters had a saying: "Having found him, yet we seek him still." In other words, now is a time to press on towards and into Christ and to enjoy now what the new life in Christ will be on that Great Day. Now is the season for celebrating our lives which are "pressed down, shaken together and running over" (Luke 6:38). And finally, we are to renew our commitment to the fulfilment of God's kingdom by drawing on the power of heaven in our earthly ministry to others. Living out of a daily, moment-by-moment communion with Christ that is rich and real enables us to "touch" the lives of others with the word, love, gospel and power of Christ. When the world to come "merges" with this world—and the Christian spiritual reality is no longer just something imagined but is "more real than real"—we are on the verge not simply of the eighth day, but of eternity itself.

26. Embodiment

"We are not human beings having a spiritual experience. We are spiritual beings having a human experience."[113] A common tendency is for us to think in *either-or* terms . . . we are either physical creatures or we are spiritual creatures. Somehow, we cannot be both. But Christianity wants to say we are *both* spiritual creatures *and physical* earthly creatures, insisting that a Jesus-shaped spirituality requires both dimensions in order to function properly. Clearly, if there is anyone who sets the pattern for our Christian spirituality, it is Jesus himself. And one of the cornerstone doctrines of our faith is, of course, the Incarnation, in which "The Word became flesh and made his dwelling among us. We have seen his glory can the glory of the One and Only, who came from the Father, full of grace and truth" (John 1:14). In the words of the Nicene Creed, we confess:

> We believe in one Lord, Jesus Christ, the only begotten of the Father . . . For us and for our salvation he came down from heaven, was incarnate by the Holy Spirit of the Virgin Mary and became truly human. For our sake he was crucified under Pontius Pilot; he suffered death and was buried. On the third day he rose again, in accordance with the Scriptures; he ascended into heaven and is seated at the right hand of the Father. He will come again in glory to judge the living and the dead, and his kingdom will have no end.

Begotten . . . born . . . incarnate . . . truly human . . . suffered death . . . resurrected . . . ascended . . . this sequence of "body language" demonstrates that Jesus was a thoroughly embodied person. During his earthly ministry Jesus was both "spiritual" (in that he lived perfectly in the power of the Holy Spirit), and "physical" (in that he inhabited a human body). The biblical record tells us that Jesus ate, slept, walked, talked, served and cared for the bodies and souls of other people, and ultimately, he died a human death because the life contained in his body was extinguished. The outcome of Jesus' physical crucifixion was his glorious resurrection. At his ascension, it was in his embodied form that he entered Heaven and thus took his humanity into the presence of God. And it remains Christ's physical body—broken and resurrected—that forms a central part of his continuing spiritual ministry through the sacrament of Holy Communion: "This is my body, given for you" (Luke 22:19).

---

113. Attributed to Pierre Teilhard de Chardin in Furey, *Joy of Kindness*, 138.

As God's obedient Son, Jesus put the divine plan of redemption into action by means of the instrumentality of his physical body. We are wrong to think it necessary to separate spirit and flesh. By doing so, we fall into the trap of *dualism*. God intentionally binds these two things together. The God who dwells as Spirit (John 4:24) may have decreed salvation from the halls of heaven—but until Jesus came to earth and took on flesh to put the divine command into action through his physical obedience, God's salvation plan would have remained un-executed. Throughout salvation-history, God's Spirit makes a habit of co-opting flesh to achieve its ultimate goals. That is most clearly evident in Jesus. Further, since "Jesus was man, as God intended man to be,"[114] . . . this pattern of embodied life lived in the power of the Spirit has become *the* pattern for emulation among Jesus' followers ever since.

As Jesus' disciples today, we must, "Work out our salvation with fear and trembling" (Phil 2:12). Since flesh is the locus, sign and agent of the Spirit, if we are to be true to the way of Jesus, we are called to "sell all we have," "take up our cross," "lay down our lives," and "forfeit our very selves" as the outworking of our decision to follow him. As spiritual people, we are to put our spirituality "into action" through our bodies. Ironically, one of the first priorities of the Christian spiritual life is to care for the bodily needs of other people. Jesus was concerned for peoples' bodies because he perfectly understood that humanity is both body and spirit, temporal and eternal, natural and supernatural. Note that his miracles during his earthly ministry were usually targeted towards people's physical ailments: healing from disease, curing blindness, and raising people from the dead in order to demonstrate his power over life and death. As a result, people were compelled to make spiritual judgments about Jesus' identity as Lord, leading many to repent and "sign over" their allegiance and their bodies to him through conversion.

So, there is an important link between the physical and the spiritual in Christian spirituality. According to Michael Casey, "The spiritual life is not so interior that it can survive without the body."[115] Likewise, in my book *Ordinary Saints*, I observe that:

> Saints' lives are testimonies in sign language, written in the cursive style of hands clasped in prayer, faces turned upwards in worship, arms reaching out in welcome to friends, neighbours

---

114. Spader, *Walking as Jesus Walked*, 39.
115. Casey, *Fully Human, Fully Divine*, 26.

and enemies in hospitable embrace. Despite our tendency to define spirituality as a non-material practice, the physical body continues to press its case. Spirituality that is removed from embodied practice becomes other-worldly, distant, dispassionately removed from the real world. It is a matter of great irony that the Christian spiritual life may well originate in ecstatic third-heaven encounters. . . But it can never be removed from the living, breathing, moving, feeling person and their embodied state. This makes Christian spirituality a lived experience that is a joint venture between the mind, the body and the soul of the human being that is in its totality a *homo spiritualis*—a fundamentally spiritual being.[116]

27. Epektasis

Epektasis is a biblical word found in the Greek text of Philippians 3:13–14, where St. Paul writes, "This one thing I do: forgetting what is behind and straining toward what is ahead, I press on [*epektasis*] towards the goal to win the prize for which God has called me heavenward in Christ Jesus." Today, *epektasis* has become a cornerstone concept of the Christian spiritual life, following the theological thought and spiritual reflections of Gregory of Nyssa (335–95). Although not commonly spoken of in Protestant theological formulations, *epektasis* has played a central role in the rich tapestry and spiritual practices of both the Orthodox and Roman Catholic traditions. There is good reason for believers of all persuasions to embrace the term.

Etymologically, *epektasis* literally means "endeavor." In its application, the word implies an effort on the part of the actor to "stretch out, to strain towards something."[117] In its metaphorical connection to a running race, the term conjures an image "of the body of the racer bent forward, his [sic] hand outstretched towards the goal, his eye fastened upon it."[118] As a formal theological doctrine, *epektasis* signifies humankind's unceasing inclination and evolution towards God, expressed in the upward movement of the soul towards apprehension of God and participation in the divine life, which is humankind's true goal and fulfilment. Gregory of Nyssa pays particular attention to the faith that must

116. Devenish, *Ordinary Saints*, 99.
117. Arndt and Gingerich, *Greek-English Lexicon of the New Testament*, 284.
118. Reinecker, *Linguistic Key to the Greek New Testament*, 212.

be activated by the mortal human creature, as it continually presses into God's perpetually self-renewing existence. In his commentary on *The Life of Moses*, Gregory writes:

> Once [the soul] is released from its earthly attachment, it becomes light and swift for its movement upward, soaring from below up to the heights. If nothing hinders . . . it's upward thrust . . . the soul rises ever higher and will always make its flight yet higher—by its desire of the heavenly things straining ahead for what is still to come.[119]

Focusing on the vision of God to come, Gregory continues:

> This truly is the vision of God: never to be satisfied in the desire to see him. But one must always, by looking at what he can see, rekindle his desire to see more. Thus, no limit would interrupt growth in the ascent to God, since no limit to the Good can be found nor is the increasing of desire for the Good brought to an end because it is satisfied.[120]

As Liviu Petcu points out, "Moses never ceases from his climb, and doesn't set a limit to it, but, once he has set foot on the ladder (of ascent) he never stops climbing it, going higher and higher. The Christian should never give up what he [sic] has gained, but must continuously affect what he has started."[121] Lucas Mateo-Seco has noted the three moments in the biblical text that attracted Gregory's attention to the life of Moses: "That of the burning bush (Ex 3:1–15), that of Mount Sinai (Ex 19:16–25) and that of the splitting of the rock (Ex 34:6–19)."[122] At their core, each of these moments are instances of fear and trembling, of approaching God's holy and awe-inspiring presence, and of Divine power.

In his article, "Becoming Men, Not Stones," Warren Smith discusses *epektasis* in Gregory's commentary on the *Song of Songs*. Under the heading "Humanity's Eternal Becoming," Smith proposes that the soul has a "bottomless thirst for God"—it is thirsty, it is hungry for God, it runs after him who is its lover and its very life.[123] Searching for words that attempt—however inadequately—to describe God's beauty and glory, Smith (following Gregory), says that God's magnificence and glory

---

119. Gregory, *Life of Moses*.
120. Gregory, *Life of Moses*, 116
121. Petcu, "Doctrine of Epektasis," 775.
122. Mateo-Seco, "Epektasis," 265–66.
123. Smith, "Becoming Men, Not Stones," 345.

transcend our human capacity to understand or describe it, and yet "each successive experience of God—whether mystical, prayerful, or exegetical—re-forms the mind with new and greater knowledge of God, and thus the mind's eternal 'increase and growth' follows upon the eternal progress of 'God's self-disclosure' in the process of 'always becoming.'"[124]

Warren Smith expands upon this idea, writing:

> The theory of *epektasis* rests on two principles, one theological, the other anthropological. The theological principle is God's infinity . . . Finite humanity cannot know all there is to know about God . . . The anthropological principle is humanity's inherent mutability (changeableness). Unlike God who is eternal, humanity is a creature that by God's power and grace came into existence from nothing . . . As the intellect contemplates the Divine, God becomes the content of its thoughts; thus, the soul acquires a likeness to the Divine object of its thought. Since God's goodness is infinite, the soul's desire to see and know more of God is insatiable.[125]

In summary, we now articulate five practical implications of *epektasis* in the life of the practicing Christian today. (1) *Epektasis* describes the movement "outwards" from the soul for re-connection with God expressed as a kind of longing, or deep desire. This outward movement corresponds to the Philippians 3 reference to a "stretching and reaching" action towards God. (2) *Epektasis* represents a movement "upwards" in the desire to participate in the life of God, which is the key capacity of the soul embedded in the human imagination as a movement towards God. As Everett Ferguson puts it, "The soul grows by participation in what transcends it."[126] (3) *Epektasis* represents a movement "forwards" activated by the soul, as it reaches for God who is its *telos*, it's final fulfilment. Reconnection and re-unification with God is the soul's most urgent desire. (4) *Epektasis* represents a reaching towards completion or perfection in the midst of human imperfection and chaos. Perfection is an ongoing process that "does not consist in reaching an end, but in running without end" out of a continuous desire to "be with" and to "be in" the divine presence.[127] And (5) *epektasis* represents an ongoing process that is continuous, active, consciously undertaken, and projects beyond

---

124. Smith, "Becoming Men, Not Stones," 349.
125. Smith, "Gregory of Nyssa: Formed and Re-Formed in God's Image," 154.
126. Ferguson, "God's Infinity and Man's Mutability," 62.
127. Mateo-Seco, "Epektasis," 267.

this life into the eschatological future. The "habit" of the soul in reaching for God in this life becomes an ongoing and sustained practice into the next life as an act of realized eschatology. Hans Boersma cites Gregory in his *Embodiment and Virtue in Gregory of Nyssa* as saying:

> There is no other way to go up to God but by constantly looking upwards and having an unceasing desire for sublime things, so as not to be content to stay with what has already been achieved, but to regard it as loss if one fails to achieve what lies above.[128]

Essentially, *epektasis* is a mystical reality because it strives to "touch" God and seeks to merge with his Being. This is put into practice by striving to grow in faith, virtue, purity, spiritual vision and connection with God, so that such striving becomes the prevailing purpose and intention of one's entire life. As Jean Danielou says:

> Spiritual life is thus an everlasting transformation of the soul in Christ Jesus in the form of a growing ardour, a thirst for God growing as participation in Him increases, which is accompanied by a growing stability, the soul becoming simple, and fixed ever more firmly in God.[129]

28. Experience (the centrality of)

After a season of anxiety about drawing on experience as an authoritative source for spirituality because of a preference for objectivity over subjectivity, and the potential for experience to be falsified . . . confidence has returned regarding the place of personal experience in the spiritual life. Following the postmodern "turn to the subject," "turn to experience," and "turn to interiority," experience is now receiving fresh attention in the academy, the church, and in personal spiritual practice. Luke Timothy Johnson has observed that there exists "two worlds of religion."[130] At the front of the typical church, where preaching, teaching and the sacraments are offered, "correctness of doctrine, morality, authority and procedure" are emphasized. There, the concern for *truth* is paramount. But at the back of the church, a second religious world comes into play. "Another religious world thrives . . . [where] the parish book of [prayer] needs, with

---

128. Boersma, *Embodiment and Virtue in Gregory of Nyssa*, no page number.
129. Danielou, *Plationisme and Theologie Mystique*, 306.
130. Johnson, *Religious Experience in Earliest Christianity*, 1.

its catalogue of pains and anxieties and desires" presides. In the second case, it is not truth that is of foremost concern—but *power*! People pray for deliverance from evil, inviting God's guidance for life's big decisions, healing from sickness, and aspirations for their future. Importantly, the form of power people have in mind here is not "a power in their control (as with paganism) . . . but rather controlling them, a power that derived from the crucified and raised Messiah Jesus."[131]

In this regard, three things regarding early New Testament Christianity bear mentioning. First, first-century Palestine was a place and time rife with competing claims to power—the military might of Rome, the religious authority of Judaism, the influence of Greek and Roman pantheon of gods, as well as the demons that were everywhere present. What is noteworthy about early Christianity is its relativizing of these worldly power struggles through the presence and power of the Holy Spirit. While the incarnation and the ascension bookend the earthly life and ministry of Jesus, laying the foundations for the inauguration of the kingdom, it is the coming of the Holy Spirit at Pentecost that marks the birth of the church. "For Paul the Spirit is a power," and his ministry is accompanied by "his experience of the power and depth of spiritual inspiration."[132] The Church did not lack power—it was simply a different form of power from the predominating, brutalizing, military might and religious authority of other regimes.

Second, we must take note of the centrality of Jesus as a personal figure. As Bonnie Thurston suggests:

> What the New Testament 'talks about' is the human experience of God mediated by the person of Jesus of Nazareth, and any study of New Testament spirituality must begin with the fact that the texts are a record of the human experience . . . Christianity revolves around the distinctive experience of the person of Jesus Christ . . . The New Testament is the early church's considered reflection on the experience of meeting Jesus . . . Put differently (it) is a record of human beings' experience of communication between themselves and God in and through the person of Jesus Christ. The New Testament . . . records spiritual experience. This presumes that 'spiritual experience' is 'real.'[133]

---

131. Johnson, *Religious Experience in Earliest Christianity*, 184.

132. Gunkel, *Influence of the Holy Spirit*, 170–71; cited by Johnson, *Religious Experience in Earliest Christianity*, 16.

133. Thurston, "New Testament in Christian Spirituality," 55.

And third, we ought to note the unexpected re-focusing of Christianity's transcendent and otherworldly spirituality to the narrow confines of an earthly, this-worldly domain. This unexpected move represents a seemingly unwarranted narrowing of Christianity's spirituality to the *material*—unwarranted in the sense that it appears to limit the glory and "excess of being" of which the Divine is fully capable of producing. In fact, however, it does the opposite—it raises mortality up to the level of immortality, our temporal, finite existence to the level of the eternal and the infinite.

Michael Gorman has explored this theme in detail, arguing that since Jesus' incarnation is so central to Christology, the visceral and emotional feelings arising from our embodied experience of such things as miracles, healings, and the redemptive aspects of our embodied existence must be taken seriously.[134] Gorman's exploration takes into account the four aspects of (1) the transfiguration accounts in the Synoptic Gospels; (2) Paul's journey to the third heaven in 2 Corinthians 12; (3) the resurrection and ascension of Christ in Colossians 3; and (4) John the Seer's journey to (or vision of) the heavenly throne room in Revelation 4–5.

The implications of the preceding analyses for contemporary believers can be summarized in three statements. First, because we are physical creatures, salvation is not simply focused towards the otherworldly, transcendent realm, but must include the materiality of our bodies. Second, the bodily experience of spiritual realities—such as forgiveness, healing, wholeness, restoration, and the Divine embrace—must necessarily be accompanied by physical sensations, tremors, and reactions. To expect otherwise is to place an impossible distance between our bodies which are the centerpiece of our earthly lives and our spiritual perception of what is ultimately real. And third, that spiritual understanding and awareness of the divine comes to us by way of what Calvin referred to us the *sensus divinitatus* (a sense of the divine), a way of knowing that properly involves one's whole being—body, mind, soul, and spirit. This makes spirituality not only something deeply believed, but also something to be deeply felt/experienced.

Following on from this, the question of *if* and *how* religious experience differs from spiritual experience is a valid one. Stephen Pretorius has distinguished between these two ideas, defining "experience" first of all as "a form of knowledge, accompanied by emotions and feelings, that

---

134. Gorman, "This-Worldliness of the New Testament's Otherworldly Spirituality."

is obtained as a result of direct reception of an impression of a reality (internal or external), which lies outside our control, that has an impact on our reaction or consciousness and being."[135] Subsequently he argues, "A religious experience . . . refer[s] to an experience [arising] as a result of participation in the rituals of religion such as worship [and] prayer."[136] In contrast, Pretorius writes, "A spiritual experience in general refers to a personal, meaningful self-transcendence and a search for the sacred or the 'inner self.'"[137]

By way of conclusion, we offer three insights that sum up the necessary experiential inter-dependency between the material body and the immaterial soul. First, William Hocking has stated, "Religious truth is founded upon experience . . . If there is any knowledge of God, it must be in some way a matter of experience."[138] Second, we now have a new raft of research methodologies capable of explicating and validating the body-brain connection from a scientific and psychological/neurological perspective. Just one example and resource is David Yadan and Andrew Newburgh's *The Varieties of Spiritual Experience*.[139] Future research into this field will inevitably open up new avenues for thinking and experiencing the spiritual elements of our human lives. And lastly, in a world that is becoming increasingly evidence-based in its judgements, any exclusion of experience from the realm of religion and spirituality reverts to a form of reductionism that breaks the rules of both naturalistic enquiry, but also transgresses Christianity's expectation that experience will be accepted as a valid measure of the existence that "something spiritual is happening."

29. Experts in Humanity

In 1985, Pope John Paul II delivered an address to the sixth Symposium of the Council of European Episcopal Conferences of the Roman Catholic Church. The task of the Symposium was to discuss "Secularization and Evangelization today in Europe." Summarizing the deliberations of the Symposium, Pope John Paul declared:

---

135. Pretorius, "Understanding Spiritual Experience in Christian Spirituality," 148.
136. Pretorius, "Understanding Spiritual Experience in Christian Spirituality," 149.
137. Pretorius, "Understanding Spiritual Experience in Christian Spirituality," 151.
138. Hocking, *Meaning of God in Human Experience*, 154–55.
139. Yaden and Newberg, *Varieties of Spiritual Experience*.

> The Church is called to *give a soul to modern society* ... And the church must infuse the soul not from above and from without, but by passing *within*, making herself close to the man [sic] of today. Therefore, the active presence and intense participation in the life of man is essential ... Heralds of the Gospel are needed who are experts in humanity, who know the heart of today's man in depth, share in its joys and hopes, anguish and sadness, and at the same time be contemplatives in love with God. For this we need new saints. The *great evangelizers of Europe* (in the past) *were the saints*. We must beg the Lord to increase the spirit of holiness of the Church and to send us new saints to evangelize the world today.[140]

The phrase "experts in humanity" is what we are working with in this entry. Two significant documents lie behind the Pope's statement. First, the Pastoral Constitution of the Church, *Gaudium Et Spes* ("Joy and Hope"), which was the fruit of the reflections of Vatican II (1962–1965). And second, the Apostolic Exhortation *Evangelii Nuntiandi* ("On Evangelization in the Modern World"), first proclaimed in 1975.[141]

The phrase "experts in humanity" is addressed in the first instance to the bishops, priests, catechists and lay-Christians who comprise the Catholic Church—but in effect it applies to all believers regardless of their affiliation within the Christian "family." Further, extrapolating from the Pope's remarks, the commission calls for all Christian witnesses to become "experts in humanity" highlights three interrelated concerns regarding spiritual formation: (1) the need for all Christian witnesses to develop a strong connection with the humanity that comprises their audience; (2) their ability to embody in their own person and character the substance of Christian faith and teaching; and (3) to develop a capacity to teach and "pass on" the faith to others in ways that are relevant, convincing and passionate.

First, when it comes to developing a strong connection with the humanity of their audience, Christians who are called to bear witness to their faith must do so through the instrumentality of a passionate commitment to their fellow human beings. Their focus is to be on:

> The joys and the hopes, the griefs and the anxieties of the men [sic] of this age, especially those who are poor or in any way afflicted, these are the joys and hopes, the griefs and anxieties

---

140. Paul VI, "Secularization and Evangelization Today in Europe," §13.
141. Paul VI, *Evangelii Nuntiandi*, 28–31.

of the followers of Christ. Indeed, nothing genuinely human fails to raise an echo in their hearts. For theirs is a community composed of men.[142]

Everything that is genuinely human stirs up a passionate response in their hearts. They are to show their love for God by loving their neighbors who are their fellow creatures under grace. It is not with angels (whose lives shine with complete perfection) that Christian witnesses must connect and communicate, but simply ordinary people who are filled with doubts and struggles and imperfections. Likewise, Christian witnesses themselves bring their own imperfections, incompleteness and struggles to the task of communicating the faith. Christian witnesses, therefore, must "know the heart of today's man [and woman] in depth, sharing in their joys and hopes, anguish and sadness."[143] The adjective "experts" indicates that such people are to possess a special knowledge, a critical insight, and be effective in dealing with their own humanity as well as that of their unbelieving or seeking neighbors.

Second, the effective Christian witness will have an ability to embody in their own life, person and character, the substance of Christian faith and teaching. The first great task in the mission of proclaiming the gospel is precisely this:

> The first means of evangelization is the witness of an authentically Christian life, given over to God in a communion that nothing should destroy and at the same time be given to one's neighbor with limitless zeal . . . 'Modern man listens more willingly to witnesses than to teachers, and if he does listen to teachers, it is because they are witnesses.'[144]

According to Michael Gorman, "To participate in Christ is both to benefit from God's mission of liberation and reconciliation and to bear witness to this divine mission—thus furthering it—by becoming a faithful embodiment of it."[145] The life of the living witness to faith becomes a living exemplar and impresario of the good news, thus providing a form of living commentary and an interpretive hermeneutic of their own message concerning what it means to believe and participate in the new reality.

---

142. Paul IV, *Gaudium et Spes*, §1.
143. Paul VI, "Secularization and Evangelization Today in Europe," §13.
144. Paul VI, *Evangelii Nuntiandi*, §41.
145. Gorman, *Becoming the Gospel*, 36.

And third, the Christian witness must develop a capacity to teach and "pass on" the faith to others in ways that are relevant, convincing, and passionate. The experts in humanity we are speaking of must also be experts in divinity, knowing how to teach the spiritual life in a way that con-joins the natural life of our humanity with the super-natural life of the Christian sacred, thus embodying a new form of life that transforms and transfigures that which is ordinary. In order to do that—suggests Pope Paul VI—it is necessary for witnesses to become saints. Christianity has always relied upon its apostles, preachers, pastors, priests, prophets, seers, mystics and holy men and women to represent the genius of the gospel. As it was in the past, so it is in the present. As Dietrich Bonhoeffer keenly observed, "The primary confession of the Christian before the world is the deed which interprets itself."[146]

To a significant extent, "believing souls" who aspire to become "experts in humanity" must also be experts in themselves. That is, aware of their calling, their gifting, their character, their needs and what they bring as a peculiar contribution to the kingdom of God and their particular way, place and moment in history. This means that their self-awareness in terms of how other people "read them," how they function in a one-on-one ministry setting, as well as in groups . . . is of paramount importance.

30. Fullness

The concept of spiritual "fullness" discussed in this entry arises from Charles Taylor's extended treatment of secularization in Western culture in his book *A Secular Age*.[147] In answer to the question, "What does it mean to say that we live in a secular age?" Taylor spent the next 800 pages defining secularism and the processes of secularization, detailing why he is unhappy with standard approaches to the topic, and offering reasons why he thinks it necessary to retain religion and spirituality as foundational building blocks in Western culture. His project aims to "define and trace" the changes that have taken us "from a society in which it was virtually impossible not to believe in God, to one in which faith, even for the staunchest believer, is one human possibility among others."[148] In tracing this transition, Taylor identifies three distinct kinds of secularity. In

---

146. Hauerwas, "Dietrich Bonhoeffer's Political Theology," 19.
147. Taylor, *Secular Age*.
148. Taylor, *Secular Age*, 3.

secularity1, religion is "everywhere," co-existing alongside other spheres of social activity such as the political, the economic and various other mundane (and hence secular) vocations. While conceptually distinct from the secular domain, religion is virtually inseparable from it, and there is a very clear sense that it is from within the secular realm that the sacred reveals itself. In secularity2, "Secularity consists in the falling off of religious belief and practice, in people turning away from God, and no longer going to Church." Thus, there is not only a separation of religious belief from other aspects of life, but also a clear tendency towards disaffiliation and unbelief on the part of the general population. And in secularity3, "Belief in God is no longer axiomatic. There are alternatives."[149] Even the deeply committed believer recognizes this and must deal with the possibility and implications of the wider loss of faith unfolding in society.

That background prepares us for Taylor's claim that despite the changing conditions that prevail in the West—dictated by cultural sensibilities and rational predilections—our underlying human condition nevertheless means that we hunger for something more than our ordinary lives are capable of offering. Taylor calls that longed-for something "fullness." He writes:

> We all see our lives, and/or the space wherein we live our lives, as having a certain moral/spiritual shape. Somewhere, in some activity, or condition, lies a fullness, a richness; that is, in that place (activity or condition), life is fuller, richer, deeper, more worthwhile, more admirable, more what it should be. This is perhaps a place of power: we often experience this as deeply moving, as inspiring, perhaps the sense of fullness is something we just catch glimpses of from afar off; we have the powerful intuition of what fullness would be, were we to be in that condition, e.g., of peace or wholeness; or able to act on that level, of integrity or generosity or abandonment or self-forgetfulness. But sometimes there will be moments of experienced fullness, of joy and fulfilment, where we feel ourselves there.[150]

For Taylor, regardless of the age or *epoch* in which we live—whether it be the pre-modern, the modern of the post-modern—the moral/spiritual "shape" of human consciousness causes us to hunger and thirst for spiritual substance and fulfilment which can only be offered by the "fullness" he describes. Sources of fullness include philosophy, the other

149. Taylor, *Secular Age*, 3.
150. Taylor, *Secular Age*, 5.

world religions and spiritual movements, and even certain social and political systems. However, as a convinced Christian, Taylor points his readers to the fullness which the Christian faith is capable of offering. In the New Testament, Jesus tells his listeners that, "The thief comes only to steal and kill and destroy; I have come that they may have life and have it to the full" (John 10:10). And St. Paul says of Christ that "in Christ all the fullness of the Deity lives in bodily form" (Col 2:9). And this very fullness is what "you have been given in Christ" (Col 2:10).

The fullness mentioned in these biblical passages is rendered by the Greek word *pleroma*, meaning a fullness or abundance of divine power. In Christian terms, this means an exceptional quality of life that flows from God the Creator, through Christ the Redeemer, into his human creatures, "filling up" any and every perceived "lack" and so elevating them to the level of God's own superabundant life. This is what enables Christians to live their human, earthly lives out of the resources of the divine, heavenly life. This notion merges with the idea of *theosis*—that the redeemed believer may come to appropriate godlike qualities, thought-processes and a super-sensate mode of existence in the limited constraints of their finite lives. Summing up the gist of Taylor's overall argument, Andrew Lincoln writes, "Just as through the power of the Spirit, Jesus experienced fullness from God, so through the same Spirit believers experience the divine fullness that Jesus experienced in his humanity and are enabled in community to share in the communication of God's plenitude to others and to the world."[151]

At the close of *A Secular Age*, Taylor looks forward anticipating two possible futures. The first follows the logic of standard secularization theory where religion diminishes to such an extent that it becomes no more than a museum piece rejected by Western culture on the grounds that it has outgrown its usefulness.[152] But the second future contains the vision of a quickening of religion now manifested as a full-blown form of spirituality. This is because—as McKenzie states:

> There is no escape for humans to seek some version of [fullness] 'for any livable understanding of human life, there must be some way in which this life looks good, whole, proper, really being lived as it should. The utter absence of some such would leave us in abject, unbearable despair.'[153]

151. Lincoln, "Spirituality in a Secular Age," 78.
152. Taylor, *Secular Age*, 768.
153. McKenzie, *Interpreting Charles Taylor's Social Theory on Religion and*

The question becomes one of where is fullness to be found? Is it located in the transcendent realm of classical (Christian) formulations of religion and spirituality, where God is experienced as the beneficent Other, and the fulfilment of oneself and the longings of one's own soul? Or is it located in the imminent realm of material nature, or even one's own innate relational and sexual motivations? These two apparently opposing and competing orientations are made to play off against one another as if they were complete strangers to one another and competing ideological positions. McKenzie summarises Taylor's categorizing of religious life in the 'age of authenticity' as of necessity "something to be lived," where "experiences and emotions are much more important than any notion of theological correctness", but where "the link between Christian faith and [the] civilizational order has been severed, specifically in regard to sexual ethics."[154] That means a Christian-sponsored transcendental form of spiritual life will need to pay significant attention to conversion—a topic to which Taylor gives significant attention at the close of his *A Secular Age*. Ultimately, Taylor states that "The religious life or practice that I become part of must not only be my choice, but it must speak to me, it must make sense in terms of my spiritual development as I understand this."[155] Could it be that Christian spirituality encapsulated within a "Christian spiritual education" offering becomes the new norm for genuine seekers into the future?

31. God's Workshop

In this entry we discuss several principles that have their origins in the monastic Rule of St. Benedict (450–547), the acknowledged patriarch of Western monasticism. In his Rule, Benedict offers instructions intended to regulate the lives of those who have committed themselves to a monastic way of life. In Chapter 4 of the Rule, Benedict describes the tools that produce good works and contribute to the faith and character of Benedictine communities. Those communities may consist of either formally declared monastics, or everyday believers who live beyond the walls of the monastery in secular society. In either case, those who aspire

---

Secularisation, 61.

154. McKenzie, *Interpreting Charles Taylor's Social Theory on Religion and Secularisation*, 45.

155. Taylor, *Secular Age*, 486.

to keep the Rule are admonished to replace pride with love, deceit with truthfulness, and to overcome temptation and seduction with maturity and godly character. The 'tools' described in the Rule of St. Benedict are virtue, harmony, good works, peacekeeping, humility, obedience, and respect. Such outward practices are aimed at producing inward godliness. In closing Chapter 4, Benedict writes:

> These, then, are the tools of the spiritual craft. When we have used them without ceasing, day and night, and have returned them on judgment day, our wages will be the reward the Lord has promised... The workshop where we are to toil faithfully at all these tasks is the enclosure of the monastery and stability in the community.[156]

Taking up this theme, Rowan Williams in a chapter entitled 'God's Workshop',[157] has spelled out the implications of the concepts of "tools" and "workshops" in conceiving of spiritual formation as a kind of "craft." He invites the reader to imagine a scene—a literal workshop. The tools are hammers, planes, chisels, a brace drill and corkscrew bits for working with wood. The scene before us is that of the tradesman who knows his or her tools so well that they sit comfortably in the hand, the fluid movements of their sinewy hands arising from long-practiced muscle memory, work skilfully to achieve their goal of making a chair, a table, an ox-harness, or a roof gable. The heft of the tools, the smell of the wood, the cut of the blade all requires persistence and attention to detail. But the image of the workshop is not intended merely to evoke the sights, sounds and smells of a medieval workroom. Rather, in Benedict's Rule, the image serves as a metaphor for the workshop of the human soul. The "spiritual craft" referred to in the Rule is intended to assist the human soul in educating its emotions, passions, and intentions as it seeks to cooperate with the Divine Spirit for the purpose of producing a human copy of the sacred model located in the life of Christ. Williams puts it this way:

> The holy life is one in which we learn to handle things, in businesslike and unselfconscious ways, to 'handle' the control of the tongue, the habit of not passing on blame, getting up in the morning and not gossiping. A monastic lifetime is one in which these habits are fitted to our hands. Simone Weil wrote somewhere about how the tool is for the seasoned worker the

---

156. Benedict, *Rule of St Benedict*, 63.
157. Williams, *Holy Living*, 53–69.

extension of the hand, not something alien. Benedict's metaphors prompt us to think of the holiness that is like that, an 'extension' of our bodies and our words that we have come not to notice.[158]

What we learn by putting the Rule into practice is that *we are the work*. In our activity-driven lives, where our to-do list exceeds the number of hours available, it is inevitable that we think of ministry as a set of outward tasks that are measured by time, monetary value and key performance indicators-based report cards. Ultimately, however, spiritual formation is the inner work we are called to . . . both in our own lives, and that of others. The fact is, *we are the work individually*, and the workplace is the depth dimensions of our own interior soul-spaces.

And equally important, *we are the work communally*, and the workplace is the right-functioning of our shared life together. One of the great contributions of the Rule of St. Benedict is its invitation to implement one's spirituality in the context of community. And one of the foremost measures of one's spiritual maturity is how one treats one's fellow human beings, including one's fellow believers, for we are indeed "our brother's/sister's keeper" (Gen 4:9). While many of us do well in the Bible-knowledge stakes and other forms of standard religious behaviors, our performance in offering care, nurture and soul-nourishment to others within our community is often less than ideal. Further, this is not simply something we must do as a matter of kindness and sheer obligation. Rather, what is sought is genuine spiritual care of the "other," properly regarded as our fellow companions on the way. Williams describes the promises we are to make to one another as a part of implementing our mutual obligation to one another within the holy community:

> I promise that I will not hide from you—and that I will also at times help you not to hide from me or from yourself. I promise that your growth towards the good God wants for you will be a wholly natural and obvious priority for me; and I trust that you have made the same promise [to me and others].[159]

A correlation exists between the quality of the life of the Christian exemplar, or *impresario* (agent, working-model, maestro, organizer), and the faith that gives that person's life meaning, purpose, direction, and narrative shape. If Christ himself is the messenger, the message, and the

---

158. Williams, *Holy Living*, 53.
159. Williams, *Holy Living*, 61.

working model of authentic Christianity, then those who follow him will manifest the same qualities and characteristics in their lives as they see expressed in his life. As Williams observes of the monastic exemplar: "The monk must be *transparent*; the monk must be a *peacemaker*; the monk must be *accountable*."[160]

The exact same principles are true for every Christian believer (not just those called to holy orders within an actual monastery), whoever and wherever they are, and whatever work they are engaged in. The monastic ideal is becoming increasingly popular in twenty-first century life, where for the average citizen, lack of self-control is a fundamental problem in an unregulated and unruly age. Beverly Lanzetta points out how many modern-day mystics—herself included—have had an encounter with the divine leading to a greater affinity with monastic spirituality:

> My affinity with monasticism was unformed until one October day in 1976 when a series of revelatory events changed my life and set me on the path of devotion. It was on this day that Divine Mystery broke into my world, transforming my whole being and opening me to a previously unimagined sacred realm. Nothing in my life since compares to the profound changes that took place in my heart and soul that day.[161]

Since that initial, critical intervention of the Sacred into her life, Lanzetta has been actively involved in interpreting the wonder, mystery and beauty of the divine "Other" and sharing her insights with her would-be fellow spiritual travelers. As a way of life, that is not an easy "sell," especially in contrast to the default set of values and outlooks held by most citizens of the Western world, what Carl Trueman has labelled "expressive individualism."[162] Commenting on Trueman's work, Carter Snead explains how expressive individualism amounts to an individual's dethroning of all forms of external authority (God, community, culture and ethical norms), and the enthroning of the individual's articulation of their own self, on the grounds of their own self-authority.[163]

In closing, the following statement from Rowan Williams underscores the idea of the church as the Body of Christ, and reaffirms the Rule of St. Benedict as a way worthy of monks in every generation: "Holiness

---

160. Williams, *Holy Living*, 55–56.
161. Lanzetta, *Monk Within*, 12.
162. Trueman, *Rise and Triumph of the Modern Self*.
163. Snead, "Anthropology of Expressive Individualism."

is a much-patched cloth, a smooth-worn tool at least as much as it is a blaze of new light; because it must be finally a state we can live with and in, the hand fitted to the wood forgetful of the joint."[164] With its central image of the spiritual workshop, the monastic traditions may continue to inform our thinking about holiness as a communal endeavour, creative and constructive in nature yet undertaken by imperfect people in an imperfect world. Quite simply, St. Benedict encourages those who live by the Rule to:

> Carry out God's commandments in what you do every day. Embrace chastity. Hate no one. Do not be jealous or given to feelings of envy. Do not take pleasure in disputes. Avoid pride, respect your elders and care for those younger than yourself. Pray for your enemies in the love of Christ. Before the day's end be reconciled with anyone with whom you have a disagreement. Never despair of God's mercy.[165]

32. Habitus

In recent years, James K. A. Smith in his *Cultural Liturgies* series has been instrumental in bringing the notion of *habitus* to the attention of readers. Here, I will draw from his first two books to enlarge on the theme of habitus with reference to its significance for spirituality in general and Christian spirituality in particular.[166] Habitus can be understood as an underlying substrate of values and pre-rational *knowings* that provide a person's or a community's ultimate values and reasons-for-being. In the spiritual life, unsurprisingly, people draw from this sub-surface level in order to locate their springboard for being and action. The following enquiry into habitus will be guided by three main questions: (1) What is habitus?; (2) How is it formed in human persons?; and (3) What is its role in the spiritual life?

In describing a Christian understanding of habitus, Smith develops two emphases in particular. The first is how worship serves to educate the Christian soul; and the second is the impact that cultural "liturgies" have on how people (religious and otherwise) think and act. Liturgies are performances that have life-shaping influence. One of Smith's core claims

---

164. Williams, *Holy Living*, 69.
165. Benedict, *Rule of St Benedict*, 63.
166. I refer to Smith, *Desiring the Kingdom*, and Smith, *Imagining the Kingdom*.

is that "liturgies—whether 'sacred' or 'secular'—shape and constitute our identities by forming our most fundamental desires and our most basic attunement to the world."[167] Above all, it is what we love—more than what we think—that makes us the people we are at our core. This goes against the grain of a rationalistic philosophy which emphasizes analytical reasoning towards established facts and mental maps. Smith makes the counterclaim that, "We are what we love, and our love is shaped, primed and aimed by liturgical practices that take hold of our gut and aim our heart to[wards] certain ends."[168] Education, then, should not become fixated on the transmission of facts and information, or the application solely of abstract reasoning and "critical thinking." Rather, Smith re-frames our attention away from thinking *per se*, towards a renewed emphasis on our imaginative, intuitive, and sensory faculties. The emphasis now is on the shaping power of subjectivity. The epistemological imperative of mathematical certainty (expressed in Descartes's famous maxim, "I think, therefore I am") is replaced by an emphasis on the human subject as one fundamentally primed for relationship: "I love, therefore I am." We are not so much "thinking" creatures as "desiring" creatures who are more shaped and directed by our hearts than by our minds. At root, this idea is based on St. Augustine's argument that if one truly wants to understand something, one must first love it.

Concerned that many Christians are shaped more by consumer culture than they are by the faith they profess to believe, Smith tries to understand how worship works, and what it takes to foster a new habitus in people who are at the beginning of their faith-journey (or to re-energize the habitus of the Christian already on the path of faith). To that end, Smith tells us that education and liturgy both play a central role, often borrowing from social theorist Pierre Bordieu to stock his "theoretical toolbox."[169] We learn that there is a connection between the body and the desires of the heart in forming powerful and convictional ways of knowing. This is not an entirely new discovery, but one that warrants renewed consideration, especially in an educational context. According to McGilchrist:

> Emotion and the body are at the irreducible core of experience: they are not there merely to help out with cognition. Feeling is

---

167. Smith, *Desiring the Kingdom*, 25.
168. Smith, *Desiring the Kingdom*, 40.
169. Smith, *Imagining the Kingdom*, 29.

not just an add-on, a flavored coating for thought: it is at the heart of our being, and reason emanates from that central core of the emotions, in an attempt to limit and direct them, rather than the other way about.[170]

Such a pedagogy of the emotions calls for what Smith describes as a "dynamics of persuasion."[171] The trick is not so much to change the mind as to change the heart. And this means Christian education is equally targeted toward the *erotic* (the body and its senses) and the *imaginative* (the heart and what we love) as it is towards the intellect and its cognitive functions.

The training and re-training of our desires and loves requires a different kind of pedagogy, as Smith suggests: "The acquisition of a habitus, then, is described by Bordieu as a slow process of co-option, initiation, and incorporation."[172] The liturgies our culture embeds in us through shopping malls, TV programs, going to the football (or baseball or cricket), art, fashion and entertainment, all teach us what is inherently "valuable." At base, we want freedom, happiness, a voice, authenticity and ultimately to be loved. The "military-entertainment complex" in which we live tries to provide all these things—but all it succeeds in doing is enlarging the "hole within us," failing dismally to provide that which satisfies and fills up the human heart and soul. As a result, most people lack the meaning, validation and purpose they crave. And the end-result is not fulfillment but distress; not love but rage; and not meaning but banality. Mental illness, addiction and dysphasia result. Such is the result of our mis-placed worship and praise.

According to Walter Brueggemann, "Praise is not a response to a world already fixed and settled, but it is a responsive and obedient participation in a world yet to be decreed and in process of being decreed through the liturgical act."[173] Brueggemann continues:

> It is the act of praise, the corporate, regularized, intentional, verbalized, and enacted active praise, through which the community of faith creates, orders, shapes, imagines, and patterns the world of God, the world of faith, the world of life, in which we are to act in joy and obedience.[174]

---

170. McGilchrist, *Master and His Emissary*, 35.
171. Smith, *Imagining the Kingdom*, 19.
172. Smith, *Imagining the Kingdom*, 93.
173. Brueggemann, *Israel's Praise*, 11.
174. Brueggemann, *Israel's Praise*, 25–26.

In Christian education, therefore, the old worlds of Babylon, of self, of twenty-first century secularism, and our cult of the ego are "cast out" and replaced with the new world of the God who loves, the God who is, the God who calls, and the God who transforms. As Jean Corbon writes of worship:

> In the liturgical celebration the church remembers all the saving events which God brought about in history and which had their climax and fulfilment in the cross and resurrection of Christ. But the Paschal event, which occurred only once in history, is contemporary with each moment of our lives, for now that Christ is risen he has broken through the wall of mortal time. The liturgy is a 'memorial' of an utterly new kind. We do the remembering, but the reality remembered is no longer in the past, it is here: the Church's memory becomes presence.[175]

In conclusion, to return to James K. A. Smith, "Liturgies are covert incubators of the imagination because they play the strings of our aesthetic hearts."[176] Smith says further that:

> Worship needs to be an incubator of the imagination, inviting us into 'the real world' by bringing us aesthetic olive leaves from the kingdom that is coming, helping us to then envision what it would look like for God's will to be done on earth as it is in heaven.[177]

33. [When] the Holy Spirit Meets the Human Spirit

Throughout the biblical record, we find repeated moments when the Holy Spirit connects with the human spirit in flashes that can only be described as "holy trysts." Think of Moses at the burning bush; Isaiah's vision of Yahweh in the heavenly temple; the visitation of the angel Gabriel with the Virgin Mary in Nazareth; the Risen Jesus' commissioning of the Apostle Paul on the road to Damascus; and the ascended Christ's revelation to the Apostle John in a vision of the untainted brilliance of heaven, accompanied by the command: "Write on a scroll what you see and send it to the seven churches" (Rev 1:11). In such moments a co-mingling occurs between the Holy Spirit and the human spirit, in both first-time

---

175. Corbon, *Wellspring of Worship*, 5–6.
176. Smith, *Imagining the Kingdom*, 137.
177. Smith, *Imagining the Kingdom*, 178.

encounters (as in conversion), and subsequent encounters (as when the Lord met with Moses "face-to-face," Ex 33:11).

At Pentecost (Acts 2:1–13) "All of them were filled with the Holy Spirit." "Amazed and perplexed, they asked 'What does this mean?'" (Acts 2:12). Pentecost is the archetypal 'moment' when the Holy Spirit comes into contact with the human spirit. As a result, there is disturbance, excitement, uplift, bewilderment—and clarity. In that moment when the Holy Spirit meets the human spirit, two certainties must eventuate. The first is that those experiencing the encounter must be persuaded of the convincingness of these events with a force of certitude big enough to commence bearing witness to the fact that Jesus Christ is God (on the basis of their previous encounters with Christ), and that this moment of power and authority is a demonstration of this urgent fact, under the inspiration of the Holy Spirit. The second is that worship and obedience must be the outflow, not simply for those testifying to these facts, but for the audience who are hearing this news for the first time. Such was the response of St. John in the book of Revelation: "I turned to see the voice that was speaking to me . . . When I saw him I fell at his feet as though dead" (Rev 1:12–17). To be ravished by God and to know the illumination that arises from the loving and convincing encounter with the Divine is enough in itself. But there are some who—for the sake of wanting to explore and explain such moments of mystery to themselves and to others—wish to go further. They want to capture something of the mystery by attempting to describe it. As William Hocking has offered, "He [sic] who has had a profound spiritual religious experience must become a teacher or else a hermit or an outcast."[178]

Thankfully, for the teachers among us, Edith Humphrey has provided considerable insight into this most amazing of all encounters.[179] The categories of "communion" and "union" with God can be found everywhere in the literature of Christian spirituality—but few writers have demonstrated the willingness and ability of Humphrey to translate the profound "atom-splitting" moment when God's Spirit merges with and re-writes the DNA of the human spirit. Humphrey's working definition of Christian spirituality is simply, "the study and experience of what happens when the Holy Spirit meets the human spirit."[180] Desperate to avoid the pitfalls of a shallow individualism and a wrongheaded quest

---

178. Cited by Wach, *Comparative Study of Religion*, 60.
179. Humphrey, *Ecstasy and Intimacy*.
180. Humphrey, *Ecstasy and Intimacy*, 17, italics in the original.

for "a religion of *pure experience*" (citing Dupre and Wiseman),[181] Humphrey locates Christian spirituality in the human encounter with God in human form: firstly the man Jesus of Nazareth during his earthly ministry; and secondly with the Risen Christ who—although ascended to heaven—continues to relate to the created order by his diffused presence in the form of the Holy Spirit. The person of the God-man, Jesus Christ, is the place where God and humankind can encounter one another. It is there that the glory of the divine can be infused into the unembellished and under-developed sacred inherent in the human so that the original divine spark placed in human beings at creation can be quickened and re-made *via* the process of redemption. Thus, redeemed humanity comes to have a share in God's person, life, kingdom and mission on earth.

Humphrey begins her discussion of this phenomenon with George Herbert's poem "Love," which reads:

> Love made me welcome: yet my soul drew back, guiltie of dust and sinne, but quick-eye'd love, observing me grow slack . . . Drew nearer to me, sweetly questioning if I lack'd anything. . . You must sit down, says Love, and taste my meat: So I did sit and eat.[182]

Having had the "offence" of our sin removed and been con-joined to God as "sons (and daughters) of God" in a second act of creation (now conceived as re-creation), we have had the mind of Christ revealed to us (1 Cor 2:16). And now that the Spirit of God has made his habitation within us, the human person in the confessing community has been made alive in Christ, baptized and re-birthed into the kingdom of God. They/we have now become "citizens of heaven" (Phil 3:20), and the "mysteries" and secret-things of heaven have been made known and manifest to us here on earth. An awareness of sacred time, sacred presence, sacred place, sacred purpose and sacred meanings is now given to us through a process of *theodidaktos* ('those who are taught by God').[183] This is the role of the teaching Spirit who is given to "teach us all things" (John 14:26).

All this has direct implications for the way Christians are to live in the world. Humphrey concludes with a reflection on the christological hymn found in Philippians 2:5–11 which she translates into a contemporary vernacular:

---

181. Dupré and Wiseman, *Light from Light*, 23.
182. Humphrey, *Ecstasy and Intimacy*, 11.
183. Humphrey, *Ecstasy and Intimacy*, 130.

Let this hymn seize you and change you: what God offers you is the mind of Christ. That same mind which is in Christ Jesus is yours, for you are in him. Look: Jesus had the highest status imaginable, and he gave it up, completely, to become one of us, to become a man who died on a *cross*. Down to humanity and death, and the grave, and up to the highest place, to be worshipped by every creature everywhere! Learn, mark, inwardly digest, let this invade your imaginations—then you will shine, you will no longer complain and argue, you will look out for each other, and be completely loving, just as Jesus was and is and always will be. Let the Lord of Glory change you as you praise him![184]

34. Imitation

Jesus commenced his earthly ministry with a call to discipleship: "Come, follow me" (Mark 1:17). This invitation inaugurated the kingdom of God on earth and opened for us a way to God in the form of the Christian spiritual life. Jesus' disciples are called to "copy his life" by reproducing his likeness in their own lives. A Christian is *de facto* a "little Christ." What is more, according to Julien Smith, "to be transformed into the image of Christ is to be restored to the human vocation, to become truly human."[185]

The Greek word *mimeomai* (meaning to copy or to reproduce) is one of the key words for discipleship in the New Testament epistles. The Apostle Paul is very specific about copying the pattern of Christ's life in our lives. In Philippians 2:5 he writes, "Your attitude should be the same as that of Christ Jesus." Similarly, in Ephesians 5:1, Paul declares, "Be imitators of God therefore, as dearly loved children, and live a life of love, just as Christ loved us and gave himself up for us." Echoing Paul, Scot McKnight concludes, "We are formed by [Christ's] life, by his death, and by his resurrection and ascension. You are not only to believe the gospel but also to embody it . . . Christoformity is rooted in Christ's own words and life."[186]

The Apostle Paul put the principle of "imitation" into action in his own life, and made it a pillar of his ministry by inviting his audience to imitate his faith, saying, "Follow my example, as I follow the example of

---

184. Humphrey, *Ecstasy and Intimacy*, 276.
185. Smith, *Paul and the Good Life*, 101.
186. McKnight, *Pastor Paul*, 4.

Christ" (1 Cor 11:1). Rodney Reeves has taken the liberty of re-phrasing Paul's words in this way:

> Want to know what the gospel looks like? You are looking at it. My life displays the crucifixion of Christ. I am buried with Christ through baptism. I am raised with Christ to walk in this new life. All things are passed away in my life; everything is becoming new because the Spirit of Jesus is in me. If you follow me, you will be following Jesus—the man you've never seen, but see in me.[187]

In the long history of Christian spirituality, there have been many devotional manuals. One of the most significant of those has been Thomas à Kempis's small booklet entitled *The Imitation of Christ*.[188] First published in 1580, *The Imitation* was the most popular devotional book in the fifteenth century and has been one of the most continuously published and frequently re-published books in history. Writing for a primarily male monastic audience, à Kempis adopted the role of a spiritual director. Perhaps he was imagining himself speaking in the role of an Abbot whose task it was to oversee the spiritual lives of his flock. Marko Rupnik styles this as "spiritual fatherhood"—a title that can be adjusted to "spiritual motherhood" for a female audience, both lay and religious.[189] à Kempis's advice is not that given by a priest, confessor, scholar or judge. Instead, he writes as a fellow traveler—the wise soul who has traveled far in the spiritual life, and who knows God as the fruit of participating in the long pilgrimage they have taken together. He addresses his brother-monks in a style that is real, direct and un-patronizing. The advice is offered in the context of a monastic community, where monks were occupied with a schedule of prayer seven times daily, and with responsibilities for the running and provisioning of the monastery, caring for the needs of its members and often the wider community. This has the potential to create a gap—ecclesial, communal, cultural, and linguistic—between the fifteenth century monk and the twenty-first century reader. And yet the advice is plain enough for those with ears to hear.

Here are some examples of the advice given by à Kempis: "If a man [sic] wants to understand Christ's words fully, and relish the flavor of them, he must be one who is trying to fashion his whole life on Christ's

---

187. Reeves, *Spirituality According to Paul*, 15.
188. à Kempis, *Imitation of Christ*.
189. Rupnik, *In the Fire of the Burning Bush*.

model."[190] "If only we could die to self altogether and enjoy complete interior freedom! Then the rest would follow; we should be able to taste the flavors of the spiritual life, and have some experience of what is meant by heavenly contemplation."[191] "This world is not a native country of yours; go where you will, you are only a foreigner, only a visitor in it. Nothing will ever bring you rest, except being closely united to Jesus."[192] "The higher a man rises in the ways of the spirit, the weightier he will often find his crosses becoming. That is because the more his love of God grows, the more painful he feels the state of exile from him."[193] And he concludes with a prayer; "Lord Jesus . . . A disciple is no better than his master, a servant than his Lord. Let this servant of yours make your life his constant study; it is there that I find my salvation and real holiness. Anything else that I read or hear of can neither feed my soul nor delight me so fully."[194]

The Christian spiritual life has as its primary goal the imitation of the life of Christ. Sometimes this involves the afflictions of Christ, sharing in his cross, the shedding of blood and the woundedness of human suffering. But it also has its consolations, living by the energies of the Spirit, resonating with the life of God, the love of Christ, and the perfections that the soul desires to "put on." It is God who decides what we will and will not suffer—according to his will for us. But in the end, there is joy in heaven to be anticipated, and the assurance of God's abiding love for us in this life and in the world to come, as St. Paul reminds us:

> I am convinced that neither death nor life, neither angels nor demons, neither the present nor the future, nor any powers, neither height nor depth, nor anything else in all creation, will be able to separate us from the love of God that is in Christ Jesus our Lord (Rom 8:37–39).

35. Imperfection (a spirituality of)

Christianity stands or falls on the quality of the people it produces. It makes sense that those outside the faith will want to test or assay the

---

190. à Kempis, *Imitation of Christ*, 19.
191. à Kempis, *Imitation of Christ*, 32.
192. à Kempis, *Imitation of Christ*, 70.
193. à Kempis, *Imitation of Christ*, 92.
194. à Kempis, *Imitation of Christ*, 197.

value of the Christian faith by the authenticity of the lives of those who profess its teachings. This makes the living out of the Christian faith a matter of utmost importance since the lives of believers serve either as living proofs or decisive dis-proofs of Christianity as a spiritual pathway. From its earliest history, Christian believers have found it difficult to live up to Jesus' exhortation to "Be perfect . . . as your heavenly Father is perfect" (Matt 5:48). For example, Peter denied Jesus, Judas betrayed him, the apostle Paul called himself the "worst of sinners" (1 Tim 1:16), the two women Euodia and Syntyche fought like terriers (Phil 4:2), the early Church splintered into factions, the first Jewish Christians resented the Gentile believers, the eucharist deteriorated into a drunken farce (1 Cor 11), false apostles arose in opposition to those that had been appointed, and the first missionary team was characterized by deep conflict between Paul, Silas and John Mark.

It doesn't take very long in life to discover that, "The human heart is the most deceitful of all things, and desperately wicked. Who really knows how bad it is?" (Jer 17:9, KJV). Even the apostle Paul recognized and confessed his inescapable sinful nature: "The good I want to do I cannot do, and the evil that rises up within me, I cannot resist" (Rom 7:14–20). The difference between the defeated "wretched man" of Romans 7 and the Spirit-empowered "overcoming" Christian in Romans 8 is chalk and cheese. Phyllis McGinley writes that even the great saints, "lost their tempers, got angry, scolded God, were egotistical and impatient in their turns, making mistakes and regretted them . . . (nevertheless) they went on doggedly blundering their way toward heaven."[195] In each case, the process of "growing up into Christ" is open-ended and an ongoing life-project that requires energy, attention and application.

Believing souls can waste a lot of time and energy on self-recrimination for committing those lingering sins that cling to them like mud, year in and year out. We claim such verses as, "If we confess our sins, he is faithful and just to forgive us our sins and purify us from all unrighteousness" (1 John 1:9). Yet "Catholic guilt" and "Protestant shame" remain with us because we routinely fall back into the same persistent sins and find it so difficult to grow into true holiness and maturity in Christ. We need a circuit breaker to transition from the defeat of a Romans 7 to the confidence and overcoming mentality of a Romans 8 life. Spiritual perfection is an ideal we cannot achieve by ourselves; it is the gift of the Holy

---

195. McGinley, *Saint-Watching*, 5–6.

Spirit, the reception of which requires an arduous process of "un-selfing" that entails competent practice and habituated skills and attitudes, as if we were spiritual athletes. Perfectionism is one of the great mistakes of the spiritual life because it is based on an impossible dream. But striving to live perfectly before God despite our human brokenness is an aspirational goal we are encouraged to make the central concern of our lives.

In his book *People of the Lie*, Scott Peck offers some challenging insights into the true nature of evil. In particular, he suggests that if one is looking for genuine evil, one had best look first within the synagogue and the church, since it is the nature of evil to "hide among the good."[196] Even after undergoing spiritual conversion and the process of sanctification that follows, saints retain their "clay feet" and so must remain imperfect in this life as saints-in-formation until they are glorified. The reality is, as James Howell writes:

> The friends of God are not superhuman. Saints do not possess an extra layer of muscle. They are not taller, and they do not sport superior IQs. They are not rich, and their parents are not more clever than yours or mine. They have no batlike perception that enables them to fly in the dark. They are flesh and blood, just like you and me; no stronger, no more intelligent. And that is the point. They simply offer themselves to God, knowing that they are not the elite, fully cognisant that they are inadequate to the task, and their abilities are limited and fallible.[197]

Furthermore, as Ben Myers suggests:

> We religious believers are, as a rule, pretty unexceptional. Only with the greatest difficulty and inconsistency do we ever manage to align some bits of our lives with what we profess to believe. What can we say? We are sorry! We have been to all the rehearsals! We wish we could do it better! But the great mass of unexceptional believers should be judged ultimately not by its weakest cases but by its strongest: St Francis, Dietrich Bonhoeffer, Mother Theresa.[198]

Martin Luther, too, was deeply aware of the flawed nature of humanity—even redeemed humanity—describing Christian believers as being *simul justus et peccator* (Latin for "simultaneously sinners and saints").

---

196. Peck, *People of the Lie*, 263.
197. Howell, *Servants*, 17.
198. Myers, "In Praise of Bad Art (and Bad Saints)," 2014.

What is needed to navigate this paradoxical life lived between realities is a "spirituality of imperfection." Ernest Kurtz and Katherine Ketchum have provided exactly that, recognizing that brokenness is a part of the human paradox. They write that, "Spirituality teaches us, or has taught most of us, how to deal with failure. We learn at a very young age that failure is the norm of life . . . Errors are part of the game; part of its rigorous truth."[199] Likewise Henry Nouwen, one of the giants of twentieth century Christian spirituality, spoke of being "broken with psychological wounds, physical limitations, and emotional needs."[200] Commenting upon Nouwen's spirituality of imperfection, Will Hernandez observes:

> Through his endless struggle with life itself, Henri Nouwen was a model of fidelity. Many of the struggles proved brutal and were unceasingly determined to debilitate him. The mounting tension inside and around him could at times be overwhelming, beyond any kind of coping on his part. The presence of darkness could be both intimidating and paralysing. Yet faithfulness was the single outstanding trait he exhibited to the very end. Henri Nouwen, without a doubt, epitomizes a decidedly different brand of spirituality that does not obsess over perfection but willingly confronts reality as it is, with its ugly sides—including all traces of imperfection.[201]

The key, therefore, is to be patient with ourselves and with others, and to recognize that both good and bad travel on parallel tracks that have a habit of arriving together. If God in Christ chooses freely to forgive us of our sins, then we must choose freely to forgive ourselves and others. Frederick von Hügel's observation that,

> *Christianity is a heroism.* People seem sometimes to think Christianity is a dear darling, a not-to-be-grumpy, not-to-be-impatient, not-to-be-violent life; a sort of wishy-washy sentimental affair. Stuff and nonsense! Christianity is not that. Christianity is an immense warning; a tremendous truism. A tremendous heroism.[202]

. . . reminds us that Christianity calls us to heroic living, which requires us to go to places we never expected or intended, sometimes by sufferings and sometimes by great delight. But thanks be to God—there is a way

---

199. Kurtz and Ketham, *Spirituality of Imperfection*, 1.
200. Nouwen, *Wounded Healer*, xvi.
201. Hernandez, *Henri Nouwen*, 134.
202. Green, *Letters from Baron Frederick von Hugel to a Niece*, xix–xx.

out of this glorious mess, into the grace of God and the new beginnings we are called to in Christ. And that way is the path of heroic faith and spiritual submission.

36. Lex Orandi

When asked, "What thing most fully defines the Christian faith?"—many contemporary Christians are likely to reply, "Its creeds, doctrines and confessions." But there exists an older mode of thought that offers the alternate view that what most defines the Christian faith is its liturgy and worship that provides substance to its life and faith. According to Scott Aniol:

> The Christian religion is more than its theology . . . one of the most accurate indicators of the central convictions of a church or movement is the way it worships. A dynamic and often unrecognised relationship exists between Christian religion and Christian liturgy.[203]

This more ancient mode of thinking is captured in the Latin phrase, *lex orandi, lex credendi, lex vivendi*, meaning "As we pray, so we believe, and so we live." The phrase is thought to have originated with Prosper of Aquitaine (c. 390–c. 455), who was a disciple of St. Augustine. The principle of these three 'laws'—the first being *lex orandi*, or the originating source of Christian faith; the second being *lex credendi*, or the creedal and confessional element of Christian faith; and the third being *lex vivendi*, or the way Christians live in the world via their moral and communal lives—has played an important part in the history and development of Christian theology, worship, and spirituality. In this entry we will explore *lex orandi* through three 'lenses', keeping in mind that our purpose is not to rehearse the long and convoluted history of the term, but to equip the twenty-first century reader to understand its relevance to the practice of Christian worship and spirituality in the contemporary setting.

The first "lens" is the relationship between theology and worship. Two key considerations for early thinkers in the formative period of Christian history were the need to exclude heretical doctrines in order to maintain orthodox beliefs; and secondly, given the rapid spread of Christianity, to establish uniformity of liturgical rites and practices. But this brought a third dynamic into play—the church's control over the liturgy via its Magisterium. Intended or otherwise, this made worship a tool

---

203. Aniol, "Changed from Glory to Glory," 48.

of politics and controversy—something which continues today. George Tyrrell writes:

> Devotion and religion existed before theology, in the way that art existed before art-criticism; reasoning, before logic; speech, before grammar. Art-criticism, as far as it formulates and justifies the best work of the best artists, may dictate to and correct inferior workmen; and theology, as far as it formulates and justifies the devotion of the best Catholics, and as far as it is true to the life of the faith and charity as actually lived, so far as it is a law and corrective for all. But when it begins to contradict the facts of that spiritual life, it loses its reality and its authority; and needs itself to be corrected by the *lex orandi*.[204]

In the theology versus worship debate, both are needed. The critical question is the order in which they proceed. According to Jesus, the fault of the Samaritan worshippers was that they "worshipped what they did not know," whereas Jesus stated that, "We [Jews] worship what we [do] know" (John 4:22). And for Christians who profess Jesus to be the Son of God as our Lord—we also know whom we worship and why we do so. We have clear knowledge of his life, words, works, miracles, his death and resurrection, and because we have encountered him for ourselves, we have come to believe in him as the Son of God. Because we have met him for ourselves through faith—we may only then proceed to the secondary process of what St. Anselm called "faith seeking understanding." Both theology and worship are needed for us to be properly Christian; but a lively, ecstatic, and love-filled faith life precedes the journey by which the mind seeks to understand what the heart already knows. *Lex orandi* arising from the originating encounter with Christ, underwrites *lex credendi* which is the point at which the creedal element of Christian faith comes to birth.

The second "lens" is the relationship between church and worship. The role of worship in the church is to provide a place and a process by which the people of God can encounter the power and presence of God in its life This occurs as the church remembers God's ancient promises that "I have called you by name" (Isa 43:1); "I have carved you on the palm of my hand" (Isa 49:16); "I will never leave you nor forsake you" (Deut 31:6); "I have loved you with an everlasting love" (Jer 31:3). The purpose of worship is to lead God's people into sacred presence, sacred

---

204. Tyrrell, *Through Scylla and Charybdis*, 221.

time, sacred place, via sacred story . . . leading to that moment when we encounter God for ourselves all over again, week after week. Like Moses, we must take off our shoes for "we are standing on holy ground" (Ex 3:5), and like the disciples who witnessed the transfiguration of Christ and "fell facedown to the ground" (Matt 17:6). The liturgy provides us with the place, the time and the opportunity to meet God again in both corporate and personal worship.

But worship is too-often made a pawn in the power game of lesser things. In the worship wars, church leaders and emergent "brands" of church make their own style of worship a way of marketing their distinctives and competing with other church 'brands'. Western "expressive individualism"[205] is applied to worship in the form of an appeal to Western individualism, offering a spiritual "sugar hit" more akin to shallow devotionalism than it is to authentic corporate worship. Robert Webber observes that cultural perceptions and expectations influence the way we understand worship:

> If *how* we worship shapes *what* we believe, then it is imperative that we pay attention to how we worship. If worship is shaped by culture, it will result in a culturally conditioned faith. If worship is shaped by narcissism, it will result in *me*-oriented consumer faith.[206]

For Webber, "Worship does truth . . . [the] truth about Jesus."[207] And for that reason, Webber poses two questions to pastors and worship leaders: "What does the order of worship [in your church] actually communicate?"; and "How does it inform our faith and shape our spiritual lives?"[208] The order or flow of the three "laws" must become one in which *lex credendi* always points towards and acknowledges a debt to the *lex orandi* which underwrites and precedes it.

And finally, the third "lens" is the relationship between how worship works and spirituality. According to James K. A. Smith, "Human beings are 'liturgical animals,' creatures who can't not worship and who are fundamentally formed by worship practices."[209] Even people who live in a secular world, have a habit of worshipping anything and everything. Why

---

205. Trueman, *Rise and Triumph of the Modern Self*.
206. Robert Webber, *Ancient-Future Worship*, 89.
207. Webber, *Ancient-Future Worship*, 89.
208. Webber, *Ancient Future Worship*, 89.
209. Smith, *Imagining the Kingdom*, 3–4.

is that? It is because we have "hungry hearts" that even our consumer economy knows how to fully exploit such hungers. We cannot dismiss *lex orandi* as something limited to fifth century patristic debates or the sixteenth century Catholic-Protestant controversies at the Reformation. *Lex orandi* is fundamental to the Christian faith because worship works in such a way that it "re-frames" our imagination, our worldview, our way of thinking, and our most basic orientations in life.[210]

Following the thought of Hans von Balthasar, Sigurd Lefsrud writes that worship is the process of "beholding the living God," who is the "object of faith and worship" rather than some vague sense of the divine.[211] When we worship as Christians, we place ourselves in the universal story of God's unfolding love for the world, centered above all else on the person of Jesus Christ who has "loved us and given himself for us" (Eph 5:2).

In closing, we refer to the work of Robert Taft who makes a distinction between two different kinds of theology. He writes:

> It is important to differentiate between *theologia prima* and *theologia secunda*. *Theologia prima* is the personal, evocative expression of experiential faith, particularly as conveyed in the liturgy. It comes prior to intellectual enquiry and the systematization of truths into doctrinal propositions, which is *theologia secunda*. Liturgical language [on the other hand], the language of *theologia prima*, is typological, metaphorical, more redolent of Bible and prayer than of school and thesis, more patristic than scholastic, more impressionistic than systematic, more suggestive than probative. In a word, it is symbolic and evocative, not philosophical and ontological.[212]

37. Logic of the Spirit

The concept of the "Logic of the Spirit" stems from the work of James Loder (1931–2001). Loder was an influential teacher, writer, and practitioner in the fields of theology, science, psychology, education, and philosophy. The author of many books, including *The Transforming Moment* (1989), *The Knight's Move* (co-written with Jim Neidhardt, 1992), and *The Logic of the Spirit* (1998), Loder left a substantial legacy of thought and

---

210. My abbreviated summary of Smith, *Imagining the Kingdom*.

211. Lefsrud, *Kenosis in Theosis*, 191.

212. Taft, "Mass without the Consecration?" cited by Lefsrud, *Kenosis in Theosis*, footnote 45, 191.

innovation to Christian teachers and practitioners with special reference to spiritual education.

In *The Logic of the Spirit*,[213] Loder undertook an expansive and wide-ranging analysis of human development. He did so at a time that might be called the "high" period of twentieth century theological reflection, when theologians such as Karl Barth, Thomas Torrance, Richard Niebuhr and Wolfhart Pannenberg had completed writing their great theological tomes. This period was also the "high" period of psychological exploration when such greats as Carl Jung, Erik Erikson, Jean Piaget, James Fowler, and Carl Rogers developed and wrote their great psychological theories. These two streams came into contact at the point at which their points-of-interest coincided—most significantly addressed towards human development. The conversation between theology and psychology has continued from that time until now. If anything, that conversation is becoming more and not less important. This is the point where Loder's theory of a spiritually shaped psycho-developmental model is best located. According to Loder, his main aim in *The Logic* was "to demonstrate the overall context that a Christian theology of the Spirit provides for the study of human nature, and especially for issues of purpose and meaning implicit in and often insufficiently articulated through the facts and theories of human development."[214]

As is often the case with Loder's work, biographical insights and case studies lighten the more complex theory-laden discussion. Loder describes his response to the birth of his daughter as one of wonder, and questioning. He notes how if his daughter had died at birth, the family would have asked "Why?"—but having been born alive and healthy, the same question of "Why?" still needed to be asked. Loder reflects the existentialism of Albert Camus in signalling the importance of such questions as: "What is a lifetime?" "Why do I live it?" and, "Does life deserve to be lived?" Loder set about asking and answering such questions in *The Logic*. He discusses traditional and emerging models of human development, bringing them into contact with the transformative aspect of the inward work of the Holy Spirit in the life of the person undergoing development. Kenneth Kovacs describes Loder's work as "relational phenomenological pneumatology," which he summarizes as follows:

---

213. Loder, *Logic of the Spirit*.
214. Loder, *Logic of the Spirit*, xiii.

> The Christian life is preeminently relational, distinguished by a relationship with God constituted by Jesus Christ, and sustained by the Holy Spirit. The relation, Loder claims, takes place in and through the life of the Holy Spirit who operates within a complimentary relationship with the human spirit, in what he describes as the *analogia spiritus*: an intimate, transformational interrelation of the Holy Spirit and the human spirit. The Holy Spirit, intimately connected to the person and work of Christ, takes up and extends the work began in the incarnation by enfleshing the presence of Christ in the life of the individual, in ways that are transformationally Christomorphic. What makes Loder's work unique is the way he articulates a theology of the Holy Spirit that incorporates a firm grasp of the way the self participates in and comes to have knowledge of itself, in the world, and God. It is precisely the logic of this dynamic, I would argue, that has extraordinary implications for the way we articulate the Christian experience.[215]

All this to say that, for Loder, human development (through the stages of infancy, toddler, school-age, adolescent, young adult, middle years and beyond) has its origins and wellspring in the spiritual life, and is not simply reducible to the schematic biological, mental and emotional stages posited by most secular, scientific and psychological models. By contrast, Loder's in-depth reading of Søren Kierkegaard's philosophical anthropology places the (embodied, psychological, spiritual) self in a lifelong conversation with God in response to what Loder calls the "negative absurd" on the one hand, which points to the tragic futility and meaninglessness of life and gives rise to despair, and on the other hand the "positive absurd," whereby human nature, redeemed by God in Christ, enters into the life of God to become what Kierkegaard called the "God-man" of faith.[216]

Loder's central argument is that spirit, both human and Divine, is a key element in human life, one that provides a transformative component which possesses the power to transfigure the mundane and natural into the quintessential and the supernatural. Only when the human spirit is brought into contact with the Holy Spirit, is the purpose of human existence properly fulfilled. Loder concludes with the words: "As each life unfolds, gets torn open, stripped to its survival techniques and its passing

---

215. Kovacs, "Relational Phenomenological Pneumatology of James E. Loder," abstract.

216. Loder, *Logic of the Spirit*, ix.

pleasures, and discovers itself as spirit, then it appears from under the surface that we have been created for nothing less than the pure love of God, whose universe is our home."[217]

For Loder, the central moments of human development—including psychological, emotional, character and spiritual development—are dependent on the inner work of the Holy Spirit which is a vital shaping force for the human journey. Growth of all kinds is not a linear and rational process, but implies an ongoing process of learning, discovery, formation, and re-formation. Loder's concept of the "logic of the Spirit" invites believers to embrace the Spirit as a partner on life's unpredictable journey, and to consider those seasons of threat, risk and change as opportunities for growth, invitation to wholeness, and resilience. These are the moments when transformation is most likely to occur, and when the Holy Spirit is most powerfully present to support, inform and resource our ongoing human and spiritual journey.

38. Maladies of the Spiritual Life

We do not know ourselves as we ought as spiritual creatures, and there are few schools for the heart where we can learn the art of *godfaring*. As a result, much wrong-thinking and many maladies creep into the spiritual lives of those who seek to follow Christ in this world. The list that follows represents a sample of what Alan Jones dubs the "Christian neuroses."[218]

1. **Perfectionism**. Many who set out on the spiritual journey make the mistake of adopting impossibly high standards for themselves and others, often based on such biblical texts as, "Be perfect, therefore, as your heavenly Father is perfect" (Matt 5:48). Imposing God's ideal character on earth-bound human creatures is a load that is often too heavy to bear. As a result, the "gentle yoke" of Jesus is made into the heavy burden of legalistic expectation, producing a false sense of guilt generating an unwholesome fear of God in would-be seekers. And yet, God-being-our-helper, it is possible to achieve a balance between human frailty and an almost-perfection.

2. **Spiritual Sweet Tooth.** Because we are naturally attracted to sweet things, many spiritually alive people fall victim to the adrenaline

---

217. Loder, *Logic of the Spirit*, 342.
218. Jones, *Soul Making*, 35–59.

rush that arises from the God-encounter. The felt-presence of God is as real and deeply felt as any drug-induced effect. St. John of the Cross deplored those people who sought out the "sugar hit" arising from the spiritual life. He rejected such candy-cane versions of spirituality, preferring that people carry their cross, deny themselves, and live lives of "nakedness of spirit" before God and neighbor. While there is undoubtedly a certain ecstasy to be had, it is a by-product of the God-encounter and not the thing itself.

3. **Distraction.** Jesus asked his disciples, "Could you not keep watch with me for one hour?" (Matt 26:40). We poor citizens of the twenty-first century, overwhelmed by the speed at which we live our lives, distracted by our smartphones, and preoccupied with the trappings of consumer culture, find it hard simply to "Be still and know that I am God" (Ps 46:10). At its heart, the spiritual life requires us to slow down, to connect deeply with God, self, and others. All this takes undivided time . . . and careful attentiveness. One metaphor for the soul spiritual life is that of a garden. Plants take time to germinate, grow, flower and fruit. And so the soul in its long, slow journey must be given time to do its best work. Hurry is what is most destructive. Slowness and careful listening is what is most constructive.

4. **Idolatry and false worship.** Although we do not always name it as such, worship is something we do naturally as people. C. S. Lewis tells us that "men [sic] spontaneously praise whatever they value and urge us to join them in praising it."[219] Even religiously attuned Israel fell victim to idolatry, worshipping the golden calf in place of Yahweh. John Calvin described the human heart as "an idol making factory." To worship God is good; to worship what God has made as if it were a god, is evil. This requires us to beware what we praise and most value, since God alone is our first love.

5. **Faulty Compass.** Those who go exploring on land have their compasses and those who take to the sea have their sextants. But we poor, blind creatures who seek to explore God and our own internal workings, have no such reliable instrument. We lack the guiding compass we need to avoid the pitfalls that so-often plague the spiritual life. What is needed is a compass that points to "true north" if we are to retain our sense of orientation as spiritual creatures living in

---

219. Lewis, *Reflections on the Psalms*, 80.

a material universe. In most cases, following the lead of our physical appetites is a good thing, since they are given by God and designed to sustain life in its fullness. But there are times when a cartography of the spirit requires us to follow higher desires that must be learned and re-learned, if we are to attend to our true nature, and to attend to the soul-journey which is our primary purpose in life.

6. **Loss of Fervor.** There are times in our spiritual lives when the fire that burns in our souls begins to dim. The apostle Paul entreats us to, "Never be lacking in zeal, but keep your spiritual fervour" (Rom 12:11). The Greek word *zeontos* lies behind the word "fervor." It refers to a blazing fire or a pot of boiling water. Paul exhorts his readers in first century Rome—and we in the twenty-first century—to stoke the fire of our spiritual lives through regular prayer, worship, brotherly and sisterly love, service toward others, patience in tribulation, and charitable works with hospitality. Lazy souls expect the Holy Spirit to do their work for them. The awakened soul understands that it must take responsibility for its own spiritual life by partnering with the Spirit and stoking the fire within.

7. **Mistaking Style for Substance.** We Westerners often live on the surface of life. Our tendency is to value external appearances more than internal things such as truth and substance. As a result, Eugene Peterson argues, "given our ancient predisposition for reducing every scrap of divine revelation that we come across to a piece of moral/spiritual technology that we can use to get on in the world . . . we have proven, time and again, that we are not to be trusted in these matters." Instead, Peterson argues, what is needed is a voluntary return to childlikeness to remedy the situation.[220] He writes, "We do not progress in the Christian life by becoming more competent, knowledgeable, virtuous or energetic." We must instead, "Go back to square one . . . [where] we are always beginners."[221] Attending to depth not surface, and substance not style is the way forward for us.

8. **Avoidance.** After Adam ate the fruit of the tree of the knowledge of good and evil in the garden, he tried to hide from God. But it was hopeless. God found him and called him to account. In the New Testament, the Apostle Paul wrote that no matter where you go—whether to the heights of heaven, or to the depths of the

---

220. Peterson, *Subversive Spirituality*, 30–31.
221. Peterson, *Practise Resurrection*, 30.

earth—God is always present (Rom 10:5–13). To avoid God is impossible; likewise, trying to avoid one's fellow Christians is a grave mistake. Rowan Williams invites us to consider the need to remain open and accessible to others. We are, after all, our brothers' and sisters' keeper. Williams counsels transparency, inviting us to make the promise that, "I will not hide from you—and that I will also at times help you not to hide from me or from yourself. I promise that your growth towards the good God wants for you will be a wholly natural and obvious priority for me; and I trust that you have made the same promise [to me]."[222]

9. **Doctrinal Terrorists.** Edith Humphrey has observed there is a certain form of Christian micro-truth-accounting which has in its arsenal the weapon of critical doctrinal orthodoxy, such that in situations of debate when the Christian faith comes under threat, they become "doctrinal terrorists."[223] Humphrey recommends putting aside such "wrong-headed" strategies and adopting instead the first-order principle of dealing with Jesus himself. He is the starting point of every Christian spiritual conversation—and the endpoint to which every conversation ends in worship, prayer, and praise rather than division, judgment and rancor.

39. Martyr Moment

From its earliest beginnings, Christianity has lauded self-sacrifice and martyrdom as an accompanying feature of Christian witness. The model for such behavior began with Jesus—the Lord of the Church—whose crucifixion and humiliation demonstrated the core of Divine self-giving "for the sake of the world." Jesus' teaching, "Blessed are you . . . when they persecute you . . . on account of me. Rejoice and be glad!" (Matt 5:11), further validated the role of suffering in Christian discipleship. Servais Pinckaers has observed that "the early Christians commonly thought of martyrdom as a reproduction of the Passion of Jesus," something which caused them to explicitly connect the death of the martyr and the death of Christ in their martyrologies.[224] The archetype of martyrdom is also

---

222. Williams, *Holy Living*, 61.
223. Humphrey, *Ecstasy and Intimacy*, 213.
224. Pinckaers, *Spirituality of Martyrdom*, 47.

located in the life of St. Paul, whose apostolic mission meant that he was exposed to constant danger and opposition (2 Cor 11:26). Although not recorded in the biblical narratives, tradition has it that Paul was beheaded during Nero's persecutions in A.D. 64–67.

As Paul Fouracre has argued, "between the apostolic age and the arrival of monasticism, "the archetypal saint was a martyr."[225] Prior to the theological disputes that led to the formalizing of Christianity's orthodox creeds and confessions at the Council of Nicaea (A.D. 325), much of the literature of the early church concerned itself with martyrs and martyrdom. Selected examples of such literature include: *The Martyrdom of Polycarp*, Tertullian's *Apologeticus* (where the phrase "the blood of the martyrs is the seed of the church" is found), *The Martyrdom of Ignatius*, and *The Martyrdom of Perpetua and Felicitas*. Invariably it was not the literary form of martyrdom, but the actual flesh-and-blood example of the martyrs themselves that offered a convincing demonstration of the authenticity of Christian faith.

Martyrdom is an act of "blood witness," in which the martyr's testimony involves suffering and a courageous death. But in the age that followed the martyrs, a second, less costly but equally demanding, form of witness predominated. As Linda Coon explains, "If the martyrs were God's exceptional dead, then the saints were the Creator's miraculous living."[226] In place of the courageous death came the heroic life. Discipleship is a costly calling. It demands an hourly and daily counter-cultural decision that requires modern-day disciples to transgress the normative cultural conditioning bequeathed to them by their culture to instead "choose Christ." Daniel Misdom[227] has observed that citizens of Western consumer-society have, from childhood, been imbued with personal freedoms, economic prosperity, a comfortable and convenient life, bodily health, a liberal education, and an innate belief that their happiness lies in this world rather than the next. But in order to fulfill Christ's invitation to become his disciples, to "Come, follow me" (Mark 1:17), and participate in his mission to the world as his agents (John 20:21–22), contemporary disciples are often required to make decisions which Misdom characterizes as "reckless." He writes:

---

225. Fouracre, "Merovingian History and Merovingian Hagiography," 13.
226. Coon, *Sacred Fictions*, 4.
227. Misdom, "Spirituality of Self-Sacrifice in Trainee Missionaries."

> This *recklessness* sees trainee missionaries (and by implication all genuine disciples) having to make the uncomfortable choice to overthrow their culturally entrenched predispositions towards self and self-interest, to achieve the higher goal of bearing witness to Christ, which is a missionary's foremost interest and joy in the context of their relationship with Christ and their understanding of the obligation of the gospel.[228]

Christian disciples must develop a Christ-centered imagination that is larger and more "real" than anything offered by Disney and Vegas. They must "curate" their wants, passions and loves to focus on Christ, and not be "taken over by the distractions and entertainments and the chatter of the world [where] we trade one sort of self-alienation for another that gives the illusion of homely comfort."[229]

And for that to happen, every moment, of every day of every sanctified life, the believing soul is confronted with their own martyr-moment, in which they/we are invited to choose for God, for good, for wholeness, for holiness, for the sake of the world, and for the sake of their own souls—to deny themselves and their lesser passions, in order to choose Christ and his "upward way." This is what Pinckaers means when he speaks of a "spirituality of martyrdom" in the twenty-first century. What is being imagined is not an unhappy death, but a flourishing life, lived not for oneself but for God and for others. And it requires us to keep ready to hand an ethics of self-sacrifice that makes sense of life when seen from a God's-eye-point-of-view. For this reason, in his training of early-career missionaries, Misdom has found "The Martyr's Oath" to be an important tool. The Oath reads:

> As Christ has given his life for me, so I am willing to give my life for him. I will use every breath I possess to boldly proclaim his gospel. Whether in abundance or need, in safety or peril, in peace or distress, I will not—I cannot—keep quiet. His unfailing love is better than life, and his grace compels me to speak his name even if his name costs me everything. Even in the face of death, I will not deny him. And should shadow and darkness encroach upon me, I will not fear, for I know he is always with me . . . I have taken up my cross; I have laid everything else down. I know my faith could cost me my life, but I will follow and love Christ until the end, whenever and however that may

---

228. Misdom, "Spirituality of Self-Sacrifice."
229. Smith, *On the Road with St Augustine*, 41.

come. Should I die for Jesus, I confess that my death is not to achieve salvation but in gratitude for the grace I have already received. I will not die to earn a reward in heaven, but because Jesus has already given me the ultimate reward in the forgiveness of my sins and the salvation of my soul. For me to live is Christ; for me to die is gain. Amen.[230]

Since the turn of the century, the persecution of Christians globally has been on the rise. Martyrdom as "blood witness" is now commonplace in many places around the world, most notably the Middle East, north and middle Africa, North Korea, and increasingly in India.[231] Persecution of Christians in Western countries is now also an emerging reality. Christian disciples in the twenty-first century will need to learn what Dana Wright has called a "marturological anthropology," which needs to be modelled, taught, learned, and applied as something intrinsic to discipleship.[232] To this end, Howard Thurman's vision of the eternal should serve as a powerful call to courageous decision-making when it comes to Christian witness in those moments when believers are called to give an account of the faith within them:

> There is in every person an inward sea, and in that sea there is an island and on that island there is an altar and standing guard before that altar is the "angel with the flaming sword." Nothing can get by that angel to be placed upon that altar unless it has the mark of your inner authority. Nothing passes "the angel with the flaming sword" to be placed upon your altar unless it be a part of the "fluid area of your consent." This is your crucial link with the Eternal.[233]

40. Metanoia

The word *metanoia* (Greek, meaning "repentance" or "a higher consciousness") is used extensively throughout the New Testament as the keyword for both conversion and repentance. Select examples include: "Repent and believe the good news!" (Mark 1:15); "Repent and be baptized, every one of you, in the name of Jesus Christ for the forgiveness

---

230. Moore, *Martyr's Oath*, x.
231. See Sookhdeo, *Hated without a Reason*, among others.
232. Wright, "Tactical Child-Like Way of Being Human Together," 328.
233. Thurman, *Meditations of the Heart*, 14.

of sins. And you will receive the gift of the Holy Spirit" (Acts 2:38); and "Remember, therefore, what you have received and heard; obey it, and repent" (Rev 3:3). According to J. Goetzmann, in the transition from the Old to the New Testament, "Repentance is now no longer obedience to a law but to a person. The call to repentance becomes a call to discipleship. So repentance, faith and discipleship are aspects of the same thing."[234]

At its root, *metanoia* means four things. First, it means repentance, which is a recognition of one's guilt before God, and the need for forgiveness from and reconciliation with the God who—in Christ—has "loved us and given himself for us" (Eph 5:2). The recognition that one's sin has caused offense against a righteous God, and one's acceptance of God's gracious act in sending Christ to the cross to reconcile us to himself (John 3:16–17), is the starting point for the journey of fundamental change of attitude and becoming "right with God" through faith in Christ.

Second, *metanoia* entails a fundamental change of allegiance from one's previous commitments, life-orientations, and defining beliefs. For example, in first-century Palestine, Jesus' audience were called not only to turn away from their sins, but to turn to Christ from their pagan, Jewish, Greek, Roman, civic, and household gods. Henceforth they were to direct their allegiance to Christ exclusively, renouncing all other objects and centers of belief, to embrace Christ alone. According to Alan Kreider, "In Christianity's early centuries conversion involved changes in belief, belonging, and behavior—in the context of an experience of God that . . . must have been very powerful."[235] This call to a fundamental reorientation on the part of the convert—which is archetypal for the spiritual life—meant that *metanoia* was a fundamental experience for Christians in the early church, as it is for Christians and those "undergoing God" in the twenty-first century and beyond.

Third, *metanoia* has a therapeutic aspect to it. It represents a change in what one loves and a new orientation of the heart at the level of its deepest hungers and drives. "Metanoia literally [means] a 'change of heart', about [people's] view of themselves, and their world and [a move] to a less alienated state and deeper awareness of themselves and others."[236] A form of Christotherapy takes place at conversion in which the convert transitions from someone previously excluded from the life and purposes of God to someone who is now included in those things. One of the

---

234. Goetzmann, "Conversion-Metanoia," 358.
235. Kreider, *Change of Conversion and the Origin of Christendom*, xv.
236. Salter, "Spirituality," 160.

foremost signs of such inclusion is the indwelling of the Spirit, who is the source, originator and energizer of the spiritual life.

And fourth, *metanoia* involves a fundamental change in one's imagination and what one takes to be *the real,* in one's pre-rational subconscious as well as one's developed thinking; in other words, one's entire worldview. In the moment of the Apostle Paul's conversion, we are told scales fell from his eyes (Acts 9:18), and the possibility of something other than a Jewish Torah-shaped reality coming into being. Confronted with the reality of Yahweh addressing him in the person of the Risen Christ, Paul was forced to radically reconceive Judaism as he had previously understood it, transfiguring it into a new interpretive system in which Christ has fulfilled the teachings of the Torah as God's appointed Prophet, Priest and King. From the time of St. Paul in the first century onwards, every Christian has been invited to receive a new interpretive system based on a creation-fall-election-redemption-apocalypse-consummation meaning string, which places Christ at its center.

Metanoia as repentance, as a change of allegiance, as healing towards inclusion in God's purposes, and as the receiving of a new worldview, comprises a central element in initially turning to Christ, subsequently remaining in him, and growing in him. Richard Niebuhr describes this as a "permanent revolution" or the ongoing transformation of human life under Divine initiative: "God's self-disclosure is that permanent revolution in our religious life by which all religious truths are painfully transformed and all religious behavior is transfigured by repentance and new faith."[237]

The idea of a "palimpsest" captures something of this radical transformation. The word derives from ancient forms of teaching and writing, and refers to a wax tray, vellum parchment manuscript, or chalk-board that has been scraped clean or erased in order to be written over and used again. Whatever content, truth or claim that was once written there, has now been erased and written over with fresh content. A more apt description for the twenty-first century is the over-writing of a hard drive on a computer. The old content is removed, and fresh content is now the predominating feature. In effect, this is what happens in Christian conversion, where the entire person (body, mind, and soul) is "written over," re-engraved, re-scripted. A new mind has arrived, seemingly ready-made, as a form of pre-packaged truth arising out of the epistemology given by the biblical metanarrative distilled as

---

237. Niebuhr, *Meaning of Revelation,* 133.

creation-fall-election-redemption-apocalypse-consummation. Such a reconfiguring of the self enables the Christian neophyte believer to perceive the world from an alternative (and elevated) point of view—as a *hierophant* (someone who sees the world as new, as if for the first time, this time with God at its center). The renewal of mind that accompanies Christian conversion comes as a result of an upward spiritual movement, one that is transformative in nature, from flesh to spirit, from death to life, and from darkness to light.

41. Mystagogy

In this entry, we define *mystagogy* (a composite word from the Greek *musterion*, meaning something hidden, an enigma; and *pedagogos*, meaning one who teaches or instructs) as the task of those who serve as catechists, instructors, and teachers (referred to as *mystagogues*) in the church who assist those confessors under their care to grow in the spiritual life towards maturity.

In ancient Greece, mystagogues played an important role in temples, shrines, and places dedicated to the worship of pagan deities. Their role was to explain the nature of the gods and what was involved in serving and worshiping the lesser gods of the pre-Christian world.

> They revealed what was hidden from human sight but experienced by those who were involved in the service of that god. The mystagogue who had been initiated into the mystery 'led' others into the mystery. In classical Greek 'mystagogy' was the term for the initiation of people into the experience of the mystery.[238]

When the Apostle Paul wrote about becoming a "servant" of the mysteries of God in Colossians 1:25–28, he effectively describes himself as a mystagogue, which is "a person who initiates others into a mystery."[239] Paul believed that his mission and ministry were to reveal the secret mysteries of God as they were found in Christ to an audience that were used to receiving mysteries from the pagan priests, and who now—in the context of the Christian gospel of Christ—were to receive those things which up until now, "no eye had seen, no ear had heard, and no mind had conceived" (1 Cor 2:9).

---

238. Kleinig, "Mystery of Christ and the Divine Service," 2.
239. Kleinig, "Mystery of Christ and the Divine Service," 2.

Kees Waaijman situates mystagogy within the practice of spiritual accompaniment in the community of faith.[240] He argues that there have traditionally been four mystagogical "moments" in the life of the Christian church. First, liturgical spirituality, where people not only participate in the liturgy and sacraments, but also come to see themselves as participating in the heavenly life as they enact God's theo-drama by taking part in ritual worship. Second, biblical spirituality, where people learn and recite the narrated story of salvation-history through reading the Scriptures—both corporately and individually—and learn the lexicon of faith and how to participate in that story for themselves. Third, spiritual formation, in which teachers and learners travel together on a pilgrimage of discovery so that their souls are enlarged, and they are brought closer to Christ with their hearts and minds made ready to embrace him for his great love. And fourth, mystical accompaniment, where those who have ascended higher in the spiritual life make it their goal to assist novices and new initiates in the faith to go deeper in their knowledge of Christian spirituality, and to rise higher in their experience of Christ towards sanctification and glorification. But note that mystagogy is not an individualistic practice—it has its roots in the corporate life of the church in the form of the sacraments and the liturgy and in the catechism where instruction takes place in groups of novice learners. According to Jean Daniélou, "Sacramental life is truly conceived as a *mystagogy*, as a progressive initiation which leads the soul to the summit of mystical life, to *sober drunkenness*."[241]

According to John Chrysostom (347–407), those who are being initiated into faith should be taught, regarding the sacrament of the Eucharist, so that "what we believe is not the same as what we see, but we see one thing and believe another."[242] That is, the bread becomes the body of Christ, the wine becomes the blood of Christ, and the carnal present is transmuted into the sacred future. Being taught to "see" lies very much at the center of spiritual accompaniment and mystagogical instruction in the church, seen as a community of alternative interpretation. When it comes to baptism, confirmation or chrismation, and the Eucharist (the "sacraments of initiation") one first learns the teaching and then undergoes the transformation it points towards. Through baptism, one not only learns about the "new birth" from passages such as Romans 6, but

240. Waaijman, "Mystagogic Research," 869–945.
241. Maspero, "Cant/In Canticum Canticorum," 123.
242. Pallikunnel, "Mystery, Mystagogy and Mysticism," 211.

one actually experiences it by participating in the new birth and being raised from death to life. And in the experience of the Eucharist/Communion, the reception of the bread and the wine do not simply imply participating in the ritual, but entering *de facto* into the sacred reality of the Divine presence and not simply thought of as a symbolic exchange. "Salvific experience can only be enjoyed through a mystical participation in the Mysteries [by] entering into the Mystery of Christ . . . So a Christian is, by his [sic] very call, a mystic, a participant in Christ, the union of God and man[kind]."[243]

Traditionally, a mystagogue is the person who accompanies the initiate on his or her entrance into that which was externally performed, leading the initiate to the point "when they discover within themselves that what has been said is true."[244] The validation of the integrity of such insights arises from the authenticity of the life of the mystagogue, who has him or herself undergone the relevant transformation resulting from their encounter with Christ, and can therefore speak with conviction of his own conversion and awakening to insight.

Waaijman insists that mystagogy rests most properly in the practice of spiritual accompaniment, where the mystagogue is basically a "thinker"—one who is willing to translate their own visceral experience of transformation and re-visioning, making these things both conceptually and practically available to the novice believer's understanding. Mystagogy requires that the spiritual teacher put into words their own inward experience in a way which is consistent with Scripture and the larger Christian spiritual tradition. "Mystagogy is the discursive sharing of the transcending, intimate and personal experience of God."[245]

But the thinking done by mystagogues/teachers is not hyper rational. It is for the purpose of applied pastoral and spiritual explanation. John Kleinig warns that the over-intellectualisation of the Christian faith—in particular by Christian teachers—does a great deal of damage to the credibility of their role as mystagogues.

> I fear that we orthodox Christians may, in the past, have all too often, misrepresented the faith by rationalising it and explaining it away. Yet we Christians are not called to present the gospel to others by explaining it, let alone explaining it away; we are called to be mystagogues, people who initiate them into the mystery

---

243. Pallikunnel, "Mystery, Mystagogy and Mysticism," 212.
244. Augustine, "Teacher (De Magistro)," 100.
245. Citing M. Ofilada Mina, Waaijman, *Spirituality*, 921.

of Christ and his gospel, the mystery of God's kingdom. And there's nothing secret about that. It is open for all who have ears to hear and hearts to receive it.[246]

42. Ordo Amoris

The concept of *ordo amoris* (Latin, meaning "the order of love") originates in the thought of the German ethicist and philosopher Max Scheler (1874–1928). *Ordo amoris* refers to a right ordering of the emotions and desires, bringing them into accord with the love and will of God.

Antecedents for the concept lie in the writings of French mathematician Blaise Pascal (1623–1662) and his attributing to the heart an authoritative yet intuitive way of knowing, as exhibited by his statement "the heart has reasons the mind knows nothing of." The concept of *ordo amoris* can be traced back to a much earlier period, in St. Augustine's belief that the proper understanding of a thing is dependent on the perceiver having a love-relationship with it. In the modern era, the notion of *ordo amoris* resonates in Scheler's phenomenology of the emotions ordered around a set scale of values. In summing up Scheler's approach to the *ordo amoris*, Eugene Kelly states:

> The human being comes to inhabit a world of value-objects that he [sic] may grasp in themselves as objects only insofar as he loves and hates. Hence, each human being, as a distinct spiritual person, possesses an *order* of loves and hates that, for Scheler, is innate, or formed in early infancy, and takes a unique form in each of us. He does not speculate on the mechanics of its construction. He calls this universal order that founds our spiritual life the 'objective' *Ordo amoris*. It is an order of the heart that intends and loves values according to their objective relative worth. Out of it emerges the basic moral tenor of a person, the ethos of his community, and the norms to which he submits.[247]

Further:

> Ordo amoris refracts the objective order of values ... Hartmann agrees with Scheler and Pascal that the uniformity in humankind's sense of the relative value of things is almost enough to

---

246. Kleinig, "Mystery of Christ and the Divine Service," 2.
247. Kelly, *Material Ethics and Value*, 44.

justify St Paul's idea of a *nomos agraphos*, an objective law of loving and hating written upon the human heart.[248]

The purpose of *ordo amoris* as a discreet category is to assist human persons to learn what love is and how to "attune" their interior worlds away from resentment and the idolatry of improper infatuations towards a proper ordering of love within their core-being.

Scheler intended to write a book on the right ordering of love, but his untimely death cut the project short, leaving it to later scholars to complete. Manfred Frings took up the challenge and developed the concept extensively in numerous authoritative published papers and books.[249] Frings captures the essence of Scheler's concept when he writes, "Whoever grasps the *ordo amoris* of a man [sic], has hold of [the] man himself"; it is love and not "knowledge or will that deserves to qualify as the core of man as a spiritual being;" because "Love is the 'mother and awakener' of all knowledge and willing" in the human person.[250] Humankind frequently suffers from many kinds of "disordered love" and falls victim to negative emotions.[251]

According to Frings, Pascal was able to see Christ as "the example *par excellence* of *ordo amoris*."[252] Thus Christian life lived before God in the form of a saint, the spiritual genius who has learned the art of ongoing intentional formation in the person and the faith-community, was a continuation of the life of Christ. If Scheler is correct, "love and value-perception precede knowledge" as a kind of ontological commitment that is foundational for the entirety of one's inward and outward life. All that to say that the concept of *ordo amoris* is of central importance to the project of spirituality as a lived venture. Since it unfolds within the human person, each individual is obliged to nourish and nurture the interior life within themselves and others, in awareness that we all live *coram Deo* ("before the face of God").

Tapio Puolimatka proposes that whereas animals live in a "closed system" of impulses, humans possess an "open system" of values including the possibility of ethical love which must be able to undergo a process

---

248. Kelly, *Material Ethics and Value*, 45.
249. Frings, "'Ordo Amoris' in Max Scheler," 40–59.
250. Frings, "'Ordo Amoris' in Max Scheler," 40.
251. Frings, "'Ordo Amoris' in Max Scheler," 53.
252. Frings, "'Ordo Amoris' in Max Scheler," 55.

of change through moral education.²⁵³ Learning to love rightly is a necessary pedagogical goal, even if it frequently remains un-addressed in the educational curriculum. Education along these lines is not simply about generating or transmitting information but is more vitally engaged in the process of helping students appropriate the virtues, which are central to what it means to be a human person. According to Puolimatka:

> Scheler differentiates various basic types [of persons] by the way values are expressed in human personalities; the saint, the creative person, the courageous and honourable person, the genius, the hero, and the leading spirit and *bon vivant* . . . According to Scheler, the highest of these is the saint, who was devoted to values of holiness. A person devoted to holiness is characterised by her focus on person-oriented values instead of the values related to performance.²⁵⁴

Thus, educators of all kinds—secular and post-secular, religious and spiritual—should be aiming to develop in their students the qualities of emotional maturity that arise from the *ordo amoris*, or the order of the heart. This is a central characteristic of the task of the Christian catechist, mystagogue, and spiritual educator.

Scheler's concept of the "ordo amoris" contributes to Christian spirituality insofar as it provides a hierarchy of values which are focused on the centrality of love as a predominating element in the human-Divine relationship. The "ordo amoris" provides Christian spirituality with a moral compass, directing individuals and faith-communities to align their desires with the will of God. It challenges any distortions caused by misplaced loves and promotes a transformative journey towards a God-centered existence.

43. Paroikos

Paroikos is a Greek word meaning a *stranger*, or "an alien, one who lives in a place that is not their native home." The Apostle Paul uses the word in its plural form (*paroikoi*) to refer to followers of Jesus whose "citizenship is in heaven" (Phil 3:20), who live on the earth out of the resources of heaven and who are guided by the ethic of a Divine and not an earthly agenda. Other similar references from the New Testament include Acts

---

253. Puolimatka, "Max Scheler and the Idea of a Well Rounded Education."
254. Puolimatka, "Max Scheler and the Idea of a Well Rounded Education," 379.

7:6 ("Your descendants will be strangers in a country not their own, and they will be enslaved and mistreated for 400 years"); Ephesians 2:19 ("Consequently, you are no longer foreigners and aliens, but fellow citizens with God's people and members of God's household"); and 1 Peter 2:11 ("Dear friends, I urge you, as aliens and strangers in the world, to abstain from sinful desires, which war against your souls)."

From the New Testament records, we learn that the earliest disciples of Jesus referred to themselves in a variety of ways. Examples include: "followers of the Way" (Acts 15:14); "saints" (Acts 9:13 et al.); "the brethren" (Acts 11:26); and "Nazarenes" (Acts 24:5). When the designation "Christian" first came into use (as described in Acts 11:26), it was likely used by the enemies of the emerging Christian movement as a term of derision. The link between *Christian* and *cretin* is easily made both linguistically and rhetorically. When we ask, "What did the early believers call themselves, and how did they think about themselves?" One probable answer is that they thought of themselves as *paroikoi* or "resident aliens." This usage is confirmed by Hebrews 13:14, "For here we do not have an enduring city, but we are looking for the city that is to come." However, as Keith Hardman notes, it is probable that, "by the middle of the second century [the term "Christian"] had been taken up as one of jubilant testimony by those who might have expected martyrdom if they admitted to being a follower of Jesus Christ."[255] The non-canonical *Epistle to Diognetus* describes the Christians as being "no different" from other people "in terms of their country, language or customs."[256] Christians, in other words, make their home in whichever country they find themselves residing in:

> They share their meals but not their sexual partners. They are found in the flesh but do not live according to the flesh. They live on earth but participate in the life of heaven. They are obedient to the laws that have been made, and by their own lives they supersede the laws. They love everyone and are persecuted by all.[257]

Additionally, when commenting on the early period of Christianity, Wendy Pullan observes:

> When taken over into Christianity [the terms *paroikos* and *polites*] were a kind of 'constitutional terminology', applied to heaven, earth and the city of God. *Paroikia*, meaning 'the stay

---

255. Hardman, "Christian," 220.
256. *Epistle to Diognetus*, 139–40.
257. *Epistle to Diognetus*, 141.

or sojourn of one who is not a citizen in a strange place', became 'parish ... a community of strangers', the permanent earthly status of Christians in the basic unit of the Christian Church ... But Ephesians 2:19 distinguishes between those before conversion who were 'strangers and sojourners' to Christianity, and those after conversion who are 'fellow citizens with the saints'.[258]

Discussing Christian identity in the modern era, Stanley Hauerwas and William Willimon, in their book *Resident Aliens*,[259] describe what it means to live as a community of radicals whose task is to colonize the earth with the values and ethics of the kingdom of God. Specifically, they compare this task to setting out on an "adventurous journey"[260] to subvert the contemporary world, which Hauerwas and Willimon describe as a "supermarket of desire." All this takes seriously Jesus' teachings in the Sermon on the Mount, choosing to behave "as if" our right-living can countermand the evil generated by a godless world. Hauerwas and Willimon write: "Paganism is the air we breathe, the water we drink. It captures us, it converts our young, it subverts the church."[261] Speaking of Christian ethics in such a world, they propose that, "Learning to be moral is much like learning to speak a language."[262] One does not begin by teaching the rules of grammar, but instead by inducting learners into a community of language. It is in such a community that the ethics of faith, of purity, and of morality are learned, and that one's identity in the community originates from a meaningful narrative, a purposeful life, and a sense of belonging to something larger than oneself.

In today's post-Christian era when Christianity is increasingly becoming a religious minority,[263] it is commonplace for churches to feel marginalized and uncertain about their identity; those who minister in professional roles are often confused about their function and purpose; and many Christians are all too aware of a brooding anti-religious "mood" among the wider population. As a result, they are likely to experience anxiety about their fundamental identity, values and allegiances when measured against those of the pervading culture. James Blumenstock discusses this experience of alienation in connection with Georg

---

258. Pullan, "Intermingled Until the End of Time," 414.
259. Hauerwas and Willimon, *Resident Aliens*.
260. Hauerwas and Willimon, *Resident Aliens*, 51.
261. Hauerwas and Willimon, *Resident Aliens*, 151.
262. Hauerwas and Willimon, *Resident Aliens*, 97.
263. Austin and Daniels, *Emerging Christian Minority*.

Simmel's "marginal man" theory, further developed by Alfred Schutz.[264] Blumenstock's work focuses on Christian identity among Thai Buddhists who convert to the Christian faith. In that context he employs Everett Stonequist's model of the "marginal man" which denotes:

> One who is poised in psychological uncertainty between two (or more) social worlds; reflecting in his [sic] soul the discords and harmonies, repulsions and attractions of these worlds, one of which is often 'dominant' over the other.[265]

The "marginal man" concept accords well with the notion of *paroikos*, according to which Christians must negotiate their identity in a world in which they frequently do not feel "at home." Ultimately, Christian spiritual identity is one which originates from God and is centered "in Christ," as St. Paul frequently reminds us (Rom 8:1; & 2 Cor12:2). Despite Christians being citizens of every age, place, culture and context—they are ultimately citizens of heaven (Phil 3:20), because Christian identity takes its "home address" from the place where God dwells. If we are to identify as "Christians in an alien public arena,"[266] and to function as aliens and strangers, we had best get used to our outsider and outlier status, and to learn how to use our prophetic voice to speak from the margins. It also behoves us to realize that Western culture has developed a penchant for listening to voices who speak from the edge. One wonders whether the time will come once again when Christian voices might be heard from the margins, and whether when that time comes, Christians will be ready to speak?

44. Participation

One of the central features of a spirituality conceptualized within the classical Christian tradition, is God's invitation for the redeemed human person to have their life integrated into his own life. This is the sense of "participation" we will discuss in this entry, noting four distinct aspects of special significance for Christian spirituality in the form of: (1) participation in God; (2) participation in Christ; (3) participation in the sacraments; and (4) participation in the mission of God.

---

264. Blumenstock, *Strangers in a Familiar Land*, 5–10.
265. Stonequist, *Marginal Man*, 8.
266. Miner and Stevens, *Identifying as Christian in an Alien Public Arena*.

First, *participation in God*. The Christian understanding of God's intra-trinitarian life is that God exists as a unity in himself, in his interior economic life (pertaining to the functioning of a household) as Father, Son, and Spirit. Theologians sometimes call this the "social trinity," describing the relationship between the three distinct Persons of the Godhead by means of the metaphor of *perichoresis* (Greek, meaning "a dance"). In the early stages of the dance, when the movement is slow, the identity of each of the Divine partners can be easily observed and recognized. But as the music speeds up, the identities of the dance partners become fused so that only a single Being can be discerned and observed. The metaphor of the dance offers insight into the intra-relational existence and mutual interpenetration of each member of the Godhead. One of the great mysteries of Christian spirituality is that God invites mortal creatures in their redeemed state to participate in the Divine life. Redemption is the result of God choosing to incorporate humankind into himself. Having been "brought near" *via* God's gracious invitation, redeemed persons must choose to become active participants in the Divine life and not simply passive observers who remain at the margins—too afraid to get involved. Yet Miroslav Volf warns, "There can be no correspondence to the interiority of the divine persons at the human level," because "another human self cannot be internal to my own self."[267] Redeemed humanity is both a beneficiary of and a contributor to God's electing choice to embrace redeemed humanity into his Divine life.

Second, *participation in Christ*. The spirituality expressed by the Apostle Paul involves a "double participation" where Christ "lives in" and "works through" us, and where we make our home in Christ and willingly conform ourselves to his "image and likeness." Dallas Willard has described spiritual formation as "the process of transforming the person into Christlikeness through each part of the person."[268] In a similar vein, Scot McKnight employs the language of *christoformity*. Speaking to pastors and spiritual formaters, McKnight defines what he means by christoformity:

> We are formed by his life, by his death, and by his resurrection and ascension. We are not only to believe the gospel but also to embody it. To use the Greek and Latin terms no one uses, *bio*-formity, *cruci*-formity, and *anastasi*-formity [resurrection].

---

267. Volf, *Church as the Image of the Trinity*, 208–10.
268. Willard, *Living in Christ's Presence*, 13–14.

Add those together and you get Christoformity, but the way we become Christoform is through participation in Christ; through baptism, through faith, through indwelling and being indwelled by Christ, through the Spirit, through being clothed with Christ, through fellowship, through transformation, and through sharing in the events of Christ's life.[269]

Third, *participation through the sacraments*. Sacramental spirituality is not well understood in many Protestant churches who see themselves as non-sacramentalist, but liturgical expression through baptism, the Eucharist, and other sacramental activities such as marriage, confession, anointing of the sick for healing, reconciliation, and reception into holy orders goes back to Christianity's earliest times. According to Robert Webber, liturgical spirituality "loves the worship of the church, the memory of God's work in history, and the anticipation of God's present and future work in the world."[270] Liturgy (from the Greek *leitourgos*, meaning "the work of the people") is a ritualized re-telling of God's work in the theatre of salvation history represented in the unfolding drama of creation-fall-election-covenant-redemption-apocalypse-consummation, a narrative-history which allows worshipers to participate in a larger reality than their own small worlds. And it delivers them into a larger transcendent world which takes sacred space, sacred time, sacred story, sacred presence and sacred fire as its locus and destination-point. Thus, through the eyes of faith and the prayers of *epiclesis* (in which the priest or pastor invites the Holy Spirit to transform the elements into their heavenly form), the "ordinary is transformed."[271] Everyday items such as bread and wine become the body and blood of Christ; ordinary time becomes the "sacred moment;" and everyday life becomes the Christian form of life which has eternal implications and consequences. Hans Boersma extends Christian sacramentalism from church-based ritual to reality as a whole, speaking of a "sacramental ontology" based on the Christian sacraments, enabling human worshipers to participate in a literal way in heavenly things by means of the Eucharist as a sacramental meal; tradition as sacramental time; biblical interpretation as sacramental practice; truth as sacramental reality; theology as sacramental discipline; and spirituality as sacramental participation in the Divine life.[272]

269. McKnight, *Pastor Paul*, 4.
270. Webber, *Divine Embrace*, 182.
271. Reno, *Ordinary Transformed*.
272. Boersma, *Heavenly Participation*.

And finally, *participation in the mission of God*. In his book *Abide and Go: missional theosis in the Gospel of John*,[273] Michael Gorman discusses the relatively new discipline of "missional hermeneutics" within Christian theology. He summarizes what is meant by missional hermeneutics in three movements as: (a) the God who is love is missional and therefore has a mission, referred to as the *missio Dei*; (b) the Scriptures bear witness to God's mission; and (c) the church is called and sent to participate in that mission in God-shaped ways.[274] Gorman states:

> To participate in Christ is both to benefit from God's mission of liberation and reconciliation and to bear witness to this divine mission—thus furthering it—by becoming a faithful embodiment of it.[275]

Thus, at the risk of jeopardizing his earth-based mission, God in Christ places the fate of the gospel in the hands of a group of twelve young, untrained, unready and sometimes unwilling young men by sending them into the world with the words, "As the Father has sent me, so I am sending you," and after breathing on them, he announces, "Receive the Holy Spirit" (John 20:21–22). It can even be said that "Christianity is . . . essentially a mystery of participation."[276]

45. Recapitulation

In this entry, we discuss the concept of recapitulation under five headings: (1) St. Paul's use of the term in Ephesians 1; (2) recapitulation in Irenaeus; (3) recapitulation as an important theory of the doctrine of the atonement; (4) recapitulation in contemporary theological understanding; and (5) recapitulation as applied to spiritual formation and the Christian spiritual life.

First, St. Paul's use of recapitulation in Ephesians 1:9–10. Etymologically, the word originates in the Greek root *kephale*, meaning 'head' or origins. The word literally means "to begin again." In its Greek linguistic form, recapitulation is used only twice in the New Testament, in which Ephesians 1:9–10 holds particular significance:

---

273. Gorman, *Abide and Go*.
274. Gorman, *Abide and Go*, 2.
275. Gorman, *Becoming the Gospel*, 36.
276. Barnhart, "One Spirit, One Body," 265.

> And he [God] made known to us the mystery of his will according to his good pleasure, which he purposed in Christ, to be put into effect when the times have reached their fulfilment—to bring all things in heaven and on earth together under one head (kephale), even Christ (Eph 1:9–10).

According to J. B. Lightfoot, "The entire harmony of the universe, which shall no longer contain alien and discordant elements, but . . . all the parts shall find their centre and bond and union in Christ."[277] What is in view is the source of the brokenness of the human condition resulting from sin and exclusion, results in the restorative process of predestination, election, redemption and revelation. Paul's intent is that readers come to understand the extent of the re-creation God has brought about in Christ.

Second, the patristic church father Irenaeus (c. 115–c. 202) made recapitulation the primary theme of his theology, since it represents a restoration of a once fallen, now broken humanity, back to its original creative wholeness. It is a "putting right" of the offence of sin and the application of the benefits of redemption that results from Christ's cross to produce a restored and reconciled humanity. Augustine wrote of the negative effects of original sin and concupiscence and their impact on the human condition—whereas Irenaeus could take the opposite view by focussing on what elevated humankind and the "ascent of man" to enter God's creational design.

> Recapitulation means the inauguration of a new humanity: 'The glory of God is a living man [sic] and the life of man is now the vision of God' (*Against Heresies*, 4.200.7). Irenaeus has his own account of man as the image and likeness of God. Because the incarnate Son is the archetypical image [of God], every human possesses shape and flesh similar to him. At baptism every believer receives the power of assimilation (likeness) from the Holy Spirit as a dynamic which gradually transforms the image until it is finally perfected by Resurrection.[278]

For Irenaeus:

> . . . recapitulation names God's process for restarting humankind in Christ, renewing and restoring it to the divine image and likeness. The word recapitulation literally means 're-heading.' Christ replaces Adam as the head of mankind . . . The process of

---

277. Lightfoot, *Notes on the Epistles of St Paul*, 322; cited in Brown, "Head/kephale." 163.

278. Osborne, "Irenaeus of Lyons," 124.

recapitulation has three aspects, and Christ accomplishes all of them at once. First, it is a repetition of the creation of mankind—a new beginning—in which Christ is the new Adam. Second, it is the reversal of what went wrong in the fall. Adam messed up the first time, but Christ does it right this time and establishes a new pattern, a new kind of existence for people to follow. And third, it is a summation of all human history throughout the world, so that all people can be united with Christ in a new humankind.[279]

Third, recapitulation is one important theory of the atonement. According to Thomas Torrance, recapitulation is "The theory associated with Irenaeus . . . that Jesus in his human life summed up the human race and its history. He undid its sin and disobedience by his obedience and gathered it up as a new humanity under his headship as the new Adam."[280] Lucas Stamps locates Christ's atonement not in the transactional theory of the ransom theory, or the economic theory of propitiation, but rather in the obediential submission of Christ in his new humanity as the New Adam that achieved God's intended restoration.

> If the human will of the first Adam was instrumental in sin's inception, then the human will of the Last Adam was instrumental in sin's defeat. Christ's assumption of a human will, with all of its weaknesses and passions, makes his work of redemption and recapitulation possible.[281]

Fourth, recapitulation in one contemporary theological understanding. For reasons of time and space, we take as our single representative of contemporary Christian theologizing Frances Young's *God's Presence: a Contemporary Recapitulation of Early Christianity*.[282] There, Young rehearses historic Christianity's systematic replacement of the old with the new, using *recapitulation* as its key. Thus, Young throughout her book explores the old Adam who is replaced by the New Adam who is Christ; the old mother of humanity in Eve who is replaced by Mary as the Mother of Christ; the old covenant with its animal sacrifices which is replaced by the new covenant whose sacrifice is Christ; the Old Testament which is replaced by the New Testament; and the fate of the old humanity under law which is replaced by the destiny of the

---

279. Harrison. *God's Many-Splendored Image*, 40.
280. Torrence, *Atonement*, 261.
281. Stamps, "Atonement in Gethsemane," 156.
282. Young, *God's Presence*.

new humanity under grace which is redeemed in Christ, and made new by Christ's actual obedience. Recapitulation invites redeemed humanity's potential obedience to conform to Christ's perfect obedience. This theology of replacement is recapitulation at work, God in Christ "making all things new" (Rev 21:5). According to Young, this principle of "redemption com[ing] through recapitulation"[283] is the repeated refrain of salvation history, where every moment in the pre-modern, the modern and the post-modern timeframes are located in this one singular majestic mechanism. And it is a mechanism from which God is not separate. He himself is not only invested in the process of redemption via recapitulation, but he is also fully present by means of incarnation. He himself is the source of recapitulation.

And fifth, recapitulation as applied to spiritual formation and the Christian spiritual life. Recapitulation is not normally applied to spiritual formation—in fact I know of no instance in the literature in which recapitulation is applied to spiritual formation. But there are good reasons for recapitulation to become an important contributor to spiritual formation. I suggest there are three points of application: First, the spiritual life is not passive. We are not to wait for the Holy Spirit to do our inner work for us. Instead, the spiritual life is an active process in which Christ invites us to full participation and involvement. The verbs applied to discipleship and the spiritual life in the New Testament are all active; i.e., repent, believe, receive, go, put off, put on, serve, take up [your cross], hear, listen, obey, see, and more. Second, this leads us to believe that the recipients of Christ's salvation have a role in being "God's fellow workers" (1 Cor 3:9) in contributing our own spiritual formation, a thought which is supported by Gregory of Nyssa who developed the notion of *sunergia* (Greek, meaning "working with God") in the spiritual life.[284] And third, from a theological point of view, Jonathan Hill describes Irenaeus's theological anthropology by saying that for him, Adam and Eve were created as children who are morally immature, and who acted childishly.

> So Irenaeus thinks of [human fallenness] . . . as a childish mistake, not a terrible, catastrophic act of rebellion. It represents humanity's failure to rise to greater things, not a loss of 'original perfection'. It should be clear that this is a quite different view of the

---

283. Young, *God's Presence*, 216.
284. Ludlow, "Cappadocians," 180.

fall from that found in later Western writers, such as Augustine. Irenaeus . . . has no notion of original sin or inherited guilt.[285]

Thus, attending to our own spiritual formation is to cooperate with God's Spirit and to participate in our own spiritual rising/elevation.

46. Sanctity: on being a Saint

We humans are granted a life comprised of physical, mental, and spiritual elements, for which we are given no readily accessible map or guidebook. It's meaning and purpose must be carefully investigated and ferreted out. The question is—what will we do with it? Mary Oliver frames the question well when she asks, "Tell me, what is it you plan to do with your one wild and precious life?"[286] One possibility among a great many others is to become a holy person—but in an age which has lost its moral compass and when ethical existence has all but disappeared,[287] becoming a saint is not everyone's cup of tea. In our era, sanctity is thought of as a ridiculous idea because it doesn't serve any instrumental purpose in our mechanized and monetized society.

George Orwell, when speaking of the possibility of Mahatma Gandhi being thought of as a modern-day saint, wrote, "Many people genuinely do not wish to be saints, and it is probable that some who achieve or aspire to sainthood have never felt the temptation to be human beings."[288] This same scepticism about sanctity and sainthood applies today, when so many of our cultural heroes and heroines are not holy people, but are instead wicked, selfish anti-heroes who have fallen in love with evil. François Meltzer and Jaś Elsner wrote in their book *Saints, Faith without Borders*, "The modern (scientific, materialist) world has abolished the figure of the saint or at least dismissed it as some sort of primitive throwback."[289]

Yet in recent years, a fresh wave of literary interest has erupted pertaining to saints. Martin Poorthuis and Joshua Schwarz sketch the ethical profile of the saint, arguing that saints continue to have an unexpected relevance today which is (unfortunately) not widely recognized. They write:

---

285. Hill, *History of Christian Thought*, 25–26.
286. Oliver, "Summer Day," 316.
287. Willard, *Disappearance of Moral Knowledge*.
288. Orwell, in Pai, "Orwell's Reflections on Saint Gandhi," 69.
289. Meltzer and Elsner, *Saints*, ix.

> A holy life is a life in which compassion for the Other is central. The saint's story is extremely modern and contemporary, or can be, because it speaks of self-denial and the primacy of the Other in such a way that readers and hearers experience the motives that impel the holy man or holy woman.[290]

Depicting a holy life is a difficult thing to do. Fyodor Dostoevsky (1821–1881) writes, "There is a thought that has haunted me for a long time . . . It is to portray a wholly good man [sic]. Nothing is more difficult . . . Especially in our time."[291]

Edith Wyschogrod provides a literary definition of sanctity when she writes:

> The saint—the subject of hagiographic narrative—*is one whose adult life in its entirety is devoted to the alleviation of sorrow (the psychological suffering) and pain (the physical suffering) that afflicts other persons without distinction of rank or group or, alternatively, that afflicts sentient beings, whatever the cost to the saint in pain or sorrow.*[292]

But because this definition of the saintly life is restricted to the moral domain, it fails to take into account that other dimension which is even more fundamental to sainthood; namely the transcendent realm with its requirement of purity and holiness that sees the saint standing before the presence of God.

It is worth noting that even the Christian faith has difficulty with the concept of being a saint—despite Christianity being a religion of saints and witnesses. Does the Church 'make' saints as in the case of the Roman Catholic Church's Congregation for the Causes of Saints in its beautification and canonization of designated holy people? Or is it something else? Eugene Peterson reminds us:

> 'Saint', as it turns out, is Paul's noun of choice for the people of God—men and women who, no longer lost, follow Jesus in the cosmos. Throughout every letter Paul wrote, 'saint' is his word for us. [Only] in subsequent centuries [did] 'Christian' come to supplant 'saint' as the common designation.[293]

---

290. Poorthuis and Schwarz, *Saints and Role Models in Judaism and Christianity*, 405.

291. Cited without source by Wyschogrod, *Saints and Post-Modernism*, 1.

292. Wyschogrod, *Saints and Post-Modernism*, 34, italics in the original.

293. Peterson, *Practice Resurrection*, 77.

In the New Testament, the Greek word for 'saint' *hagios* is used some 40 times and remains one of the most important categories in sacred theology from New Testament times until today. Biblically speaking, it is God who makes saints, and he does so by co-opting ordinary people to voluntary participation in the extraordinary process of sanctification and growth towards Christlikeness. According to Søren Kierkegaard, the genius of the Christian faith is its capacity to turn "sinners into saints."[294]

In his autobiography, *The Seven Storey Mountain*, Thomas Merton recounts how he once told his friend Bob Lax that he wanted to become a good Catholic. "What you should say," said his friend in reply, "is that you must want to be a saint." Merton later reflected on Lax's reply, writing:

> A saint? The thought struck me as a little weird. I said: 'How do you expect me to become a saint?' 'By wanting to,' said Lax, simply . . . 'All that is necessary to be a saint is to want to be one. Don't you believe God will make you what he created you to be, if you consent to let him do it? All you have to do is desire it.'[295]

Sanctification is that process in which the human soul yields itself in trusting surrender to the will and purposes of God, knowing that the sometimes-painful process of divine hammering on the anvil of purification is intended to reproduce the life of Christ in the life of its human image. It is a process which cannot be imposed from the outside—it must be activated from the inside and requires a partnership in which the believing soul directly invites, submits to, and cooperates with the inward work of the Holy Spirit. It may well feel like a strange work of spiritual alchemy where base metal is being turned into gold, but it is the destiny of every human being to be re-made in the forges of God to reclaim our unique creational design of total humanity, absolute godlikeness, and reclaimed self-hood. Christ has done the work of redemption through his cross and his crown. Now the human part in the process of sanctification that follows, is to work with his indwelling Spirit as the junior partner in the glorious process of Christotherapy by retro-fitting Christ's life and character to our own. And above all, it requires being in love with goodness.

> Saints march into a world full of danger and uncertainty, with no resources other than their faith, their sanctified lives, and their awareness of the presence of Christ in the form of the Spirit

---

294. Kierkegaard, *Journals*, 59.
295. Merton, *Seven Storey Mountain*, 238.

working in and through them. The only weapons they have at their disposal are the force of their moral lives and the slender apparatus of prayer, righteousness, compassion and mercy. They are to overcome evil by living out of a countercultural reality that posits the goodness of God as the source and destiny of all existence. To that end they bend their bodies, minds, wills, and resources to establish what William Willimon called 'colonies' of heaven on earth. By the way they live, through their example of justice, mercy, and truthfulness among themselves and with their neighbors, they not only announce the presence of the kingdom of God but they "inaugurate" that kingdom through the efficacy of their persons and the communities of faith in which they live. Goodness, mercy and love are a saint's 'stock in trade.' The power they wield is nothing more (and nothing less) than the power of a transformed life.[296]

47. Second Naïveté

The concept of "second naïveté" arises from the writings of Paul Ricœur, and is discussed most fully in his *Symbolism of Evil*.[297] The state of second naïveté implies the confidence to return to one's previously secure faith and conviction after the foundations of one's belief have been eroded by the arguments of others (from outside), and the doubts in our own minds (from inside). Ricœur observes that many Christians are aware of the grounds on which the Christian faith can be critiqued using an Enlightenment way of thinking. This "destruction of the foundations" (Ps 11:3) of faith has been promoted by that group of scholars Ricœur refers to as the "masters of suspicion," in Karl Marx, Friedrich Nietzsche and Sigmund Freud, and the ruminations of the new atheists such as Richard Dawkins, Sam Harris, Christopher Hutchens, and others. It is likely that Christians who live in the twenty-first century know more reasons why they should *not* believe, than why they should. To combat this situation, believers must move from the child-like faith of a "first naïveté" which is vulnerable to being undermined by secular arguments—due to the often shallow, presumptive, or unreasoned grounds on which one's early faith

---

296. Devenish, *Ordinary Saints*, 169.

297. Ricœur, *Symbolism of Evil*, and augmented by Davidson's *Companion to Ricœur's Symbolism of Evil*.

is built—to a second naïveté that is capable of withstanding critique and sustaining people of faith in challenging times.

Eli Gotlieb defines second naïveté as follows:

> What is second naïveté? It is the innocence that some people recover after learning to be critical. It is a more complex, richer kind of empathy, to which they return after critique. For example, after being exposed to higher biblical criticism or social-scientific accounts of religion, it is difficult to continue to believe and behave as a religious person. Second naïveté appears when a person discovers the limits of critique, and seeks a way back to the pre-critical experience—not in a way that nullifies the critique, but in a way that respects it and reconciles with it.[298]

Ricœur rehearses the three phases of believing, doubting and re-believing when reading the Scripture in Western contexts. The *first phase* is what Linards Jansons calls the "pre-critical" stage,[299] marked by a presumed and taken-for-granted overlap between the world of the Bible, the supernatural, and one's own life, where God is thought of by persons influenced by cultural Christianity in a spirit of innocence or naïve realism. The second, "critical stage," is where a certain dissonance creeps in under the banner of an encroaching "hermeneutic of suspicion"—prompted by cultural pressure to apply the apparatus of critical reason in a way that undermines faith rather than supports it. Doubt, questioning, and a "stripping of the altars" is the end-result. The question is what can be believed—is everything simply myth and symbol, or does something *real* underwrite their external appearances? Ricœur himself states, "We are in every way children of criticism, and we seek to go beyond criticism by means of criticism, by a criticism that is no longer reductive but restorative."[300] This leads to what Jansons labels the third, "post-critical" moment where, as a result of careful interpretation, the believing soul goes "beyond the desert of criticism" to the place where they are capable of re-appropriating the grounds of faith and to again feel the full force of convictional belief. The grounds for this third stage are explained by Ricœur, who writes:

> For the second immediacy that we seek and the second naïveté that we await are no longer accessible to us anywhere else than in a hermeneutics; we can believe only by interpreting. It is the

---

298. Gottlieb, "Second Naiveté."
299. Jansons, "What is the Second Naivete?"
300. Ricœur, *Symbolism of Evil*, 350–51.

'modern' mode of belief in symbols, an expression of the distress of modernity and a remedy for that distress.[301]

Ricœur's invention of the second naïveté enables believers to re-appropriate the grounds of faith on which they stand . . . *as if for the first time*. In the third, post-critical, phase, believers are able to "re-feel"[302] the weight, veracity and credibility of faith and so to be convinced anew by it. The benefit now is that we have in our possession a clear understanding not only of those things that both oppose faith, but also those things that build it up, underpin it and demonstrate its veracity. That being the case, the state of mind of one living under the power of the second naïveté is far preferable to that associated with the first naïveté. Indeed, Mark Williams brings his work on second naivete to a close with these words:

> The true telos of a theological hermeneutic of the second naïveté [is] what Ricœur calls 'putting the Word to work' to allow the texts that I have loved and interpreted to be a poetics of my liberation in a concern for others, in solidarity with the planet, and in discipleship to the God of the biblical message. What this interpretive task offers is the remarkable possibility of a second hermeneutical innocence to the claims of Scripture, the hope that the mystery of the Bible can be construed as speaking again to the cultured despisers among us; indeed, the expectation, as Ricœur says, that 'by interpreting we can hear again.'[303]

Finally, concerning the relevance of the second naïveté to Christian spirituality, I offer two illustrative examples. The first is from James Fowler's psychological exploration of the "stages of faith," in which he recounts how learning to apply the intellectual apparatus of the academy to matters of faith was ultimately able to nurture faith. Concerning his own journey in Ignatian spirituality, Fowler writes:

> The Ignatian approach did not require me to give up or negate my critical skills, but it did teach me to supplement them with a method in which I learned to relinquish initiative to the text. Instead of my reading, analyzing and extracting the meaning of a Biblical text, in Ignatian contemplative prayer I began to learn

---

301. Ricœur, *Symbolism of Evil*, 352.

302. Ricœur, *Symbolism of Evil*, 27, referring to philosophers, but the sensation applies equally to believing souls.

303. Wallace, *Second Naivete*, 124–25.

how to let the text read me and to let it bring my needs and the Spirit's movements within me to consciousness.[304]

The second example comes from Ronald Rolheiser, arising from his reflections on childhood belief in Santa Claus:

> If you ask a naïve child: 'Do you believe in Santa Claus?' he [sic] replies 'Yes!' You ask a bright child the same question, he replies "No!" However, if you ask an even brighter child that question, he replies 'Yes!' [Previously] I described our need for what I termed 'revirginization,' our need to again say 'yes' to the question of Santa Claus. But how do we revirginize? How do we move towards a second naivete? We do it by touching the nerve of novelty, by purging ourselves of the illusion of familiarity. We must, as Chesterton once put it, 'Learn to look at things familiar until they look unfamiliar again.' We do this by making a deliberate and conscious effort at assuming the posture of the child before reality. We must work at regaining the primal spirit, a sense of wonder, the sense that reality is rich and full of mystery, that we do not yet understand that we must read chastely, carefully, and discriminately, respecting reality's contours and taboos. Concomitant with this effort comes the deliberate and conscious attempt at purging ourselves of all traces of cynicism, contempt, and all attitudes which identify mystery with ignorance, taboo and with superstition, and romance and ideals with naivete.[305]

Faith is a precarious affair in the twenty-first century. What is required is a knowing that facilitates the move from a condition of first naïveté to a second naïveté, followed by a knowledge of how to do so. Only in this way can one know oneself to be "called again" to faith "as if" for the first time.

48. Self-Implicating

The idea that spirituality is a "self-implicating" practice arises from the work of Sandra Schneiders. Schneiders's extensive body of work on spirituality in general, and Christian spirituality in particular, is well-known. The setting in which the self-implicating nature of spirituality comes into focus is the academic study of the topic by students who have an expressed interest in spirituality, and who take courses in that topic in

---

304. Fowler, *Stages of Faith*, 186.
305. Rolheiser, "Saying 'Yes' to Santa Claus."

an institution of higher learning (whether religious or non-religious). Schneiders writes:

> Students who choose to study spirituality are usually personally involved in the search for God. What goes on in the seminar room and the library, in preparing examinations and writing a dissertation, is often profoundly transformative. Faith is stimulated, vocations are renegotiated, self-knowledge is deepened, appreciation of other traditions is broadened, commitment to service is consolidated. The quiet or dramatic interaction between study and personal growth is probably the most important aspect of the self-implicating character of the field of spirituality. As Socrates knew, one cannot wrestle with ultimate truth without becoming a different person.[306]

Celia Kourie has observed that although spirituality is an "old" discipline for the church, it has recently experienced a re-birth in both church and society, and as an emerging academic discipline in institutions of higher education. She writes, "Spirituality can no longer be considered a 'Cinderella' discipline; on the contrary it has returned to its rightful place and is exerting considerable influence both within and outside the walls of the University."[307] Kourie also notes the recent coming-of-age of spirituality in the disciplines of psychology, the health professions, business, education, sociology and the human potential movement—with a growing number of international conferences, publications and academic journals giving sole attention to its subject-material.[308]

Given that scientific rationalism with its demand for objectivity and abstract reasoning has proved a driving force in Western education, one might suppose that those students engaged in the study of spirituality should be excluded from this kind of learning on the basis of a conflict of interest. The demand for objectivity could be seen as being cancelled out by the subjective nature of the topic of enquiry—i.e., those intangible processes occurring within the self. The *question* becomes, "How is it possible to enquire into those deeply subjective processes can take place within the human self in a way that produces objective outcomes?" Only the *believing soul* who has undergone the transformations of conversion, the spiritual encounter with Christ, and the elevation of consciousness that arises from them, could even begin to know where to look and how

---

306. Schneiders, "Approaches to the Study of Christian Spirituality," 31.
307. Kourie, "Spirituality and the University," 148.
308. Kourie, "Spirituality and the University," 148–50.

to apprehend the mysteries to be found there. As Robert Doran states, "... The data on men and women as selves will be understood not by studying physics, chemistry, biology, or even sensitive psychology, but by questioning the data of human consciousness itself (vis-à-vis) experiencing one's own experiencing, understanding, judging and deciding..."[309]

Regarding Christian spirituality as an academic discipline, Bernard McGinn asks three key questions: "What is spirituality?" "Should spirituality be taught?" and—if so—"How should spirituality be taught?"[310] In answer to the first question McGinn traces the historic confessional twists and turns of spirituality, to give Rowan Williams's reply, "If spirituality can be given any coherent meaning, perhaps it is to be understood in terms of... each believer making his [sic] own that engagement with the questioning of the heart of faith which is so evident in the classical doctrines of Christian belief."[311] In answer to the second question—how should spirituality be taught?—McGinn answers by appealing to the full retinue of biblical, theological and spiritual history arising from the long tradition of Christian salvation history, but also insisting that "the study of spirituality requires a desire to try to appreciate how religious people actually live their beliefs."[312] And thirdly—how should spirituality be taught—he replies "in a way that [ensures] the personal appropriation of Christian faith."[313]

To return to Schneiders, the self-implicating nature of spirituality does not exclude the academic rigor necessary for carrying out research in the academic field of spirituality. Indeed, she writes:

> To understand, theoretically and practically, the lived experience of God and try to clarify this phenomenon in all its multiplicity and uniqueness and power... [It is] concerned with the conditions of possibility of such experience, its actual occurrence, the variety of religious experience, the structure and dynamics of such experience, the criteria of adequacy of such experiences, the effect of social context and theological milieu

---

309. Doran, *Psychic Conversion and Theological Foundations*, 18.
310. McGinn, "Letter and the Spirit," 29.
311. Williams, *Christian Spirituality*, cited by McGinn, "Letter and the Spirit," 33–34.
312. McGinn, "Letter and the Spirit," 37.
313. McGinn, "Letter and the Spirit," 39.

on religious experience in literature, art, and social construction and so on.[314]

We conclude by offering four observations. Firstly, studying spirituality as a "formal object" may be completely un-interesting to the person who has yet to grasp the reality of a two-world hypothesis in which God lovingly invades this world, and who is unaware of the sacred as a mode of existence which has both substance and validity. But for the person who has had an encounter with the Divine, the study of spirituality brings with it deep resonances and holds potential for discoveries that hold eternal significance. Secondly, exploring one's own beliefs, values and experiences acts as a stimulus to curiosity and further exploration. Students who come to the classroom with a lively and dynamic faith-experience are likely to progress deeper into their studies than other less-motivated pupils. The kind of enquiry that encourages "faith seeking understanding" is to be encouraged and certainly not discouraged. Thirdly, on the question of critical self-reflection, one of the dangers of fully-engaged "converts" is that they have yet to discover an appropriate method for identifying the tools of critical analysis and interpreting spiritual experiences provided by the wider tradition of Christian spirituality as a discreet tradition, and not simply through their own ecstatic experiences. One of the key objectives of spiritual teachers and soul guides ought to be to introduce disciples to the ancient ways of interpreting the scriptures, enabling students to account for the interior life, and for expressing it in liturgical and ritualized ways. This will require the teaching and learning of methods for developing critical self-reflection in students. And fourthly, once spiritual explorers have obtained an awareness of the wider discipline of one's own spiritual tradition and the broad perspectives it offers, the possibility of and necessity for engaging in the processes of dialogue, mission, witness, and service with other spiritual travelers who are likewise engaged in the spiritual journey is likely to require that the Christian advocate has a thorough working knowledge of the classical Christian spiritual pathway, and of themselves as travelers on that "way." It was John Calvin who stated in his *Institutes*, "Without knowledge of the self there is no knowledge of God. Nearly all the wisdom we possess . . . consists of two parts: the knowledge of God and of ourselves."[315]

---

314. Schneiders, "Spirituality as an Academic Discipline," 12.
315. Calvin, *Institutes of the Christian Religion*, 35.

49. Self-Transcendence

In this entry we explore the term "self-transcendence" under four headings; (1) in humanistic psychology; (2) in theological anthropology; (3) in Christian spirituality; and (4) in the lived experience of human persons engaged with the spiritual life as a lived practice.

First, in humanistic psychology. Viktor Frankl wrote that human existence is characterized by self-transcendence. He states that the self-transcending quality of human existence "Is a constitutive characteristic of being human [in] that it always points, and is directed, to something other than itself."[316] Abraham Maslow in his revised hierarchy of human needs, realized that his earlier classification which included psychological, safety, belonging-intimacy, and self-esteem needs . . . was inadequate and required the additional element of self-actualization. For both Frankl and Maslow, self-actualization pointed towards the greater category of self-transcendence. As Crino Zappala states, "Maslow's self-actualization model is self-transcendence."[317] Martin Seligman and the Positive Psychology movement have prioritized personal well-being and flourishing as the goal of human existence. But Paul Wong offers the critique that such ego-centeredness is a misunderstanding of the true nature of self-transcendence which by-passes self-interest to reaffirm Frankl's maxim that "meaning comes from commitments that transcend personal interests . . . reaching beyond the self toward causes that serve other people."[318]

Second, in theological anthropology. Jeff Astley argues that self-transcendence "Is reported by mystics and those undergoing more ordinary religious experiences . . . in which their view of themselves and the world is 'radically transformed', has been described as a 'consequence . . . of self-transcendence' and is often associated with self-surrender."[319] With reference to Christian theology, Bernard Lonergan, in *Method in Theology*, observes that the human person "achieves authenticity in self-transcendence."[320] For Lonergan, self-transcendence can either be cognitive or moral. But it can never be taken for granted. It is always related to love, and "self-transcendence is ever precarious" because it is

---

316. Frankl, "Self-Transcendence as a Human Phenomenon," 97.
317. Zappala, "Well-Being," 64.
318. Wong, "Viktor Frankl's Meaning-Seeking Model and Positive Psychology," 158.
319. Astley, *Religious and Spiritual Experience*, 76.
320. Lonergan, *Method in Theology*, 104.

never quite finished.[321] For Lonergan, "Being in love with God is an ultimate fulfilment of man's capacity for self-transcendence . . . [in which] God is conceived as the supreme fulfilment of the transcendental notions, as supreme intelligence, truth, reality, righteousness, goodness."[322]

Third, in Christian spirituality. Sandra Schneiders writes that:

> Spirituality is the actualization of the basic human capacity for transcendence and will be defined . . . as the experience of conscious involvement in the project of life-integration through self-transcendence toward the horizon of ultimate value one perceives.[323]

But once again it comes with a warning. As David Benner points out in *Spirituality and the Awakening Self*, authenticity is costly:

> Self-transcending authenticity always involves a cost; we, like the person in the parable of the pearl told by Jesus (Matt. 13:45–46), must have our eyes and heart so set on the pearl of inestimable value that we will be prepared to do anything to get it. Because of the immense value of the pearl of authenticity and self-transcendence that we see, no price is too high.[324]

As James Fowler has proposed, faith development requires a movement, a willingness on the part of the whole self to progress towards maturity, involving one's hopes, strivings, thoughts and actions towards wholeness and holiness. This means self-transcendence is not a 'thing' or a mechanism as such but an attitudinal necessity implying an openness and a willingness to participate in a movement through something like Fowler's stages of faith; via (1) intuitive faith; (2) mythic-literal faith; (3) synthetic-conventional faith; (4) individuated-reflective faith; (5) conjunctive faith; and (6) universalizing faith.[325] Benner continues by suggesting that:

> The essential dynamic of the human spirit is a radical drive for self-transcendence: a longing to be more than we are, to be all that we can be. At some deep level we seem to recognise that this "more" is not simply more of the same but that it demands deep transformation. It involves a reorganisation of the self so radical that our old self must be released before our new and larger life

---

321. Lonergan, *Method in Theology*, 110.
322. Lonergan, *Method in Theology*, 111.
323. Schneiders "Approaches to the Study of Christian Spirituality," 16.
324. Benner, *Spirituality and the Awakening Self*, 166.
325. Fowler, *Stages of Faith*, 117–211.

can unfold. We must, as Jesus taught, be prepared to lose our life if we wish to truly gain it.[326]

Fourth, in the experience of those human persons engaged in living the spiritual life. From a naturalistic and non-religious perspective—Hans Joas describes the experience of self-transcendence in the life of the fictional character Nagel from Knut Hamsun's novel *Mysteries*:

> A tremor of ecstasy ran through him. He felt himself . . . filled with an intoxicating sense of well-being; . . . Strange; he had distinctly heard someone calling him. But he dismissed the thought; perhaps he might have imagined the whole thing . . . He was in a strange, euphoric state of mind; his every nerve vibrated; music surged through his blood; he was part of nature, of the sun, the mountains; he was omniscient; the trees, the earth . . . spoke to him alone. His soul went into a crescendo, like an organ with all the stops pulled out. Never would he forget how this heavenly music would pulsate through his blood.[327]

Nagel's experience of self-transcendence is essentially an experience of ecstatic "fusion with nature" which Maslow and others have called a "peak experience." But it is not yet Christian in orientation.

And finally, we observe self-transcendence in the lived experience of one exemplary human person engaged in living the Christian spiritual life. It has been suggested that the life of Etty Hillesum (1914–1943) is a case study in self-transcendence. Born into a Jewish family in Holland, at the age of 23 she was arrested and interred in Westerbork, a Nazi transit camp for Jewish detainees. Etty was a social worker at Westerbork where she sought to care for her fellow detainees—many of whom were sent to Auschwitz for extermination. A psychologist-friend suggested she keep a diary of her experiences. In that diary Etty tells of her turning to faith in Christ, of her discoveries of her "inner landscape" and of her attempts at prayer—which she called "kneeling down." Etty herself was transferred there in November 1943, and is thought to have died in the gas chambers, despite the many desperate offers of escape by her friends. Her act of solidarity with the Jewish community—and indeed with all mankind—was generous in the extreme. Etty's letters and diary from Westerbork tell a story of utter degradation in the barracks. At one point she was assigned the task her of preparing young mothers and their babies for transport

---

326. Benner, *Spirituality and the Awakening Self*, 191.
327. Joas, *Do We Need Religion?* 8.

by rail from Westerbork to Auschwitz for extermination. She wrote "My God, those faces! I looked at them, each in turn . . . And I have never been so frightened of anything in my life. I sank to my knees with the words that preside over human life. 'And God made man in His likeness'. That passage spent a difficult morning with me."[328] Despite the hatred, the oppression, the abuse, the fetid stench of humanity at war with itself—Etty was able to resist the temptation to hate, but turned instead to wonder, to prayer, and to depth. She wrote:

> You have made me so rich, O God, please let me share out Your beauty with open hands. My life has become an uninterrupted dialogue with You, O God, one great dialogue. Sometimes when I stand in some corner of the camp, my feet planted on Your earth, my eyes raised toward Your heaven, tears run down my face, tears of deep emotion and gratitude. At night, too, when I lie on my bed and rest in You, O God, tears of gratitude run down my face . . .[329]

Despite her captor Klaas, who was a fellow Jew who had sold out to the Nazis, being particularly cruel, Etty wrote, "I should have liked to reach out to that man with all his fears, I should have liked to trace the source of his panic, to drive him ever deeper into himself."[330] She found herself embracing a broken humanity—friends and enemies alike—with the same equanimity and compassion that transcended the moment, enabling her to move beyond ugliness to beauty, truthfulness and hope. Surely Etty's life was a life of self-transcendence, because it was lived towards God, and it was lived for the sake of others, and against her own self-interest. Etty's life embodied self-transformation in ways that continue to shine for those who would follow her path.

50. Shadow

The psychologist Carl Jung believed there is an un-tended part of the human psyche that needs to be attended to if the human person is ever to become "whole." He wrote:

> Everyone carries a shadow, and unless it is embodied in the individual's conscious life, the blacker and denser it is. If an

---

328. Smelik, *Etty*, 644.
329. Hillesum, *Letters from Westerbork*, 116.
330. Smelik, *Etty*, 529.

inferiority is conscious, one always has a chance to correct it. Furthermore, it is constantly in contact with other interests, so that it is steadily subjected to modifications. But if it is repressed and isolated from consciousness, it never gets corrected . . . We carry our past with us, to wit, the primitive and inferior man [sic] with his desires and emotions, and it is only by a considerable effort that we can detach ourselves from this burden. If it comes to a neurosis, we have invariably to deal with a considerably intensified shadow. And if such a case wants to be cured it is necessary to find a way in which man's conscious personality and his shadow can live together.[331]

Explaining the concept further, Steven Diamond writes:

> The shadow is an unknown "dark side" of our personality—dark both because it tends to consist predominantly of the primitive, benighted, negative, socially or religiously depreciated human emotions and impulses like sexual lust, power strivings, selfishness, greed, envy, aggression, anger or rage, and due to its unenlightened nature, [remains] obscured from consciousness. Whatever we deem evil, inferior or unacceptable and deny in ourselves becomes part of the shadow, the counterpoint to what Jung called the persona or conscious ego personality.[332]

Robert Mulholland and Ruth Haley Barton in their book *Invitation to a Journey*, address the notion of the shadow-side of human personality as it applies to the task of spiritual formation.[333] In this entry, we will explore Mulholland and Barton's treatment of the shadow in spiritual formation. First, Mulholland and Barton (hereafter M&B) highlight Jung's psychological pairings. which M&B call our creation gifts—those qualities and characteristics which are given at birth. According to Jung, these basic psychological predispositions come in four pairs; 1. Extraversion (E) and Introversion (I); 2. Sensing (S) and Intuition (N); 3. Thinking (T) and Feeling (F); and 4. Judgement (J) and Perception (P). The first pairing of E & I relates to a person's preferred personal focus (i.e., internal or external). The second pairing of S & N relates to a person's preferred mode of receiving and processing information. The third pairing of T & F relates to the way people process information (i.e., either rationally or intuitively). And the fourth pairing of J & P relates to the flow of life

---

331. Jung, *Psychology and Religion*, 93.
332. Diamond, "Shadow," 836.
333. Mulholland and Barton, *Invitation to a Journey*, chapters 5, 6, and 7.

(i.e., whether one prefers to function in an ordered world, tied in with their decision-making capacity, or can manage in a messy and unfinished environment, signalling how they cope with change).

M&B—following Jung—write that people tend to fall into one of the possible 16 "types" this schema allows for. These have been described in the Myers-Briggs typologies, which many clergy and lay-leaders have been introduced to and have explored.[334] According to M&B, we should celebrate the qualities that are ours by our natural "handedness" as they are our "default-setting" and ought to be regarded as gifts rather than weaknesses. It should also be noted that M&B underline the fact that our natural personality profiles carry over into our spiritual profiles, and significantly shape styles of ministry, approaches to spiritual practice, and how we "carry" our faith within ourselves. It is to this latter tendency that we turn with special reference to spiritual formation.

According to M&B, we tend to play to our strengths, and under-emphasize our weaknesses (which become our work areas). In other words, if we are an extrovert with a sensing capacity, who feels things deeply and has perceptive abilities (ESFP), two things will happen. First, we will be very different to people with other personality profiles, such as an INTJ (an introvert, with a thinking facility, whose natural way of processing is by means of thinking and judgment). And the second is that the natural strengths exhibited by the ESFP will come to the fore, and the person will naturally tend to function out of their strength-areas. An important corollary, however, is that the unattended, "shadow" side of one's personality (i.e., the ISTJ aspects) will be left to one side. M&B suggest, "As you may suspect, at this point serious problems can arise related not only to our own psychological wholeness but also to our spiritual wholeness."[335]

M&B describe the ignored parts of our personal and spiritual preferences as the "under-nourished shadow side [that will] sooner or later, demand equal time."[336] If they are not given proper attention, there is the potential for disintegration. If we do not nurture our shadow side, there is the possibility of us falling apart as a result of our one-sided spirituality. M&B write:

> One of the special temptations for intuitive-type persons is primitive sensuality . . . One wonders . . . How many of the

---

334. Discussed by Briggs-Myers and Myers, *Gifts Differing*, among many others.
335. Mulholland and Barton, *Invitation to a Journey*, 66.
336. Mulholland and Barton, *Invitation to a Journey*, 70.

sexual aberrations of noted Christian leaders in recent years might be due in part to their being strongly intuitive types who failed to nurture the sensing side of their preference pattern?[337]

The question M&B forms for us is: "How do my patterns of individual and corporate spirituality nurture my shadow side?"[338] Worship styles, ministry styles, prayer styles, managing conflict and our "pilgrimage towards wholeness" will all be influenced by the 'shadow' sides within us. There is a responsibility on our part to carry out a balancing act. If the overdeveloped parts of us do not pay attention to the underdeveloped sides of us, sooner or later a distemper, an imbalance, will come to the surface. What is needed is a balanced spirituality—especially among leaders.

51. Sober Drunkenness

In our age—which has been called the "age of intoxication"[339]—what do drunkenness and inebriation have to do with Christian spirituality? The answer is more than you might think! Christianity has traditionally held four principled positions regarding the use of alcohol: (1) total abstention on the grounds that Christians are "Not to get drunk with wine . . . But [instead must] be filled with the Spirit" (Eph 5:18); (2) under scriptural authority, allow the use of alcohol by the poor, the perishing and dispossessed for their comfort (Prov 31:6–7); (3) offering (alcoholic) wine as the symbol of Christ's shed blood in the sacrament of the Eucharist, and to symbolize the "new wine" that Christ will drink with his disciples in the new heaven and the new earth (Matt 26:29); and (4) full and free partaking—within appropriate constraints—to demonstrate the freedom Christ's followers have to enjoy the good things that God has given them in anticipation of the glorious life to come in the Kingdom of God. This last view reflects Tony Campolo's observation that "the kingdom of God is a party."[340]

Considering the desire of some to drink to the point of intoxication, Charles Baudelaire has written that human beings have a deep need to reach beyond themselves to find interior consolation against the disturbances of life. He writes:

337. Mulholland and Barton, *Invitation to a Journey*, 70.
338. Mulholland and Barton, *Invitation to a Journey*, 84.
339. Breen, *Age of Intoxication*.
340. Campolo, *Kingdom of God is a Party*.

> You must be drunk always. That is everything: the only question. Not to feel the horrible burden of Time that crosses your shoulders and bends you earthward, you must be drunk without respite. But drunk on what? On wine, on poetry, on virtue—take your pick. But be drunk.[341]

Whereas "people are looking for the right thing in the wrong places"[342]—and no doubt in all the wrong ways—the Christian preference is always towards situating the source for the much-needed consoling *elixir* in Christ rather than in alcohol, drugs, and other pick-me-ups present in society. In an article in *Christian Century* entitled "Soul-altering Substances: What implications does this psychedelic renaissance have for faith and spirituality?" Ron Cole-Turner[343] discusses research carried out by the Johns Hopkins School of Medicine on the impact of *psilocybin* (an extract from so-called "sacred mushrooms") on the spiritual encounters of Christian clergy with God, mystery and the sacred. As Cole-Turner reported, one Episcopal priest experienced the hallucinogenic *psilocybin* making a positive contribution to his faith, causing him to see it as a way of connecting spiritually hungry people with "a direct experience with the Beloved."[344] However, Cole-Turner expresses doubts about the value of psychedelic drugs as a genuine and long-lasting way of assisting modern-day seekers to connect with God, since the source of the spiritual life has always originated through the agency of the Spirit in the Christian spiritual tradition. Instead, he argues for a more orthodox approach, since "it is always the light of the Spirit that makes us spiritual."

The "better way" (1 Cor 12:31) offered by Christian spirituality is "sober drunkenness." It is a pathway that not only offers access to a higher level of inspiration and insight, but also avoids the loss of mental capacity, moral control, and emotional stability associated with illicit substances. Gregory of Nyssa (335–84) provides us with the concept of "sober drunkenness" as a way of connecting the human spirit with the Divine Spirit that lives within us. Borrowing the term "sober drunkenness" (sometimes "sober intoxication") from the Jewish philosopher Philo of Alexandria (a contemporary of Jesus), Gregory argued that the "proper [use of such] drunkenness is to produce an ecstasy that, in the case of spiritual drunkenness, signifies a leap from inferior realities to heavenly

---

341. Baudelaire, "Get Drunk," 1.
342. Hirsch and Nelson, *Reframation*, 209.
343. Cole-Turner, "Soul-Altering Substances."
344. Cole-Turner, "Soul-Altering Substances," 59.

realities."[345] Here, Gregory makes use of the concept of ecstasy, whose etymology from the Greek is *ek* (meaning outside), and *stasis* (meaning to stand), renders the word as meaning to "stand outside oneself." This form of ecstasy places the locus of inspiration in the Holy Spirit, and not in the human person or in external addictive substances. This positive ecstatic element provides the crucial experiential basis for Gregory's mystical theology. If *epektasis* is the generation-point of humankind's hungering and thirsting after God, the means by which it is achieved is by "sober drunkenness."

Gregory pays attention to three archetypal exemplars of sober drunkenness in the Scriptures. First, King David who danced before God in a frenzy of worship arising from an ecstasy of the Spirit. The second is St. Paul, who was literally "out of his mind" (2 Cor 5:13), as he was "caught up to paradise" and who "heard inexpressible things" while in the third heaven—pointing towards a transformative experience that laid the foundations for his apostolic ministry. And third, St. Peter who—under the inspiration of the Spirit—received a Divine vision of animals that had been designated "unclean" under Jewish law, but which under the new law of the kingdom of Christ laid the groundwork for racial equality and gender inclusivity.

To return to our guiding question, "What do drunkenness and inebriation have to do with Christian spirituality?"—Olivier Clement has offered an insightful commentary on Gregory of Nyssa's homilies on the *Song of Songs*:

> The banqueting house, the wine cellar, the must fermenting with a gurgling sound and a heavy scent rising from it, the eager mouth rejecting a cup in order to suck straight from the bung-hole of the barrel, staggering everywhere, a dark red whirlpool, breaking away from everyday restraints, inebriation with the divine *eros*. One needs to be a vine-grower to understand this text, its sparkling symbolism, its September plenty, the crushed grape, the bodies drenched in must, the new wine . . . It is the poem of a strict ascetic and a mad drunkard. It is the poem of *epektasis*, of going out of self, and when a person is wrenched away from everyday order and convention, and enters into the whole power and spontaneity of true life.
>
> The soul then says [quoting Gregory now], 'Bring me into the banqueting house, spread over me the banquet of love (Song 2:4) . . . Her thirst has become so strong that she is no

---

345. Matteo-Seco, "Sober Drunkenness," 686.

longer satisfied with the 'cup of wisdom' (Prov 9:2). The contents of the cup poured into her mouth no longer seems able to quench her thirst. She asks to be taken to the cellar itself and apply her mouth to the rim of the vats themselves that are overflowing with intoxicating wine. She wants to see the grapes squeezed into the vat and the vine that produces those grapes, and the vinedresser of the true vine who has cultivated these grapes . . .That is why she wants to enter the cellar where the mystery of the wine is performed. Once she has entered she aspires still more highly. She asks to be put under the banner of love. Now love, John says, is God.[346]

Further, the early Church Father Macarious made this observation:

> One must look on the life of the Christian (in this way). He [sic] may have fasted, kept visuals, chanted the Psalms, carried out every ascetic practice and acquired every virtue; but if the mystic working of the Spirit has not been consummated by grace with full consciousness and spiritual peace on the altar of his heart, all his ascetic practice is ineffectual and virtually fruitless, for the joy of the Spirit is not mystically active in his heart.[347]

In today's intoxicated society, where opioids and illicit substances of all kinds have devastated people's lives, what is Christianity's answer to the problem of intoxication? It is to offer the "better way" of sober drunkenness—to be drunk on God. "Intoxication with God" as taught by Macarious, is that which surpasses and fulfils all four of Christianity's standard approaches to intoxication, to offer a "better way."

52. Soliloquy

"Soliloquy" (meaning "to speak to oneself as a technique for arriving at truth through internal dialogue") plays a central part in human life. Historically and experientially, in such things as ancient prayer (e.g., the Psalms), to early biography (e.g., Augustine's *Confessions*), through the development of all forms of poetry and dramatic literature (e.g., Shakespeare's famous soliloquies), one can see the centrality of this kind of inner dialogue in human experience. But soliloquy has a special place in Christian theology and spirituality, as we shall see.

---

346. Clement, *Roots of Christian Mysticism*, 245.
347. Cantalamessa, *Sober Intoxication of the Spirit*, loc. 1993.

In a theological context, consider the intra-Trinitarian conversation within the God-*self* between Father, Son, and Spirit. Keith Putt[348] has proposed that one important way of interpreting the Apostle Paul's discussion of trinitarian theology in Romans 8:26–27[349] is to understand the Holy Spirit's prayers on behalf of God's people as a form of Divine soliloquy. The Spirit's prayer-language is uttered in "groanings too deep for words," in a relational language that binds together the hearts of those who believe, with the mind of the Spirit, and the will of God. This, Putt suggests, makes God a *soliloquist* . . . one who speaks with himself on behalf of others.[350]

In human spiritual experience, perhaps the best-known soliloquy can found in St. Augustine's book *Soliloquies* in which he debates the purpose of his life before an audience comprised of his conscience, God, and the wider world of people's thoughts and opinions.[351] Augustine writes, "For many days I had been debating within myself many and diverse things, seeking constantly . . . to find out my real self, my best good, and the evil to be avoided . . ."[352] Later, he addresses himself to the "God, who hast created out of nothing this world, which the eyes of all perceive to be most beautiful!"[353] Augustine's style of self-talk in the *Soliloquies* is extended in his *Confessions*,[354] where he "prays out aloud" his thoughts, his doubts, his fears and his passions before the God who is an audience of one.

But St. Teresa of Avila also makes extensive use of soliloquy as a primary strategy in her spiritual life:

> Oh life, life! How can you endure being separated from your Life? In so much solitude, with what are you occupied? What are you doing, since all your works are imperfect and faulty? What consoles you, O soul, in this stormy sea. I pity myself, and have greater pity for the time I lived without pity.[355]

---

348. Putt, "Too Deep for Words," 142–53.

349. "In the same way, the Spirit helps us in our weakness. We do not know what we ought to pray for, but the Spirit himself intercedes for us with groans that words cannot express. And he who searches our hearts knows the mind of the Spirit, because the Spirit intercedes for the saints in accordance with God's will" (Rom 8:26–27).

350. Putt, "Too Deep for Words," 161.

351. Augustine, *Soliloquies*, 1.

352. Augustine, *Soliloquies*, 2.

353. Augustine, *Soliloquies*, 3.

354. Augustine, *Confessions*.

355. Teresa, "Soliloquies," 375.

She continues, this time changing voice to address God directly:

> O Lord, how gentle are Your ways! But who will walk them without fear? I fear to live without serving You; and when I set out to serve You, I find nothing that proves a satisfactory payment for anything of what I owe. It seems I want to be completely occupied in Your service, and when I consider well my own misery I can see I can do nothing unless You give me this good.[356]

The transition from addressing oneself to addressing God seems like a natural progression—particularly in the light of concepts like *de Magestro* where the "self beneath the self" is thought of as God who participates in the conversation and generates the needed wisdom for the life-situation that confronts the sacred self.

If the concept of soliloquy or "self talk" is ubiquitous in spiritual experience, we can expect to find it in use in the lived experience of holy persons up to the present day as recorded in the best spiritual literature. One such example can be found in Dietrich Bonhoeffer's prison correspondence in a poem in which he interrogates himself:

> Who am I? . . . A squire from his country house; . . . I bore the days of misfortune; . . . Am I one person today and tomorrow another? . . . Who am I? They mock me, these lonely questions of mine. Whoever I am, thou knowest, O God, I am Thine![357]

And although Thomas Merton's "Prayer" is more prayer-like and less soliloquy-like than the form dictates, nevertheless it has self-referential elements to it, and therefore can be included as soliloquy, since his prayer has a dialectical, self-referential quality. He writes: "My Lord God, I have no idea where I am going, I do not see the road ahead of me. I cannot know for certain where it will end, nor do I really know myself . . ."[358]

In my own case, after a sudden and life-changing conversion experience at the age of 18, I later reflected on my inward experience, writing a poem that was (unknown to me at the time) soliloquy-like in its attempt to come to terms what had unfolded in my inner life:

> Holy Fire
> What is this impulse, this contagion of passion
> that wells up in my breast? A love that burns

---

356. Teresa, "Soliloquies," 375.
357. Bonhoeffer, *Cost of Discipleship*, 15.
358. Merton, *Thoughts in Solitude*, 70.

and bids me come closer to the flame of love
so that ablaze I light the walls of my dungeon.
With nothing but a pure heart and surrendered life
I ascend the hill of God to see his face and there
to dance for his glory while still in my place.[359]

It is a matter of great import that the "believing soul" who has been confronted with the call to follow Christ must come to grips with the challenges that the life of discipleship entails. And so, at the center of this re-negotiation of life from the "inside out," is a form of soliloquy where the sacred self asks and is required to answer the fundamental questions: What would it mean to become a follower of Christ? . . . A penitent sinner? . . . A true believer? . . . What would others think of me? This is part of Jesus' requirement to "count the cost" when he says, "Anyone who does not carry his cross and follow me cannot be my disciple" (Luke 14:27). Engaging in soliloquy enables the sacred self to explore the deep questions of one's faith, rehearsing answers to existential questions, and expressing gratitude towards God for the opportunity to enter the sacred space before his presence, to rise to think great thoughts after God, to discern their implications, and to nurture a deeply authentic spiritual life which both enables self-discovery and God-discovery—both of which are fundamental to the human person engaged in the Divine life.

53. The Soul

The soul is an essential property of the inner life of human persons. Without it we are merely animals who are less than the *homo spiritualis* that comprises our true nature. And yet—strangely—the notion of "soul" is a controversial one, leading Daniel Helminiak to state, "This matter of soul is a can of worms . . . because of its ambiguity the term soul is not useful for technical discussion, but it is very useful in poetic, suggestive and evocative contexts."[360] The philosophers, the scientists, the theologians, and the psychologists have fought wars—metaphorically speaking—over the nature of the human soul. Roughly speaking, the rational materialists find little or no evidence for an immortal soul. They typically allow a mind and a will in this life, and as for the next, something amounting to an unconscious and soul-less oblivion. Whereas the spiritual-ists

---

359. Devenish, previously unpublished poem entitled "Holy Fire."
360. Helminiak, *Human Core of Spirituality*, 27.

(those who are open to the reality of substance beyond the material, the essential nature of spirit and life after death, including Christians) believe that everything is enlivened by something variously called spirit, soul, or inspiration. For Christians, the immortal soul is something of eternal value, and is worth attending to, defending, nurturing, and educating as our "true" self. All this alerts us to the fact that any exacting definition of "soul" is fraught with danger. In this entry we will restrict our enquiry to how the classical Christian spiritual tradition understands soul. Because of word limits, no consideration will be given to Aristotle's treatment of the soul in his *De Anima*, despite it having exerted considerable influence on Christian scholastic thinkers such as Aquinas.

Biblical Sources. In the Old Testament, the Hebrew word *nephesh* denotes a "living being" (Gen 1:20) characterized by existence, movement, and breath. In the Septuagint—the Greek translation of the OT—the equivalent word is *psyche*, denoting the seat of the heart and emotions, the ego and the integrating center of the person. In the New Testament, the *psyche* is likewise the seat of life. Jesus taught, "Whoever would save his life (*psyche*) will lose it; and whoever loses his life for my sake . . . will save it" (Mark 8:35). *Psyche* also denotes will, disposition, understanding and insight. Günther Harder writes: "The soul, is the part of us which believes and is sanctified, [and] is destined to an inheritance in God's future kingdom."[361]

Theological Reflections. From earliest times, Christian theologians have wrestled with the concept of soul. Statements concerning the soul by patristic theologians are the result of an inter-mingling of Greek philosophy, Old Testament antecedents, and Jesus' teachings about the soul. Grounded in Pauline theological anthropology, patristic theologians set out to discover the implications of Christ's life, teachings, death, resurrection, and the coming of the new heavens and new earth for the human soul. François Bovon observes that early Christian writers sometimes appear "naïve and amateurish" in their writings regarding the soul in comparison with other classical writers, but that is because they were having to re-think the soul in its provenance and eternal significance from the ground up.[362] Tertullian (ca. 155–220) argues for the soul as essentially embodied spirit:

---

361. Harder, "Soul," 685.
362. Bovon, "Soul's Comeback," 394.

The soul, then, we define to be sprung from the breath of God, immortal, possessing body, having form, simple in its substance, intelligent in its own nature, developing its power in various ways, free in its determinations, subject to the changes of accident, in its faculty is immutable, rational, supreme, endued with an instinct of pre-sentiment, evolved out of one [archetypal] soul.[363]

François Bovon says of Tertullian's description of the soul:

> He [Tertullian] believes from Scripture that the soul is created by the Spirit of God. The soul has a beginning, and her birthday coincides with the body's birthday . . . Death constitutes the separation of body and soul, the temporary suspension of what Tertullian calls 'the company of body and soul.' The soul after death does not climb triumphantly to heaven . . . but goes to the realm of the dead.[364]

Whereas Origen's (ca. 185–253) understanding rejects the division of the soul into a "higher" and a "lower" as thought by Middle Platonism. Instead of seeing the soul as a "fallen mind," Origen sees the soul as:

> . . . framed less by speculative, philosophical concerns than by the hermeneutical strictures of Christian revelation, especially the moral and ascetical dynamics of the spiritual life, whereby the soul is reunited with the divine *Logos* into whose image it was created.[365]

Origen elevated the soul, saying "the soul is worthier than all bodies."[366] Arguing against the heretics who limited the survival of the soul's existence beyond death, Origen "insists that it will be our souls and our bodies both that will inherit eternal life."[367] With St. Paul, Origen agrees that "flesh and blood cannot inherit the kingdom of God" (1 Cor 15:50);

> The dying body is distinct from the living soul, the destiny of the soul in the afterlife depends on the ethical commitment of the body of this life, and a reunion of both, soul and body, is expected on the day of resurrection. This is the orthodox vision that we find in Origen's treatise on martyrdom.[368]

---

363. Green, "Soul," 81.
364. Bovon, "Soul's Comeback," 393
365. Blosser, *Become Like the Angels*, 267.
366. Bovon, "Soul's Comeback," 403.
367. Bovon, "Soul's Comeback," 392.
368. Bovon, "Soul's Comeback," 397.

Spiritual Explorations. Brian Edgar has reflected on the nature of soul as the point-of-connection between humanity and God. He coined the phrase "the theo-anthroplogical functions of the soul," arguing that the soul operates to con-join the human with the Divine, making the ensouled human person something of absolute worth.[369] According to Kees Waaijman, the soul lies at the heart of Christian spirituality.

> In the history of spirituality the human reality operative in the divine-human relational process is above all described with the word "soul". . . The soul [is] understood in light of the biblically-oriented traditions as a many-sided phenomenon; a reserved space which can open itself up but simultaneously has the ability to close itself; the source of life but with the capacity to jam up within itself; surrender and laugh but also capable of devouring one's life; it can live together in peace with the core of one's personality but also depress the inner self; it can turn inward and be beside itself. The peculiar nature of the soul is that it is multidimensional and highly mobile.[370]

Therapeutic Focus. The Western world is currently engaged in a search for health and wholeness. Thomas Moore places soul-care at the center of his therapeutic quest. He writes:

> The great malady of the twentieth-century, implicated in all our troubles and affecting us individually and socially, is 'loss of soul.' When soul is neglected it doesn't just go away; it appears symptomatically in obsessions, addictions, violence, and loss of meaning. The temptation is to isolate these symptoms or try to eradicate them one by one, but the root problem is that we have lost our wisdom about the soul, even our interest in it.[371]

But when soul loses its connection with Christ and the resources of Christotherapy available to it, it has the potential to fall to the level of shallow marketing, quackery and charlatanism.

Educational Application. Can the soul be educated? The task of spiritual education is to educate the inner-self, and to befriend its desires. This is tantamount to educating the soul, a task that relies as much on intuition, emotion, feeling and desire as it does on knowledge, awareness, facticity and perception. In his book *Soul Making*, Alan Jones introduces

---

369. Edgar, "Theoanthropological Functions of the Soul."
370. Waaijman, *Spirituality*, 436.
371. Moore, *Care of the Soul*, xi.

the reader to the Desert way of spirituality. There, amidst isolation, alone with the voices of the angels, the demons and of oneself, the death of the ego and "abandonment to God," one must "be silent, wait and watch."[372] Soul-making, therefore, is not so much creating the intangible stuff from which a soul is made, as if *ex nihilo*. Instead, soul-making is a journey towards the "real". . . a journey that usually involves a certain amount of brokenness, which Jones labels "playing poker with God."[373] It is there that we come to an end of ourselves and must deal with the gigantic questions about love, life, death, power and time. These things—says Jones—are the materials from which the soul is constructed in a process of transformative tension that re-makes the self into something completely new . . . fashioned after the image and likeness of Christ.

54. Spiritual Intelligence

In this entry we discuss the differences between three kinds of intelligence; namely IQ ("intelligence quotient"); EQ ("emotional quotient"); and SQ ("spiritual quotient"), highlighting the value and benefits of each from the literatures that define their existence, with special reference to the classical Christian spiritual tradition.

We begin with IQ ("intelligence quotient"). IQ has its origins in the work of French psychologist Alfred Binet in the field of experimental psychology. Binet and his colleague Theodore Simon sought to assess attention, memory, and problem-solving skills in individuals. As a measure, IQ is a time-and-task test intended to identify persons with either increased or decreased cognitive abilities. Stanford University devised a test to measure IQ, which has had extensive application in the fields of education, the military and leadership domains. However, IQ also has a sinister side, where people who have achieved low IQ scores can potentially have their value diminished for ideological, political and/or economic reasons. "The IQ test played a central role in the eugenics movement as a shibboleth designed to reaffirm Nordic supremacy and stratify the populous along ethnic, racial and class lines."[374] Once an IQ score is allocated to a person, it can determine their destiny, especially

---

372. Jones, *Soul Making*, 45.
373. Jones, *Soul Making*, 135.
374. Reddy, "Eugenic Origins of IQ Testing," 669

when thought of as an unchanging and "once for all" capacity, rather than something capable of being improved through education and practice.

Next, EQ ("emotional quotient"). By contrast, EQ refers to an affective capacity that harnesses the powers of human intuition and emotion. The concept was developed by Peter Salovey and John Meyer, who defined EQ as, "The ability to monitor one's own and others' feelings, to discriminate among them, and to use this information to guide one's thinking and action."[375] Daniel Goleman extended and popularized the earlier research, identifying five components of EQ *qua*: (1) self-awareness; (2) self-regulation; (3) internal motivation; (4) empathy; and (5) social skills.[376] Goleman argues that in social settings, EQ is of greater value than IQ, an idea that has found resonance and application in the leadership and human potential movements. Goleman speaks of the "emotional brain," and is disappointed that IQ which measures only the cognitive and the rational, has assumed prominence over EQ, when so much of human life is driven by our human emotions and relational capacities.

Next, SQ ("spiritual quotient") has come to prominence after Danah Zohar and Ian Marshall published their book *Spiritual Intelligence: the Ultimate Intelligence*,[377] in which they identify and explore the nature of spiritual intelligence as a form of "super intelligence," which is the "missing jewel" of the Western Enlightenment and secular humanism. They write:

> Spiritual intelligence is the soul's intelligence. It is the intelligence with which we heal ourselves and with which we make ourselves whole. So many of us today live lives of wounded fragmentation . . . SQ is the intelligence that rests in that deep part of the self that is connected to wisdom from beyond the ego, or conscious mind, it is the intelligence with which we not only recognise existing values, but with which we creatively discover new values.[378]

If IQ has specific strengths in addressing the *what* and *how* of a particular situation; and EQ addresses the *who* and *what* of a relational exchange; then SQ addresses the *why* of the *who* in question.

---

375. Salovey and Meyer, "Emotional Intelligence," 189.
376. Goleman, *Emotional Intelligence*.
377. Zohar and Marshall, *Spiritual Intelligence*.
378. Zohar and Marshall, *Spiritual Intelligence*, 9.

For Zohar and Marshall, SQ represents a form of "spiritual capital" that extends those resources found in intellectual capital, human capital and presumably economic capital/resources;[379] and is not necessarily dependent on conventional religious or transcendent spiritual sources . . . since we are all spiritual people, making SQ available to everyone, anywhere, and everywhere;[380] and like any other skill or psychological capacity, it can be measured, learned, lost and appropriated towards one's personal goals.

It should be noted that the SQ discussed by Zohar and Marshall is of a fundamentally different kind to that imagined and offered by the classical Christian spiritual tradition. Brian Draper, in his book *Spiritual Intelligence: a New Way of Being*,[381] uses the four categories of (a) awakening; (b) seeing afresh; (c) living the change; and (d) passing it on, as a template for bringing his Christian-influenced spiritual intelligence into play in the domains of business, commerce, and industry in public life.

In closing, I argue that because the sources that generate the Christian version of SQ are its Scriptures, its Christ, its Spirit, its teachings, its wisdom, and its expected outcomes in terms of holiness—it is inevitable that it will stand apart from other forms of SQ, in four ways.

First, the "Jesus quotient." In her book *The Jesus Quotient*, Jennie Harrop[382] discusses IQ, EQ and AQ ("audience quotient"—an important category for Christian communicators), describing the need for twenty-first century Christians to integrate these elements (along with SQ), in order to be prepared for the challenges of Christian witness in a rapidly changing Western world. Second, SQ derived from the Holy Spirit. The classical Christian spiritual perspective affirms that the source of its spiritual life originates from the Spirit. Since "no one knows the thoughts of God except the Spirit of God" (1 Cor 2:12), those who have been given the "mind of Christ" (1 Cor 2:16), are enlivened, taught, and informed by the Spirit. Third, the "greater" transformation resulting from Christian SQ. Christian spirit-focused SQ is not the transformation of "lesser things"—but deals instead with absolute being, total transcendence, and

---

379. The authors provide the following definition: "Spiritual capital is the amount of spiritual knowledge and expertise available to an individual or a culture, where spirituality is taken to mean 'meaning, values and fundamental purposes.'" Zohar and Marshall, *Spiritual Capital*, 27.

380. Zohar and Marshall, *Spiritual Intelligence*, 8–10.

381. Draper, *Spiritual Intelligence*.

382. Harrop, *The Jesus Quotient*, 2019.

living in the presence of God in such a way that Paul Ricœur's "excess of being" is imagined, rather than the small things of human preference and consumer choice. And fourthly, SQ as "integral" spirituality. Ken Wilbur in his book *Integral Spirituality*,[383] allocates an appreciative role to spirituality in the twenty-first century world which derives its sources from Christian models and Christian mysticism, making a strong case for arguing that those original Christian models function at an elevated level because of its transcendental subject-material.

And finally, it is important to note that there is a potential problem in how we approach SQ from a Christian point of view. Note that the capabilities and qualities injected by IQ and EQ are thought of as belonging to a person's powerbase. But from a Christian point of view, SQ belongs to God alone. What I want to say here is that every human being has the same amount of spiritual intelligence/capacity. At creation, God invested all people/persons with a form of spirit-infused existence that belonged to his own being and character, and which he gave to them at creation as a gift. No variableness of SQ can be said to exist between one person and the other because it is given by God "in full." And at redemption, God re-invested all people/persons with the same amount of possibility for living a spirit-infused "new life" which is the direct result of Christ's atoning work on the cross. Only at sanctification can there be said to be a point-of-difference in SQ. While sanctification is the work of the Spirit in the human person and is "without limit," nevertheless the one limiting and variable feature is the extent to which the human subject chooses to resist or to cooperate with the inner work of the Spirit, thereby exerting a limiting or expanding extent of the process and results of sanctification in their lives. This is a salient lesson regarding SQ as it occurs in the Christian spiritual life and prevents any assertion that I have a bigger SQ than you do as the grounds for competition in the Christian spiritual life.

55. (The) Spiritual Senses

As embodied persons living in a physical world, under normal circumstances we are gifted at birth a set of five senses to help navigate our way through life . . . our fingers for touching, our eyes for seeing, our noses for smelling, our ears for hearing, and our mouths for tasting. Each sense is perfectly adapted to savor the objects they are intended to sense and to

---

383. Wilber, *Integral Spirituality*.

transmit those sensations from our bodily organs to our brains as sentient information. This allows us to function as living organisms, as *homo materialis*, in our physical surroundings. As children we learn to use these senses, and as adults we fine-tune and apply them with expert mastery.

But in addition, as spiritual persons living in a spiritual universe, we need a variety of "spiritual senses" to enable us to navigate our way through a somewhat more veiled world where good and evil, truth and falsehood, light and darkness, mystery and obfuscation are at work. We need a set of spiritual senses that enable us to navigate our existence as human beings whose foremost mode of life is as *homo spiritualis*. If the physical senses give us access to the objects they were designed to measure and connect with—is it actually possible to see, touch and taste God with our spiritual senses? There are indications from the biblical texts that the spiritual senses may be real and are likely to function within peoples' souls . . . believers and unbelievers alike. John's first Epistle is replete with sensory language: "That which was from the beginning, which we have heard, which we have seen with our eyes, which we have looked at and our hands have touched—this we proclaim concerning the Word of life" (1 John 1:1). The disciples *did* see and touch Jesus, physically-speaking. And despite their initial unbelief, they *did* come to see and touch him in their worship, spiritually-speaking. Paul Gavrilyuk and Sarah Coakley write:

> Christian authors of all ages have used sensory language to express human encounters with the divine. In the Old Testament believers are enjoined to 'taste and see that the Lord is good' (Ps 33:9, 1 Pet 2:3); the prophets and others 'hear the word of the Lord' (Isa 1:10; Hos 4:1); the beatitude promises that 'the pure in heart will see God' (Matt 5:8); the Apostle Paul speaks of receiving the vision of God 'face-to-face' (1 Cor 15:12) and beholding the 'glory of the Lord as in a mirror' (2 Cor 2:18); . . . These biblical passages seem to point to certain features of human cognition that make perception-like contact with God possible. But how precisely should the statement be construed?[384]

How indeed? St. Paul recounts indirectly his mystical experience of being "caught up to the third heaven," daring only to identify the transcendent "moment" in order to convey the lesson learned and not the experience itself. The point of his disclosure is certainly not for his own self-aggrandizement but for the instructive benefit of others (2 Cor

---

384. Gavrilyuk and Coakley, *Spiritual Senses*, 273.

12:1–10). The lesson is that the use of the spiritual senses and the language that accords with them, must be used carefully and wisely.

Origen of Alexandria (148–253) is credited with having pioneered the doctrine of the "spiritual senses."[385] Origen's sources were primarily generated via careful exegesis of Scripture. According to Mark McInroy, Origen makes repeated use of the spiritual senses in his body of work, many of them appropriating the physical senses as the means for "seeing God with the 'eyes of the mind', hearing him via the inner 'spiritual ears', speaking to God with 'a bodiless voice' and 'breathing Christ in everything.'"[386] The outwardly focused physical senses are matched by a corresponding and inwardly focused set of parallel non-organic capacities which are more metaphorical and less literal than the physical senses. But McInroy concludes that the later Origen seeks to apply a "realist" understanding:

> The passages examined . . . describe those who have Christ before their eyes, those who speak to God with a bodiless voice, and those who delight in a variegated intelligible beauty. They describe seeing and hearing the mysteries of divine power, receiving the odour of Christ pouring himself into our senses. I propose that God is described as being present to the human being in these passages, and it is because the human being is able to discern that presence that we are justified in speaking of something resembling perception.[387]

A later contributor of note in the intellectual tradition regarding the spiritual senses is Bonaventure (1221–1274). Once again, Bonaventure references the five senses of sight, smell, taste, touch and hearing, but Gregory LaNave is careful to point out that for Bonaventure, "The heart of his doctrine is its attention to the object of the spiritual senses. God makes himself present in such a way that he can be spiritually sensed; it is when one is attentive to the presence that one understands what the spiritual senses are."[388] As was the case with Origen, in Bonaventure the "exterior sense" refers to the five corporeal senses, whereas:

> . . . the 'interior senses' 'are the acts of the soul—memory, intellect and will—that apprehends divine things. Man [sic] is

---

385. Plested, "Spiritual Senses, Monastic and Theological," 301–2.
386. McInroy, "Origen of Alexandria," 21.
387. McInroy, "Origen of Alexandria," 33.
388. LaNave, "Bonaventure," 160–61.

made to be oriented towards God. The natural functioning of his cognitive faculties brings him in touch with the divine. This is precisely what it means for man to be [made] in the image of God: 'a creature is called an "image" in so far as it has *conditiones* which point to God not only as a cause, but as an object, which are memory, intelligence and will.' Needless to say, the interior senses are philosophically and theologically significant, for if we do not understand the soul's natural orientation towards God we do not rightly understand the powers of the soul.[389]

John Calvin originated the phrase *sensus Divinitatus* by which he meant an innate knowledge or sense of God possessed by every human creature. Of this innate sense of the Divine, Calvin wrote: "The knowledge of God, as I understand it, is that by which we not only can see that there is a God, but also grasp what befits us and is proper to his glory, in fine, what is to our advantage to know him."[390] Calvin continues:

> There is within the human mind, and indeed by natural instinct, an awareness of Divinity. That we take to be beyond controversy. To prevent anyone from taking refuge in the pretence of ignorance, God himself has implanted in all men a certain understanding of his divine Majesty . . . Since, therefore, men one and all perceive that there is a God and that he is their Maker, they are condemned by their own testimony because they have failed to honour him and to consecrate their lives to his will.[391]

Calvin's argument is limited to this one central point; regardless of whether one is redeemed or unredeemed, branded on one's soul is this sense of God. Nothing more and nothing less. Paul Helm writes:

> Calvin shows little or no interest in the rationality of religious belief as such; he shows much more interest in establishing the fact that all men [sic] know God, or at least have the capacity for knowing God . . . By the [term] *sensus Divinitatus* Calvin implicitly rejects the view that unbelief or agnosticism are the natural human conditions, or that it is rational to presume atheism, but implies that belief in God is natural in the sense of being part of man's original condition, part of what it means to be really or fully human.[392]

389. LaNave, "Bonaventure," 162–63.
390. Calvin, *Institutes*, 39.
391. Calvin, *Institutes*, 43–44.
392. Helm, "John Calvin, the Sensus Divinitatis, and the Noetic Effects of Sin," 87–88.

56. Supernatural Existential

In the years preceding and leading into Vatican II (1962–65), a theological renewal movement arose within the Roman Catholic world known as *Nouvelle théologie* (the new theology). Hans Boersma describes the movement as follows:

> Reaching back past the ossified Scholasticism of the previous centuries, *Nouvelle théologie's* turn to the fathers and the medieval theologians was an effort to reintegrate faith and theology; it was an effort to go back to Scripture itself; and it was an endeavour to allow theology to speak to people's everyday lives.[393]

Karl Rahner (1904–1984) came to the table somewhat late in the process, but the concept of the "supernatural existential," which he coined to summarize one defining aspect of his spiritual theology, has made an important contribution to the goals of *Nouvelle théologie*, helping to make God's presence in the human soul thinkable, accessible, and expressible. It is this phrase "supernatural existential" that will hold our attention in this entry.

One problem we face when discussing the phrase "supernatural existential" is that Rahner provided only the barest outline of what he meant by the term, rather than developing it in any systematic way. This minimalist approach was the result of Rahner's preference for not allowing Christian discourse to become entangled in complex theological argument, and his predilection for addressing the practical needs faced by the modern-day Christian believer. One benefit of Rahner's minimalist approach is that his pregnant phrase "supernatural existential" invites twenty-first century spiritual disciples/seekers to consider how the concept of "supernatural existential" might apply to their lives in the contemporary moment.

In this entry, I propose that the Rahnerian language of the "supernatural existential" represents an important gift to the *repertoire* of the classical Christian spiritual tradition, in seven different ways: 1) the theological; 2) the philosophical; 3) the anthropological; 4) the pastoral; 5) the spiritual; 6) the personal; and 7) the experiential. First, the *theological*. In his *Foundations of Christian Faith*, Rahner identifies the "supernatural existential" as "God's absolute self-communication" of himself to

---

393. Boersma, *Heavenly Participation*, 15.

humankind as an act of transcendence and grace.[394] Commentating upon this theme, Philip Endean observes, "If Christianity is about God-with-us, then any account of how we respond to God himself will be an aspect of the doctrine of God."[395] For Rahner, God is a God of mystery, and yet his default method of working with his creation is to make himself known in such a way that his human creatures can both know and be grasped by the mystery that God is with us, in us, and for us.

Second, the *philosophical*. Rahner was a trained philosopher and theologian who believed that humankind's essence was to be "infinitely open to the infinite." He wrote:

> We are reflecting upon the concrete whole of the human self-realization of a Christian. That is really 'philosophy'. We are reflecting upon a Christian existence and upon the intellectual foundation of a Christian self-realization, and that is basically 'theology'.[396]

Rahner's "transcendental anthropology" is comprised of both philosophical and theological components—even if Rahner subscribed to the idea that philosophy must be the servant of theology and indeed spirituality, despite the fact that some of his philosophical assumptions are thought to be questionable from other philosophical perspectives.

Third, the *anthropological*. Rahner's theology has its roots in the human experience of God. Anton Losinger has observed a strong "anthropological turn" in Rahner's theological reflections, such that we most truly know ourselves when looked at from the standpoint of God's person, revelation and will. Susan Parlow further explains: "Human beings are more than creatures of time and space alone . . . We are, at root, open to universal presence, limitless Being—a dizzying incomprehensibility that the passion of faith assures us is beneficent."[397] The doctrine of the "supernatural existential" is what enables humankind to participate in grace—"grace is that which makes it possible for the movement to reach God in himself."[398]

Fourth, the *pastoral*. For Rahner, the church is the "sacrament of Christ" whose existence in the world as God's physical representation,

---

394. Rahner, *Foundations of Christian Faith*, 141.
395. Endean, "Christian Spirituality and Theology of the Human Person," 223.
396. Rahner, *Foundations of Christian Faith*, 10.
397. Parlow, "Personal Transformation in Karl Rahner's Christianity," 576–77.
398. Marmion, *Spirituality of Everyday Faith*, 169.

enables the church—despite it being a "community of sinners"—to welcome ordinary men and women into the community of the Spirit. The pastoral ministry of the church has as its primary purpose the formation, nurture and instruction of the spiritual life among its members.

Fifth, the *spiritual*. As a Jesuit, Rahner's prayer life and thought life were deeply grounded in St. Ignatius of Loyola's *Spiritual Exercises*. They, more than any philosophy or theology, were his fundamental point of reference. In his essay "Ignatius of Loyola Speaks to the Modern Jesuit," Rahner places these words in the mouth of Ignatius:

> You know that I wanted 'to help souls' . . . Therefore to say something about God, his grace, and about Jesus Christ, the crucified and risen one, so that their freedom would be redeemed in God's freedom . . . I experienced God directly and I wish to communicate this experience to others, as well as I can . . . I mean only that I experienced God, the ineffable and unfathomable one . . . One thing remains certain: a person can experience God's very own self.[399]

Sixth, the *personal*. Rahner provides a clear insight into his theological method as well as his own personal life in the following exposé of his inner world:

> When I love, when I am tormented by questions, when I am sad, when I am faithful, when I feel longing, this human and lived existential reality is a unity . . . That is not fully communicated by the idea of this reality that makes it an object to be reflected on academically.[400]

It is clear that Rahner's personal encounter with God was a key shaper of both his theology and his spirituality. The "supernatural existential" is Rahner's way of bringing together the two central themes of his overwhelming sense of God in his personal life, with his indispensable experience of self as the concrete human/existential subject.

And finally, the *experiential*. All that has gone before cannot help but be worked out in the human experience of God. The supernatural and the experiential are brought together as con-joined entities to form Rahner's description of the human experience of God. Marijn de Jong has observed that, "Whereas John Milbank holds that Rahner 'naturalises the

---

399. Cited from Egan, "Theology and Spirituality," 25.
400. Rahner *Foundations of Christian Faith*, 15–16.

supernatural,' Hansjurgen Verwyen conversely argues that he [Rahner] 'supernaturalises the natural.'"[401]

There remain two things to say in conclusion. The first is that Rahner's category of the "supernatural existential" applies not only to the Christian believer, but to humankind in general. As Rahner suggests:

> We are oriented towards God. This original experience is always present . . . This un-thematic and ever-present experience, this knowledge of God which we always have even when we are thinking or concerned with anything but God, that is [the] permanent ground from which that thematic knowledge of God emerges which we have in explicitly religious activity and in philosophical reflection.[402]

And the second thing to note regarding the "supernatural existential" is the need to make this nascent awareness fully conscious through living out the Christian spiritual life. Rahner specialist Phil Daughtry puts it this way:

> For me, the point of the 'supernatural existential' is the conviction that God is present to us as an offer of himself within the deepest, unconscious part of the human psyche, and that human experience is shaped and influenced by this presence at an unconscious level . . . When the unconscious becomes conscious, through the lens of Christian thought and belief, we have in the human person what we call Christian faith.[403]

57. Theosis

The doctrine of *theosis* (meaning "to become like God") is an ancient belief characteristic of the Christian faith that seeks to express the goal and endpoint of salvation and justification in those who believe. This entry will discuss the doctrine in outline, paying special attention to a renewed Protestant understanding of the concept, and the relevance of *theosis* to the spiritual life. The Greek word *theosis* does not itself appear in the biblical text, but the concept of god-like-ness has been a mainstay of Christian theology from the second century onwards. There is support for such thinking from the Old Testament texts: "You shall be holy, for I

---

401. de Jong, *Metaphysics of Mystery*, 128.
402. Rahner, *Foundations of Christian Faith*, 55.
403. Daughtry, personal correspondence, November 9, 2023.

am holy" (Lev 11:45); and "You are gods, children of the Most High, all of you" (Ps 82:6). And similarly in the New Testament: "God made him [Christ] who had no sin to be sin for us, so that in him we might become the righteousness of God" (2 Cor 5:21); "We, who with unveiled faces, all reflect the Lord's glory, are being transformed into his likeness, with ever-increasing glory, which comes from the Lord, who is the Spirit" (2 Cor 3:18); and "His [God's] divine power has given us everything we need for life and godliness . . . So that through them you may participate in the divine nature" (2 Pet 1:3–5). These and other founding texts regarding deification and/or union with God require a response from the contemporary believer.

Eastern Orthodox Christianity has made *theosis* the cornerstone of its doctrinal beliefs and spiritual practices, grounded in these and other biblical texts along with the writings of the Apostolic and Post-Apostolic Fathers, including Athanasius who wrote, "He [Christ] became what we are in order that we might become as he is."[404] Orthodoxy has been a strong advocate for *theosis*. Detailing the Orthodox tradition, Norman Russell defines *theosis* as follows:

> Theosis is our restoration as persons to integrity and wholeness by participation in Christ through the Holy Spirit, in a process which is initiated in this world through our life of ecclesial communion and moral striving to find ultimate fulfilment in our own union with the Father—all within the broad context of the Divine economy.[405]

Similarly, Roman Catholicism is the keeper of the spiritual tradition belonging to the Latin West, where such persons and movements as St. Augustine, St. Antony as the founder of monasticism, Thomas Aquinas and Hans von Balthasar all promote *theosis* as the pinnacle of theological orthodoxy and one of the "proofs" against heresy.[406] From a Protestant perspective, however, many people are suspicious of *theosis*, (wrongly) suspecting that it represents an unwelcome return to pre-Christian pagan ideas of *apotheosis*, or sectarian teachings (as in Mormonism) which take the position that humans literally become gods, to extremes.

---

404. Athanasius, *De Incarnatione* 54, 65.

405. Russell, *Fellow Workers with God*, 21.

406. Meconi and Olsen, *Called to Be the Children of God*, provides a particularly rich sampling of chapters on theosis from a Catholic perspective.

Considering the meaning and validity of *theosis*, Michael Gorman asks, "Kenosis is familiar to us, and justification we know, but what in the world is theosis?"[407] In answer to his own rhetorical question, Gorman writes:

> The term and concept 'theosis' or 'deification' is not well-known in many Western ecclesial circles, but it has come back onto the radar screen recently. There is no 'official' definition of the term, but it is commonly expressed in phrases such as union with God, becoming like God, sharing (or participation) in the Divine life, human transfiguration, restoration to full humanity in Christ, sharing in Christ the God-man, and even 'Christification'.[408]

Gorman defines *theosis* as, "Theosis is about divine intention and action, human transformation and the *telos* of human existence—union with God."[409]

As a theological concept, *theosis* can be understood as a Divine drama in three "acts:" firstly, at *creation*, God created humankind in his "image and likeness" (Gen 1:27), but because of sin, that image became marred and despoiled; secondly, at *redemption*, through Christ's cross, "If anyone is in Christ, he/she is a new creation, the old has gone, the new has come" (2 Cor 5:17)—on the basis that whatever offence once stood between God and broken humanity, has been removed, and a reconciliation has been put into effect; and thirdly, in *sanctification*, the indwelling Spirit of God facilitates and resources the believing soul in their desire to live out of the righteousness that Christ has won for them *via* the cross at the cost of his own life.

On a human level, *theosis* can also be seen to play out in a parallel set of three acts: firstly as *re-creation*, in which redeemed human persons endeavor to embrace the "exchanged life," where Christ's life is exchanged for their own—by submitting themselves as a partner with God in the process of being "made new" in the image of Christ; secondly, as *glorification*, in which redeemed human persons reclaim their original creational-and-now redeemed nature by submitting to the inward work of the Spirit who unites the two elements of the *supernatural* and the *existential*, as Rahner imagined; and thirdly, as *realization*, in which the poverty of human self-effort is overthrown and replaced with the

---

407. Gorman, *Inhabiting the Cruciform God*, 3.
408. Gorman, *Becoming the Gospel*, 3.
409. Gorman, *Inhabiting the Cruciform God*, 5.

victorious, conquering, mature self, described in Romans 8. At this stage of realization, whatever has been promised by God in election, by Christ in redemption, and by the Spirit in sanctification, is fulfilled and enacted to the extent that the human person actively fosters it in their lives.

We close with five theses that integrate aspects of what has been discussed up to this point. First, *theosis* is the "missing doctrine" from the Protestant theological collection, to the extent that it is the *telos* and fulfillment of all that God has promised in Christ. Second, *theosis* does not intend to convey the concept of actual godhood, but refers instead to godlikeness, where the actuality of the image of God in creation, the benefits of Christ's cross, and the existence of the Spirit's indwelling presence are fully realized in the life of the believer. Third, *the spiritual life* is one of conscious, intentional and convictional cooperation with the inward work of the Spirit through a "making real" of the Divine life in the human life. Fourth, *theosis* in this understanding has juridical, moral and relational elements, since it is through the strivings of those engaged in the spiritual life that the qualities of Christlikeness are made manifest. And fifth, *theosis* is not intended to be Pelagian (i.e., self-salvation), or reflect a hyper-holiness position (i.e., self-sanctification); rather, it designates the goal and summit of what God has offered to us in the gospel of Christ. It is Christianity pure and simple.

58. Tragic Spirituality

In a booklet entitled *Beyond Tragic Spirituality: Victimhood and Christian Hope*,[410] David Kettle explored the tragic sense of life that pervades Western society. The expectation of unending technological improvement designed to provide uninterrupted "progress" in the West has delivered a banal mode of life that neither tastes nor satisfies. In moments of cultural crisis—such as the death of Princess Diana, or the terror attacks of 9/11—people are moved to externalize their pain in collective expressions of public grief. At such significant moments in history, we reach into the emotional cupboard only to find it bare—as with the Old Mother Hubbard nursery rhyme. Kettle cites the Australian cartoonist Michael Leunig as saying:

> Something is amiss. It's like when birds suddenly can't find their flight to Alaska. We are in a particular time in history when it's

---

410. Kettle, *Beyond Tragic Spirituality*.

immensely stressful to be alive. I would say we are in the midst of a pillaging and rape of the psychological eco-system, the ecology of the soul. There is a great, delicate, interconnected ecology that goes on in people's lives. We are defiling it, exploiting it, and this will have tremendous consequences for the emotional health of society.[411]

We sit "in the ruins of neoliberalism,"[412] no longer able to believe the Western myth of unaided human reason that enables technologically driven progress towards utopian certainty that has informed our journey thus far. Now, with our heads in our hands, we wonder how we got into this mess. In that situation, many people paint themselves as "victims" of a political and economic system that has over-promised but under-delivered. This is where Leunig's image of the West's threadbare ecology of the soul has led us to.

One way people manage the psycho-spiritual stresses of victimhood is to self-medicate on the elixir of pseudo-spirituality. As these *victim-spirits* enter the all-you-can-eat candy-store of sacred delights, they presume it is their right to bring their ego-based self-interest with them. After all, taking a spiritual "trip" has to be cheaper than psychotherapy, and you remain in control at all times—right? But there is a benefit to be had and a price to be paid when one steps out on the spiritual journey.

The "tragic spirituality" discussed by Kettle seeks out the sacred as a place of safety and refuge in which to formulate one's hope for a better life, approaching the sacred as a genie in a bottle, designed to serve the interests of the ego without any real understanding of the true nature of the sacred nor any intention of submitting to its truthfulness or core-teachings. For those engaged in tragic spirituality—the statue of a Buddha in the garden, the self-help books on the shelf, the rosary in the handbag, the candle on the windowsill—do not provide the *axis mundis* ("gateway to another world") being sought. Instead, they amount to pitiable cries emitted by the immature self who demands more from life than they are willing to pay. Tragic spirituality locks people into victimhood rather than freeing them from it. It is a lantern inside Plato's cave, not the longed-for freedom of the noonday sun.

Robert Grant has explored the part that pain and suffering play in preparing us for entry to the spiritual journey.[413] As an expert in trauma,

---

411. Kettle, *Beyond Tragic Spirituality*, 12, without source.
412. Brown, *In the Ruins of Neoliberalism*.
413. Grant, *Way of the Wound*.

Grant acknowledges that Western consumers are risk-averse, avoiding pain and suffering at all costs. And yet trauma has become one of the few entry-points to the deep-places of life. Our ego is usually self-centered and introspective, but when cancer, the death of a child, a car accident or depression strike, a deep fracture occurs in the self. In situations of trauma, Grant writes, "A wound is no longer viewed by the ego as an indication of failure, weakness, or inadequacy. It is now recognized as an access to Spirit. Here, wounded individuals are not the exception—but the rule."[414] For Grant, trauma is the unexpected doorway, the unwanted teacher that takes people beyond tragic spirituality into an authentic form of spiritual life. He explains:

> Suffering is a witness to the world's need for the Spirit. It demonstrates that all people are equal (in that they all suffer and can all be broken) and that no human being, when s/he is wounded, can bear the human condition alone. Suffering exposes the need for divine and human support. It is a sacrament for those who can receive it without resentment or hatred . . . Sufferers are challenged to plunge into the human condition rather than to escape it.[415]

Kettle points to the positive capacity of the Christian spiritual pathway to reconcile us not only back to God, but also to ourselves, to sanity, and to hope. "In Jesus' life we see all goodness and justice, all blessing and promise, coming to fulfillment among us."[416] The invitation of the Christian spiritual journey is not to become fixated on a sense of the tragic in life, but rather to draw closer to the God who invites us to become his child, his beloved, his family, his guests, his redeemed People. It is hope, not despair, that is the catch-cry of Christian spirituality . . . accompanied by faith, hope and love. But it is only those who have taken the "leap of faith" and allowed themselves to pass through the portal of pain and suffering on their way to personal transformation, who are able to make this discovery for themselves. When we put aside the tragic sense of life and go beyond tragic spirituality to engage with an authentic spiritual struggle that produces transformation and "wholeness" on the other side, we realize the extent of the change we have undergone. As Frederick Buechner has pointed out:

---

414. Grant, *Way of the Wound*, 223.
415. Grant, *Way of the Wound*, 138.
416. Kettle, *Beyond Tragic Spirituality*, 21.

People are prepared for everything except for the fact that beyond the darkness of the blindness there is a great light. They are prepared to go on breaking their backs ploughing the same old field until the cows come home without seeing, until they stub their toes on it, that there is a treasure buried in that field rich enough to buy Texas. They are prepared for a God who strikes hard bargains but not for a God who gives as much for an hour's work as for a day's. They are prepared for a mustard-seed kingdom of God no bigger than the eye of the newt but not for the great banyan that it becomes with birds in its branches singing Mozart. They are prepared for the potluck supper at First Presbyterian but not for the marriage supper of the Lamb.[417]

59. Transformation

In the class notes for one of my courses on spirituality is a statement outlining the four "theses" on which the course is built: (a) Christianity is an ancient spiritual pathway based on the person and teachings of Jesus of Nazareth, whom Christians believe to be the Son of God; (b) The gospel or 'Way' he imparted is a way of wisdom that instructs people in how to live as spiritual persons by attending to how they relate to God, the world, self and others; (c) Christian spirituality represents a workable and operative pathway by which to undertake the adventure of one's life as a spiritual pilgrim in both time and eternity; and (d) authentic Christian spirituality offers its adherents a *transformative pathway* that invites spirited engagement with life and death, good and evil, hope and despair. Transformation is a recurring theme throughout the course because redemption is a form of transformation in which God in Christ makes available to his people the church, spiritual formation as a voluntary and cooperative form of self-transformation that believers enact in their lives in partnership with the Holy Spirit.

In this entry, we are working with the category of transformation, and in particular self-transformation in the context of Christian spirituality. There are two ways of approaching transformation ... as a *lesser* way and as a *greater* way. Beginning with the lesser way—Eugene Peterson observed that like the word *evangelism*, spiritual language (including transformation) can easily become a "ruined word."[418] This happens when

---

417. Buechner, *Telling the Truth*, 70.
418. Peterson, *Subversive Spirituality*, 242.

it is employed using a palette of small things. So, for example: a real estate agent spruiks the benefits of a lick of paint as a way of "transforming" a shambolic wreck of a house; or a beauty therapist describes the benefits Botox injections can produce in enhancing a young woman's appearance as something "truly transformational." In both instances the claims made grossly over-state the results of mere earthly things. What is needed is a new and elevated transcendent frame within which to conceptualise transformation.

Christian thinkers in every era have worked hard to promote the second and *greater* sense of transformation. Transformation is a large word whose boundaries are limitless and whose consequences are multi-faceted and divinely energized. In Scripture, St. Paul wrote: "And we, who with unveiled faces all reflect the Lord's glory, are being *transformed* into his likeness with ever-increasing glory, which comes from the Lord, who is the Spirit" (2 Cor 3:18). No amount of Botox can generate the glories of the transformation that comes from God's transcendent resources, when they are written large in human form, using the language of the Spirit, in the lives of saintly people. And notice that the words "ever-increasing glory" imply a transformation that is ongoing, ever-increasing, and potentially never-ending.

Christian apologists in the early periods of Christian history thought it necessary to define how fundamentally *different* Christian transformation was from those transformations conceived by and offered in classical Greek culture and thought, such as in the writings of Publius Ovid (43BC–17AD) and Lucius Apuleius (c124–c170AD)—both of whom wrote influential books entitled *Metamorphoses* (the Greek word for "transformation"). And Christian spiritual teachers in the twenty-first century will want to do the same, but they often struggle to find a language capable of naming and explaining ways in which Christian spiritual transformation transcends and supersedes those lesser transformations of twenty-first century culture in terms of drugs, sexuality, money, fame, and power.

At the heart of the Christian spiritual life are four 'conversions', each of which are deeply transformative in nature. Firstly, the conversion of the heart. James K. A. Smith has written that "we are what we love."[419] In Jeremiah 31:33, God promises to give Israel a "new heart" with which to love him and to worship him. Secondly, a conversion of the mind.

---

419. Smith, *You Are What You Love*.

No longer will God's people hanker after consumer items to satisfy their deepest desires, but their imaginations will be transformed, they will have a new mind, they will be given the "mind of Christ" (1 Cor 2:16), and they will come to think God's thoughts after him. Thirdly, the conversion of the self. The irritable, egoistic and self-righteous person who resists God's Spirit and holds out for the best 'deal' from God, willingly submits to God's embrace and desires to receive everything that God in Christ has for them. And fourth, the conversion of the hands. Instead of living for themselves, such people are willing to spend and be spent, in a spirit of kenotic 'self-emptying' that sees their best joys and their greatest achievements realized through seeking justice via acts of mercy on behalf of others, carried out in a spirit of lovingkindness. These are the four conversions of the Christian spiritual life which result in a transformation of character, reflecting the image of God who is ever good, beautiful and true.

Lewis Rambo offers a definition of conversion as, "a significant sudden transformation of a person's loyalties, patterns of life, and focus of energy."[420] Not everyone would agree with Rambo's assertion that conversion is always "sudden" because conversion is inevitably an event-process that unfolds over the course of an individual's life. But the adjective "sudden" is frequently reported in first-person accounts by people who experience conversion for themselves because the radical nature of the discontinuous change they have experienced appears to them as something instantaneous. But less controversial are the kinds of catalytic changes conversion produces in a person's life. Writing in Ephesians 1 and 2 regarding what God has done in Christ for the new People of God in first century Palestine (and subsequently), St. Paul employed some lavish language. Eugene Peterson describes that language as "God's verbs" in the form of blessed... chosen... destined... bestowed... lavished... made known... gathered up.[421] While the word transformation (*metamorphosis*) itself is not used, each of these verbs points towards and produces Christ-centered change that is transformative.

Webster's Dictionary defines transformation as a change in form and/or outward appearance; to change the condition, nature and function of something or someone, connected to the inward personality and/or character of a person or group of people. David Benner speaks about

---

420. Rambo, "Psychological Perspectives on Conversion," 22.
421. Peterson, *Practise Resurrection*, 57.

the "transformational potency" inherent in Christian spirituality,[422] suggesting that:

> The essential dynamic of the human spirit is a radical drive for self-transcendence; a longing to be more than we are, to be all that we can. At some deep level we seem to recognise this "more" is not simply more of the same but that it demands deep transformation.[423]

Jason Fout, in his book *Fully Alive: the Glory of God and the Human Creature in Karl Barth, Hans Urs von Balthasar and Theological Exegesis of Scripture*, provides two reports of interest to us here. He writes:

> von Balthasar talk[s] . . . freely about human participation and transformation in God. As he states, 'The [created] spirit's horizon is not confined to worldly being . . . But extends to absolute Being . . . and only in this light can it think, will and love . . . Being itself here unveils its final countenance, which for us receives the name of Trinitarian love; only with this final mystery does light fall at last on that other mystery: why there is Being at all and why it enters our horizon as light and truth and goodness and beauty.[424]

Fout continues:

> In Christ is found 'the logic of abundance', which brings transformation in ever-greater increase (from glory to glory). Focusing on [2 Cor 3:18], . . . Ricœur observes that 'It is to this reinterpretation of the glory of God figure through the person of Christ that Paul grafted the extraordinary theme of the transformation of the Christian into the same image. In this way he forged the central metaphor of the Christian self as christomorphic, that is, the image of the image par excellence. A change of glory, if we may put it this way—of descending glory, it must be added—is created in this way: God's glory, that of Christ, that of the Christian. At the far end of this chain, if the mediation goes back to the origin, the christomorphic self is both fully dependent and fully upstanding: an image 'always more glorious' according to the apostle.'[425]

---

422. Benner, *Spirituality and the Awakening Self*, 191.
423. Benner, *Spirituality and the Awakening Self*, 216.
424. Fout, *Fully Alive*, 188.
425. Fout, *Fully Alive*, 162.

60. True Self-False Self

This entry is focussed on the double concept of "true self-false self" as it is developed in the writings of the Trappist monk Thomas Merton (1915–1968). That is not to say that Merton is the only person to develop theories of the true self and the false self. A range of important contributions have been made to the topic by psychologists such as Donald Winnicott, Carl Rogers and Abraham Maslow—all of which are significant at a time when Western culture leans heavily towards egotism and the shadow-side located in the "false self," and when citizens of Western culture find themselves deeply impacted by a growing mental health crisis. Christian psychologists like Neil Pembroke[426] bring Thomas Merton's concept of the "true self-false self" into conversation with psychological theories of the topic, treating Merton as both a valid contributor to the field, but also as someone who has contributed to a new theory of the self.

In this entry, we will restrict our discussion to Thomas Merton's theory of the "true self-false self," and to working within the discipline of Christian spirituality. The flow of thought works best under the three sub-headings of: (1) the false self; (2) the true self; and (3) the true self in the spiritual life. To begin with, two clarifying statements are needed: first, William Shannon's observation that the new English translation of the Bible version of Matthew 10:39 is close to Merton's understanding of the "true self": "If anyone loses his life in my name, he will find his true self. What gain is there for a man to have won the whole world and to have lost his true self or what can he give to save his self?"[427] And second, an initial working definition of the "true self-false self" concept will enable readers to grasp our central concern here. The "false self" is the Promethean self who is antagonistic towards God, refusing to expose themselves to scrutiny by knitting their own defensive dress of fig leaves out of their own illusory materials; whereas the "true self" is the self who is awakened to insight regarding the life God calls them to live as their "best selves," and who is willing to work with God in co-creating the new person they were designed to become *via* inner wholeness and Christ-likeness. Now we turn to the three headings that will allow us to further explore the true self-false self concept.

---

426. Pembroke, *Moving Toward Spiritual Maturity*, from chapter 6, entitled "Conversion to the True Self," 101–11.

427. Shannon, "Thomas Merton's Theology of Self," 202.

First, the false self. Merton arrived at the concept of the "false self-true self" through his own experiences of suffering, following the death of his mother when he was six, being abandoned by his father, the death of his grandparents and his brother in quick succession, and the tragic death of his lover and their young child in the blitzkrieg bombings of London. His carousing and drinking during his university days can be read as an unsuccessful quest for personal fulfilment and true happiness. Over time, he came to understand that these efforts only created a false sense of self which was illusory. In his book, *New Seeds of Contemplation*, Merton writes:

> Every one of us is shadowed by an illusory person: a false self . . . My false and private self is the one who wants to exist outside . . . of reality and outside of life. And such a self cannot help but be an illusion.[428]

Merton continues:

> [The 'false self'] is the deep, confused, metaphysical awareness of *the basic antagonism between the self and God* due to estrangement from him by perverse attachment to a 'self' which is mysterious and illusory.[429]

And further:

> For most people in the world, there is no greater subjective reality than this false self of theirs, which cannot exist. A life devoted to the cult of the shadow is what is called a life of sin.[430]

This "false self" is the castle in the air we devote our lives to constructing to protect ourselves from outward scrutiny, in order to maintain our inward illusion of happiness and self-confidence. But the truth is, maintaining the "false self" requires everything we have to sustain the lie, which is an egotistical miscalculation.

Second, the "true self." For Merton, the "true self" is not a "thing" in itself, but is a symbolic representation of human life as it was intended to be before God which contains a certain wholeness, authenticity, relationality and internal balance to it. From the perspective of our culture, the "true self" is difficult to perceive, and even when we *can* see it, has the appearance of a form of insanity.

---

428. Merton, *New Seeds of Contemplation*, 34.
429. Merton, *Contemplative Prayer*, 122.
430. Merton, *New Seeds of Contemplation*, 34.

> Our reality, our true self, is hidden in what appears to us to be nothingness and void. What we are not seems to be real, and what we are seems to be unreal . . . The 'empty' self that is 'nothing' in our eyes . . . is our true reality in the eyes of God.[431]

Choosing to abandon the "false self" and to embrace the "true self" requires a conscious decision to do so, but it is a decision that contains much risk. What if God is not true to his promise, and intends to do us evil and not good? What if I am discovered for who I truly am—an ugly duckling? But according to Merton, "The only true joy on earth is to escape from the prison of our own selfhood . . . and enter by love into union with the Life who dwells and sings within the essence of every creature and in the core of our own souls."[432] When considering the "true self," one must ask the following questions expectantly: What kind of life does God have for me which is whole, and resplendent with his Being? What if Christ's call to follow him truly does lead through the valley of the shadow of self-emptying (which is kenosis or self-emptying), to a kind of life where my cup is filled to overflowing? Merton says: "For me to be a saint means to be myself. Therefore the problem of sanctity and salvation is in fact the problem of finding out who I am and in discovering my true self."[433] "There is only one problem on which all my existence, my peace and my happiness depend: to discover myself in discovering God. If I find Him I will find myself and if I find my true self I will find Him."[434]

And third, the "true self" in the Christian spiritual life. It is important to note with Reggie McNeil, that:

> God shapes our lives; he does not script them. Certainly he makes some unilateral decisions—like the culture of origin we are born into, what time of history we intersect, and maybe some direct interventions along the way. But his work in our hearts requires our collaboration.[435]

Progressing from the "false self" to the "true self" requires that we cooperate with God, in the name of Christ, and in the power of the Spirit—to produce in our own lives the life of Christ where joy, wisdom, sanctity, authenticity and credibility are available for all to see. Our best resource

---

431. Merton, *New Seeds of Contemplation*, 281–82.
432. Merton, *New Seeds of Contemplation*, 8.
433. Merton, *New Seeds of Contemplation*, 31.
434. Merton, *New Seeds of Contemplation*, 36.
435. McNeal, *Work of Heart*, xv.

for ministry is not which denomination we belong to, which theological degree we have completed, what position we hold in our church ministry, or what strategy or program we are putting into practice. On the contrary, our best resource for ministry is the person we are becoming, the spiritual life-force that is growing within us, the good we intend to do to ourselves and to others, the love we show towards others, and the winsomeness with which we "live out" these things before a watching world. It is this authentic witness to Christ, through the person who lives out their "true self" with conviction and courage, who is the most powerful *impresario* of the kingdom of God. "We are only really ourselves when we completely consent to "receive" the glory of God into ourselves. Our true self is, then, the self that receives freely and clearly the missions that are God's supreme gift to His sons. Any other "self" is an illusion."[436]

END

---

436. Merton, *New Seeds of Contemplation*, 42.

Bibliography

a'Kempis, Thomas. *The Imitation of Christ*. London: Burns and Oates, 1959.
Aldous, Ben. *The God Who Walks Slowly: Reflections on Mission with Kosuke Koyama*. London: SCM, 2022.
Aniol, Scott. "Changed from Glory to Glory: The Liturgical Formation of the Christian Faith," *Journal of Spiritual Formation and Soul Care* 14 (2021) 48–71.
Arndt, William F., and F. Wilbur Gingerich. *A Greek-English Lexicon of the New Testament and Other Early Christian Literature*. Chicago: University of Chicago Press, 1979.
Astley, Jeff. *Religious and Spiritual Experience*. London: SCM, 2020.
Athanasius. *De Incarnatione 54*, in *Nicene and Post-Nicene Fathers: a Select Library of the Christian Church*, Second Series, edited by Philip Schaaf and Henry Wace. Peabody, MA: Hendrickson, 1995.
Augustine. *The Soliloquies of St. Augustine*. Translated by Elizabeth Cleveland. Boston: Little, Brown and Co., 1910.
———. *Confessions*. Nashville: Thomas Nelson, 1999.
———. "The Teacher (De Magistro)." In *Augustine: Earlier Writings*, edited by J. H. Burliegh, 69–101. Louisville, KY: Westminster John Knox, 2006.
Austin, Victor L., and Joel C. Daniels. *The Emerging Christian Minority*. Eugene, OR: Cascade, 2019.
Barclay, John, M., and Simon J. Gathercole. *Divine and Human Agency in Paul and His Cultural Environment*. London: T. & T. Clark, 2007.
Barnhart, Bruno. "One Spirit, One Body: Jesus' Participatory Revolution." In *The Participatory Turn: Spirituality, Mysticism, Religious Studies*, edited by Jorge N. Ferrer and Jacob H. Sherman, 265–91. Albany: State University of New York Press, 2007.
Barrett, C. K. *The Gospel According to St John: An Introduction with Commentary and Notes on the Greek Text*. London: SPCK, 1978.
Barth, Karl. *The Doctrine of Creation*, Volume 3, *Church Dogmatics*, edited by G.W. Bromiley and T. F. Torrence. Peabody, MA: Hendrickson, 2010.
Bass, Diana B. *Christianity After Religion: The End of the Church and the Birth of a New Spiritual Awakening*. New York: HarperOne, 2012.

Batson, C. Daniel. *The Religious Experience: A Social-Psychological Perspective*. Oxford: Oxford University Press, 1982.
Batson, Daniel C., et al. *Religion and the Individual: A Social-Psychological Perspective*. New York: Oxford University Press, 1993.
Baudelaire, Charles. "Get Drunk." In *Paris Spleen: Little Poems and Prose*, translated by Keith Waldrop, 71. Middleton: Wesleyan University Press, 2009. Cited by Jean-Luc Nancy, *Intoxication*. New York: Fordham University Press, 2016.
Benedict. *The Rule of St Benedict*. Translated by Carolinne White. London: Penguin Classics, 2008.
Benner, David. *The Gift of Being Yourself: The Sacred Call to Self-Discovery*. Downers Grove, IL: InterVarsity, 2004.
———. *Spirituality and the Awakening Self*. Grand Rapids: Brazos, 2012.
Blake, Nigel. "Against Spiritual Education." *Oxford Review of Education* 22 (1996) 443–56.
Blossor, Benjamin P. *Become like the Angels: Origen's Doctrine of the Soul*. Washington, DC: Catholic University of America Press, 2012.
Blumenstock, James A. *Strangers in a Familiar Land: A Phenomenological Study on Marginal Christian Identity*. Eugene, OR: Pickwick, 2020.
Boersma, Hans. *Embodiment and Virtue in Gregory of Nyssa: an Anagogical Approach*. Oxford Early Christian Studies Series. Oxford: Oxford University Press, 2013.
———. *Heavenly Participation: The Weaving of a Sacramental Tapestry*. Grand Rapids: Eerdmans, 2011.
Bonhoeffer, Dietrich. *The Cost of Discipleship*. London: SCM, 1964.
Bowker, John. *The Sense of God: Sociological, Anthropological and Psychological Approaches to the Origin of the Sense of God*. Oxford: One World, 1995.
Bowlby, John. *A Secure Base: Parent-Child Attachment and Healthy Human Development*. New York: Basic, 1988.
Brabant, Christopher. "The Truth Narrated: Ricoeur on Religious Experience." In *Divinising Experience: Essays in the History of Religious Experience from Origin to Ricoeur*, edited by Lieven Boeve and Laurence P. Hemming, 246–70. Leuven: Peeters, 2004.
Breen, Benjamin. *The Age of Intoxication: Origins of the Global Drug Trade*. Philadelphia: University of Pennsylvania Press, 2019.
Briggs-Myers, Isabel, and Peter B. Myers. *Gifts Differing: Understanding Personality Type*. London: Davies-Black, 2010.
Brown, Brené. *Atlas of the Heart: Mapping Meaningful Connection and the Language of Human Experience*. New York: Random House, 2021.
Brown, Colin. "Head/kephale." In *Dictionary of New Testament Theology*, Volume 2, edited by Colin Brown, 2:156–63. Exeter: Paternoster, 1976.
Brown, Wendy. *In the Ruins of Neoliberalism: The Rise of Antidemocratic Politics in the West*. New York: Columbia University Press, 2019.
Brueggemann, Walter. *Israel's Praise: Doxology Against Idolatry and Ideology*. Philadelphia: Fortress Press, 1988.
Bruteau, Bearice. *The Easter Mysteries*. New York: Crossroad, 1995.
Buechner, Frederick. *Telling the Truth: The Gospel as Tragedy, Comedy, and Fairy Tale*. San Francisco: HarperCollins, 2009.
Burton, Tara I. *Strange Rites: New Religions for a Godless World*. New York: Public Affairs, 2020.

Calvin, John. *Institutes of the Christian Religion*. The Library of Christian Classics. Philadelphia: Westminster, 1984.
Campolo, Tony. *The Kingdom of God is a Party: God's Radical Plan for His Family*. Nashville: Thomas Nelson, 1992.
Cantalamessa, Raniero O.F.M. *Sober Intoxication of the Spirit: Filled with the Fullness of God*. Cincinnati: Servant, 2010.
Caputo, John D. *On Religion*. New York: Routledge, 2019.
Casey, Michael. *Fully Human, Fully Divine: An Interactive Christology*. Ligouri, MO: Ligouri/Triumph, 2004.
Cassidy, Jude, and Phillip R. Shaver, eds. *Handbook of Attachment: Theory, Research and Clinical Applications*. New York: Guildford, 1999.
Chan, Simon. *Spiritual Theology: A Systematic Study of the Christian Life*. Downers Grove, IL: InterVarsity, 1998.
Chaucer, Geoffrey. *Canterbury Tales in Modern English*. Translated by J. U. Nicolson. Garden City, NY: Doubleday, 1934.
Chittester, Joan. *The Monastery of the Heart: an Invitation to a Meaningful Life*. Katona: Blue Bridge, 2011.
Chrétien, Jean-Louis. *The Call and the Response*. New York: Fordham University Press, 2004.
Clark, Francis. *Godfaring: On Reason, Faith, and Sacred Being*. London: St Paul's, 2000.
Clement, Olivier. *On Human Being: A Spiritual Anthropology*. New York: New City Press, 2000.
———. *The Roots of Christian Mysticism: Texts from the Patristic Era with Commentary*. New York: New City, 1993.
Cole-Turner, Ron. "The Soul-Altering Substances: What Implications Does the Psychedelic Renaissance Have for Faith and Spirituality?" *Christian Century* 140.10 (2023) 54–60.
Coon, Lynda L. *Sacred Fictions: Holy Women and Hagiography in Late Antiquity*. Philadelphia: University of Pennsylvania Press, 1997.
Corbon, Jean. *The Wellspring of Worship*. New York: Paulist, 1988.
Cox, Michael. *Mysticism: The Direct Experience of God*. Wellingborough, Northamptonshire: Aquarian, 1983.
Cromer, John Mark. *The Ruthless Elimination of Hurry*. Colorado Springs, CO: Water Brook, 2019.
Csordas, Thomas J. *The Sacred Self: A Cultural Phenomenology of Charismatic Healing*. Berkeley: University of California Press, 1994.
Cutri, Mary P. *Sounding Solitude: An Approach to Transformation in Christ by Love*. Washington, DC: ICS Publishers, 2016.
Daley, Brian E., SJ. *Gregory of Nazianzus*. London: Routledge, 2006.
Danielou, Jean. "Cant/In Canticum Canticorum." In *The Brill Dictionary of Gregory of Nyssa*, edited by Lucas Fransisco Mateo-Sco and Giulio Maspero, 121–25. Leiden: Brill, 2010.
———. *Plationisme and Theologie Mystique*. Doctrine Spirituelle Saint Gregorie de Nysse. Aubier: Editions Montaigne, 1944.
———. *Prayer: The Mission of the Church*. Translated by David Louis Schindler. Grand Rapids: Eerdmans, 1996.
Davidson, Scott. *A Companion to Ricoeur's Symbolism of Evil*. Lanham, MD: 2020.
De Caussade, Jean-Pierre. *The Sacrament of the Present Moment*. San Francisco: Harper & Row, 1982.

de Jong, Marijn. *Metaphysics of Mystery: Revisiting the Question of Universality through Rahner and Schillebeeckx*. London: T. & T. Clark, 2020.
de Lubac, Henri. *The Discovery of God*. Grand Rapids: Eerdmans, 1960.
Devenish, Stuart C. *Ordinary Saints: Lessons in the Art of Giving Away Your Life*. Eugene, OR: Cascade, 2017.
———. *Seeing and Believing: The Eye of Faith in a Visual Culture*. Eugene, OR: Wipf& Stock, 2012.
Diamond, Steven A. "Shadow." In *Encyclopedia of Psychology and Religion*, edited by David A. Leeming et al., 836–37. New York: Springer, 2010.
Dickens, W. T. *Hans Urs von Balthasar's Theological Aesthetics: A Model for Post-Critical Biblical Interpretation*. Notre Dame: University Press of Notre Dame, 2003.
Doran, Robert. *Psychic Conversion and Theological Foundations: Toward a Reorientation of the Human Sciences*. Chico, CA: Scholars, 1981.
Dostoyevsky, Fyodor. *The Idiot*. Translated by Eva Martin. New York: Vintage, 2003.
Draper, Brian. *Spiritual Intelligence: A New Way of Being*. Oxford: Lion, 2009.
Dru, Alexander, ed. *The Journals of Søren Kierkegaard*. New York: Harper Torchbooks, 1958.
Dupre, Louis. *Transcendent Selfhood: The Rediscovery of the Inner Life*. New York: Crossroad, 1976.
Dupré, Louis, and Wiseman James A. *Light from Light: An Anthology of Christian Mysticism*. Mahwah, NJ: Paulist, 1988.
Eagleton, Terry. *Culture and the Death of God*. New Haven, CT: Yale University Press, 2014.
Edgar, Brian G. "The Theoanthropological Functions of the Soul." PhD diss., Deakin University, 1992.
Edwards, David. *Mystify: Operating in the Mystery of God*. Santa Rosa: School of Revivalists Ministries, 2021.
Egan, Harvey D. "Theology and Spirituality." In *The Cambridge Companion to Karl Rahner*, edited by Declan Marmion and Mary E. Hines, 13–28. Cambridge: Cambridge University Press, 2005.
Endean, Philip. "Christian Spirituality and Theology of the Human Person." In *The Blackwell Companion to Christian Spirituality*, edited by Arthur Holder, 223–38. Oxford: Blackwell, 2005.
Epistle to Diognetus. In *The Apostolic Fathers*, edited by Bart D. Erhman, 2:121–59. Loeb Classical Library. Cambridge, MA: Harvard University Press, 2003.
Ermatinger, Cliff. *St. Therese of Lisieux: Spouse and Victim*. Washington, DC: ICS Publications Institute of Carmelite Studies, 2010.
Evdokimov, Paul. *The Sacrament of Love*. New York: St Vladimir's Seminary Press, 2011.
Fanning, Steven. *Mystics of the Christian Tradition*. London: Routledge, 2001.
Ferguson, Everett. "God's Infinity and Man's Mutability: the Perpetual Process According to Gregory of Nyssa." *Greek Orthodox Theological Review* (1973) 18, 59–78.
Fiddes, Paul. *Seeing the World and Knowing God: Hebrew Wisdom and Christian Doctrine in a Late-Modern Context*. Oxford: Oxford University Press, 2015.
Fishbane, Michael. *Sacred Attunement: a Jewish Theology*. Chicago: University of Chicago Press, 2008.
Flory, Richard, and Donald E. Miller. *Finding Faith: The Spiritual Quest of the Post-Boomer Generation*. New Brunswick: Rutgers University Press, 2008.

Fouracre, Paul. "Merovingian History and Merovingian Hagiography." *Past and Present* 127 (1990) 3–38.
Fout, Jason A. *Fully Alive: the Glory of God and the Human Creature in Karl Barth, Hans Urs von Balthasar and Theological Exegesis of Scripture*. London: Bloomsbury, 2015.
Fowler, James W. *Stages of Faith: The Psychology of Human Development and the Quest for Meaning*. San Francisco: HarperSanFrancisco, 1981.
Francis, Pope. "World Youth Day Address." 2013. http://www.catholicherald.co.uk/news/2013/07/28/wyd-2013-full-text-of-pope-francisshomily-for-world-youth-days-closing-mass/.
Frankl, Viktor. "Self-Transcendence as a Human Phenomenon." *Journal of Humanistic Psychology* 6 (1966) 97–106.
Fraser-Pearce, Jo. "Spiritual Education as a Subspecies of Relational Education?" *British Journal of Religious Education* 44 (2021) 112–21.
Frings, Manfred S. "The 'Ordo Amoris' in Max Scheler." In *Facets of Eros: Phenomenological Essays*, edited by F. J. Smith and Erling Eng, 40–59. The Hague: Martinus Nijhof, 1972.
Frohlich, Mary, RSCJ. "Spiritual Discipline, Discipline of Spirituality: Revisiting Questions of Definition and Method." In *Minding the Spirit: The Study of Christian Spirituality*, edited by Elizabeth A. Dreyer and Mark S. Burrows, 65–78. Baltimore: The Johns Hopkins University Press, 2005.
Fry, Christopher. *A Sleep of Prisoners: A Play*. London: Oxford University Press, Geoffrey Cumberlege, 1952.
Fuhrer, Therese. "Ille Intus Magister. On Augustine's Didactic Concept of Interiority." In *Teachers in Late Antique Christianity*, edited by Peter Gemeinhardt et al., 129–46. Tubingen: Mohr Seibeck, 2018.
Furey, Robert J. *The Joy of Kindness*. New York: Crossroad, 1993.
Garcia-Rivera, Alejandro. "Aesthetics." In *The Blackwell Companion to Christian Spirituality*, edited by Arthur Holder, 345–62. Oxford: Blackwell, 2005.
Gaultiere, Bill. "Soul Shepherding." https://www.soulshepherding.org/the-jesus-burn-a-blessed-experience-of-gods-presence/.
Gavrilyuk, Paul L., and Sarah Coakley. "Introduction." In *The Spiritual Senses: Perceiving God in Western Christianity*, edited by Paul L. Gavrilyuk and Sarah Coakley, 1–19. Cambridge: Cambridge University Press, 2012.
Geybels, Hans. "Experience Searching for Theology & Theology Interpreting Experience: Augustine's Hermeneutics of Religious Experience." In *Divinising Experience: Essays on the History of Religious Experience from Origen to Ricoeur*, edited by Lieven Boeve and Laurence P. Hemming, 33–57. Leuven: Peeters, 2004.
Goetzmann, J. "Conversion-Metanoia." In *Dictionary of New Testament Theology*, edited by Colin Brown, 357–59. Grand Rapids: Zondervan, 1975.
Goleman, Daniel. *Emotional Intelligence*. New York: Bantam, 2006.
Gorman, Michael J. *Abide and Go: Missional Theosis in the Gospel of John*. Eugene: OR: Cascade, 2018.
———. *Becoming the Gospel: Paul, Participation and Mission*. Grand Rapids: Eerdmans, 2015.
———. *Inhabiting the Cruciform God: Kenosis, Justification and Theosis in Paul's Narrative Soteriology*. Grand Rapids: Eerdmans, 2009.
———. "The This-Worldliness of the New Testament's Otherworldly Spirituality." In *The Bible and Spirituality: Exploratory Essays in Reading Scripture Spiritually*, edited by Andrew Lincoln et al., 151–70. Eugene, OR: Cascade, 2013.

Gorringe, Timothy. *The Education of Desire*. London: SCM, 2001.
Gottlieb, Eli. "Second Naivetè." https://www.egottliebconsulting.com/single-post/2012/10/22/second-naivete.
Granqvist, Pehr. "Religion as Attachment: The Godin Award Lecture." *Archive for the Psychology of Religion* 32 (2010) 3–24.
Grant, Robert. *The Way of the Wound: A Spirituality of Trauma and Transformation*. Oaklands: self-published, 1996.
Green, Gwendolyn, ed. *Letters from Baron Frederick von Hugel to a Niece*. London: J.M. Dent & Sons, 1929.
Green, Joel B. "Soul." In *The Cambridge Dictionary of Christian Theology*, edited by Ian A. McFarland et al., 81–82. Cambridge: Cambridge University Press, 2011.
Gregory of Nyssa. *The Life of Moses*. The Classics of Western Spirituality Series. New York: Paulist, 1978.
Habermas, Jürgen. "Secularism's Crisis of Faith: Notes on Post-Secular Society." *New Perspectives Quarterly* 25 (2008) 17–29.
Han, Byung-Chul. *The Burnout Society*. Stanford: Stanford University Press, 2015.
Hand, Michael. "The Meaning of 'Spiritual Education.'" *Oxford Review of Education* 29 (2003) 391–401.
Harder, Günther. "Soul." In *Dictionary of New Testament Theology*, edited by Colin Brown, 3:676–89. Exeter: Paternoster, 1978.
Hardman, Keith. "Christian." In *The New International Dictionary of the Christian Church*, edited by J. D. Douglas, 202. Exeter: Paternoster, 1974.
Harrison, Nonna V. *God's Many-Splendored Image: Theological Anthropology for Christian Formation*. Grand Rapids: Baker Academic, 2010.
Harrison, Victoria S. *The Apologetic Value of Human Holiness: Von Balthasar's Christocentric Philosophical Anthropology*. New York: Springer, 2000.
Harrop, Jennie. *The Jesus Quotient: IQ to EQ to AQ*. Eugene, OR: Cascade, 2019.
Hart, James. *The Person in the Common Life: Studies in a Husserlian Social Ethics*. Dortrecht: Kluwer Academic, 1992.
Hauerwas, Stanley. "Dietrich Bonhoeffer's Political Theology." *Conrad Grebel Review* 20 (2002) 17–39.
Hauerwas, Stanley, and William Willimon. *Resident Aliens: A Provocative Assessment of Culture and Ministry for People Who Know that Something is Wrong*. Nashville: Abingdon, 1991.
Hays, Richard B. *The Moral Vision of the New Testament: A Contemporary Introduction to New Testament Ethics*. New York: Continuum, 1997.
Heelas, Paul. "The Spiritual Revolution of Northern Europe: Personal Beliefs." *Nordic Journal of Religion and Society* 19 (2007) 1–28.
Helm, Paul. "John Calvin, the Sensus Divinitatis, and the Noetic Effects of Sin." *International Journal for the Philosophy of Religion* 43 (1998) 87–107.
Helminiak, Daniel A. *The Human Core of Spirituality: Mind as Psyche and Spirit*. New York: State University of New York Press, 1996.
Hernandez, Will. *Henri Nouwen: A Spirituality of Imperfection*. New York: Paulist, 2006.
Hill, Jonathan. *The History of Christian Thought*. Oxford: Lion, 2003.
Hillesum, Etty. *Etty: Letters from Westerbork*. Edited by Klaas A. D. Smelick and translated by Arnold Pomerans. New York: Random House, 1986.
Hirsch, Alan, and Mark Nelson. *Reframation: Seeing God, People and Mission through Re-Enchanted Frames*. Cody, WY: 100 Movements, 2019.

Hocking, William E. *The Meaning of God in Human Experience: A Philosophic Study of Religion*. New Haven, CT: Yale University Press, 1912.
Honoré, Carl. *In Praise of Slow: How a Worldwide Movement is Challenging the Cult of Speed*. Toronto: Vintage, 2004.
Hopkins, Gerard M. *Poems of Gerard Manley Hopkins*, edited by Robert Bridges. London: Oxford University Press, 1931.
Howard, Evan B. *The Brazos Introduction to Christian Spirituality*. Grand Rapids: Brazos, 2008.
Howell, James C. *Servants*. Nashville: Upper Room, 1999.
Humphrey, Edith M. *Ecstasy and Intimacy: When the Holy Spirit Meets the Human Spirit*. Grand Rapids: Eerdmans, 2006.
Ignatius. *The Spiritual Exercises of Saint Ignatius*. Translated by George E. Ganss SJ. St Louis: The Institute of Jesuit Sources, 1992.
James, William. *The Varieties of Religious Experience*. London: Longmans Green and Co., 1902.
Joas, Hans. *Do We Need Religion? On the Experience of Self-Transcendence*. London: Paradigm, 2006.
John of the Cross. *Dark Night of the Soul*. Translated by E. Allison Peers. New York: Image Books, 1990.
———. *The Spiritual Canticle*. Translated by John Venard OCD. Newtown, NSW: E.J. Dwyer, 1990.
John Paul II, Pope. *Evangelii Nuntiandi (On Evangelization in the Modern World)*. Repr. Homebush, NSW: St Paul, 1989.
Johnson, Luke T. *Religious Experience in Earliest Christianity: A Missing Dimension in New Testament Studies*. Minneapolis: Fortress, 1998.
Jones, Alan. *Soul Making: The Desert Way of Spirituality*. London: SCM, 1986.
Jung, Carl G. *Psychology and Religion*. New Haven, CT: Yale University Press, 1938.
Kapic, Kelly. *Communion with God: the Divine and the Human in the Theology of John Owen*. Grand Rapids: Baker, 2007.
Keen, Sam. *Hymns to an Unknown God: Awakening the Spirit in Everyday Life*. London: Piatkus, 1994.
Kelly, Eugene. *Material Ethics and Value: Max Scheler and Nicolai Hartmann*. Phaenomenologica Series. Dortrecht: Springer. 2011.
Kerr, Nathan R. "From Description to Doxology: The Dogmatic Bases of Christian Vision." In *Transcendence and Phenomenology*, edited by Peter M. Candler and Conor Cunningham, 174–200. London: SCM, 2007.
Kettle, David. *Beyond Tragic Spirituality: Victimhood and Christian Hope*. Cambridge: Grove, 2005.
Klassen, Derrick, W. and Marvin J. McDonald. "Quest and Identity Development: Re-Examining Pathways for Existential Search." *The International Journal for the Psychology of Religion* 12 (2002) 189–200.
Kleinig, John W. "The Mystery of Christ and the Divine Service." Paper delivered at the Higher Things Conference, St. Louis, July 2005.
Kourie, Celia. "Spirituality and the University." *Verbum et Ecclesia JRG* 30 (2009) 148–73.
Kovacs, Kenneth E. "The Relational Phenomenological Pneumatology of James E. Loder: Providing New Frameworks for Christian Life." PhD diss., University of St Andrews, 2002.

Kreider, Alan. *The Change of Conversion and the Origin of Christendom*. Christian Mission and Modern Culture Series. Harrisburg: Trinity, 1999.

———. *Worship and Evangelism in Pre-Christendom*. Cambridge: Grove, 1995.

Kurtz, Ernest, and Katherine Ketham. *The Spirituality of Imperfection: Storytelling and the Journey to Wholeness*. New York: Bantam, 1992.

LaNave, Gregory T. "Bonaventure." In *The Spiritual Senses: Perceiving God in Western Christianity*. Edited by Paul L. Gavrilyuk and Sarah Coakley, 159–73. Cambridge: Cambridge University Press, 2012.

Lanzetta, Beverly. *The Monk Within: Embracing a Sacred Way of Life*. Sebastopol: Blue Sapphire, 2018.

Lee, Dorothy A. *Hallowed in Truth and Love: Spirituality in the Johannine Literature*. Northcote, Victoria: Morning Star, 2011.

Lefsrud, Sigurd. *Kenosis in Theosis: an Exploration of Balthasar's Theology of Deification*, Eugene, OR: Pickwick, 2020.

Lewis, C. S. *The Weight of Glory*. London: SPCK, 1942.

———. *Reflections on the Psalms*. London: Collins Fount Paperbacks, 1979.

Linards, Jansons. "What is the Second Naivete? Engaging with Paul Ricoeur, Post-Critical Theology, and Progressive Christianity." Paper delivered at the Australian Lutheran College in Adelaide, South Australia, on October 30, 2014.

Lincoln, Andrew T. "Spirituality in a Secular Age: From Charles Taylor to Study of the Bible and Spirituality." *Acta Theologica* Supplementum series 15 (2011) 61–80.

Lindbeck, G. *The Nature of Doctrine: Religion and Theology in a Postliberal Age*. Philadelphia: Westminster, 1984.

Loder, James E. *Educational Ministry in the Logic of the Spirit*. Edited by Dana R. Wright. Eugene, OR: Cascade, 2018.

———. *The Logic of the Spirit: Human Development in Theological Perspective*. San Francisco: Jossey-Bass, 1998.

———. *The Transforming Moment: Understanding Convictional Experiences*. San Francisco: Harper and Row, 1981.

Lonergan, Bernard. *Method in Theology*. London: Darton, Longman & Todd, 1972.

Lossky, Vladimir. *In the Image and Likeness of God*. Crestwood: St Vladimir's Seminary, 1985.

———. *The Mystical Theology of the Eastern Church*. Crestwood: St Vladimir's Seminary, 1976.

———. *The Vision of God*. Yonkers, NY: St Vladimir's Seminary, 2013.

Ludlow, Morwenna. "The Cappadocians." In *The First Christian Theologians: An Introduction to Theology in the Early Church*, edited by G. R. Evans, 168–85. Oxford: Blackwell, 2004.

Luhrmann, Tanya. *When God Talks Back: Understanding the American Evangelical Relationship with God*. New York: Knopf Doubleday, 2012.

Lundin, Roger. *Emily Dickinson and the Art of Belief*. Grand Rapids: Eerdmans, 1998.

Marmion, Declan. *A Spirituality of Everyday Faith: A Theological Investigation of the Notion of Spirituality in Karl Rahner*. Louvain Theological & Pastoral Monographs series. Louvain: Peeters, 1998.

Martin, James SJ. *Becoming Who You Are: Insights on the True Self from Thomas Merton and Other Saints*. New York/Mahwah: Paulist, 2005.

Maspero, Giulio. "Cant/In Canticum Canticorum." In *The Brill Dictionary of Gregory of Nyssa*, edited by Lucas Fransisco Mateo-Seco and Giulio Maspero, 121–25. Leiden: Brill, 2010.

Masson, Robert. "Personal Transformation in Karl Rahner's Christianity: Consecrated by Love." *Psychoanalytic Enquiry* 28 (2008) 570–79.
Mateo-Seco, Lucas, F. "Epektasis." In *The Brill Dictionary of Gregory of Nyssa*, edited by Lucas Francisco Mateo-Seco and Guilio Maspero, 263–68. Lieden: Brill, 2010.
———. "Sober Drunkenness." In *Brill Dictionary of Gregory of Nyssa*, edited by Lucas Francisco Mateo-Seco and Guilio Maspero, 686–87. Leiden: Brill, 2010.
May, Gerald. *The Awakened Heart: Opening Yourself to the Love You Need*. San Francisco: HarperSanFrancisco, 1993.
McClendon, James Wm Jr. *Biography as Theology: How Life Stories Can Remake Today's Theology*. Eugene, OR: Wipf & Stock, 2002.
McGilchrist, Iain. *The Master and His Emissary: The Divided Brain and the Making of the Western World*. New Haven, CT: Yale University Press, 2010.
McGinley, Phyllis. *Saint-Watching*. New York: Viking, 1969.
McGinn, Bernard. "The Letter and the Spirit: Spirituality as an Academic Discipline." In *Minding the Spirit: The Study of Christian Spirituality*, edited by Elizabeth A. Dreyer and Mark S. Burrows, 25–41. Baltimore: The Johns Hopkins University Press, 2005.
McGrath, Alister E. *Christian Spirituality*. Oxford: Blackwell, 1999.
McInroy, Mark J. "Origen of Alexandria." In *The Spiritual Senses: Perceiving God in Western Christianity*, edited by Paul L. Gavrilyuk and Sarah Coakley, 20–35. Cambridge: Cambridge University Press, 2012.
McKenzie, Germán. *Interpreting Charles Taylor's Social Theory on Religion and Secularisation: a Comparative Study*. Sophia Studies in Cross-Cultural Philosophy of Traditions and Cultures 20. Gewerbestrasse, Switzerland: Springer, 2017.
McKnight, Scot. *Pastor Paul: Nurturing a Culture of Christoformity in the Church*. Grand Rapids: Brazos, 2019.
McNeal, Reggie. *A Work of Heart: Understanding How God Shapes Spiritual Leaders*. San Francisco: Jossey-Bass, 2000.
Meconi, David, SJ, and Olsen Karl E., eds. *Called to Be the Children of God: the Catholic Theology of Human Deification*. San Francisco: Ignatius, 2016.
Meek, Esther L. *Loving to Know: Covenant Epistemology*. Eugene, OR: Cascade, 2011.
Meilaender, Gilbert. *The Way That Leads There: Augustinian Reflections on the Christian Life*. Grand Rapids: Eerdmans, 2006.
Meltzer, François, and Jaś Elsner. *Saints: Faith without Borders*. Chicago: University of Chicago Press, 2011.
Merton, Thomas. *Contemplative Prayer*. New York: Herder and Herder, 1969.
———. *New Seeds of Contemplation*. New York: New Directions, 1961/1972.
———. *The Seven Storey Mountain*. San Diego: Harvest, 1976.
———. *Thoughts in Solitude*. London: Burns and Oates, 1958.
Mircea, Eliade. *The Sacred and the Profane*. Translated by William R. Trask. San Diego: Harcourt Brace, 1987.
Misdom, Daniel. PhD Proposal with the working title of "A Spirituality of Self-Sacrifice in Trainee Missionaries." University of Pretoria, South Africa, 2023.
Monk-Kidd, Sue. *Firstlight*. New York: Guidepost, 2004.
Moore, Johnnie. *The Martyr's Oath: Living for the Jesus They Are Willing to Die For*. Carol Stream: Tyndale Momentum, 2017.
Moore, Thomas. *Care of the Soul: A Guide for Cultivating Depth and Sacredness in Everyday Life*. New York: HarperCollins, 1994.

Moser, Matthew A. "Love Itself is Understanding: Balthasar, Truth, and the Saints." PhD diss., Baylor University, 2013.
Mulholland, M. Robert, and Ruth H. Barton. *Invitation to a Journey: A Road Map for Spiritual Formation*. Downers Grove, IL: InterVarsity, 2016.
Muller, Richard A. "Concursus." In *Dictionary of Latin and Greek Theological Terms*, 76–77. Grand Rapids, Baker, 1985.
Needleman, Jacob. *Lost Christianity*. New York: Doubleday, 1980.
Niebuhr, H. Richard. *The Meaning of Revelation*. New York: MacMillan, 1941.
Norris, Kathleen. *Acedia and Me: A Marriage, Monks and a Writer's Life*. New York: Riverhead, 2008.
Nouwen, Henri. *The Life of the Beloved: Spiritual Living in a Secular World*. New York: Crossroad, 2002.
———. *The Wounded Healer: Ministry in Contemporary Society*. New York: Doubleday, 1974.
Nussbaum, Martha C. *The New Religious Intolerance: Overcoming the Politics of Fear in an Anxious Age*. Cambridge, MA: The Belnap, 2012.
O'Donnell, John. "The Logic of Divine Glory." In *The Beauty of Christ: An Introduction to the Theology of Hans Urs von Balthasar*, edited by Bede McGregor and Thomas Norris, 161–70. Edinburgh: T. & T. Clark, 1994.
O'Murchu, Dairmuid. *The Transformation of Desire: How Desire Becomes Corrupted, and How We Can Reclaim It*. London: Darton Longman and Todd, 2007.
Oakes, Edward T., and David Moss, eds. *Cambridge Companion to Hans Urs von Balthasar*. Cambridge: Cambridge University Press, 2004.
Oliver, Mary. *Devotions: The Selected Poems of Mary Oliver*. New York: Random House, 2017.
Orwell, George. Cited by Gita V. Pai in "Orwell's Reflections on Saint Gandhi," in *Concentric: Literary and Cultural Studies Journal* 40 (2014) 69.
Osborn, Eric. "Irenaeus of Lyons." In *The First Christian Theologians: an Introduction to Theology in the Early Church*, edited by G. R. Evans, 121–26. London: Blackwell, 2004.
Pallikunnel, Geo, CMI. "Mystery, Mystagogy and Mysticism: Toward a Sacramental Mysticism of the Early Fathers of the Church." In *Ascend to Holiness; Feschrift in Honour of Dr Thomas Kalayil CMI*, edited by Francis Thonippara et al., 205–20. Bengaluru: Dharmaram, 2018.
Panikkar, Raimundo. *Blessed Simplicity: The Monk as Universal Archetype*. New York: Seabury, 1982.
Parlow, Susan B. "Personal Transformation in Karl Rahner's Christianity: Consecrated by Love." *Psychoanalytic Enquiry* 28 (2008) 570–79.
Pascal, Blaise. *Pensees*. Translated by A. J. Krailsheimer. Harmondsworth: Penguin, 1995.
Pattison, George. *A Phenomenology of the Devout Life: A Philosophy of Christian Life, Part 1*. Bampton Lectures 2017. Oxford: Oxford University Press, 2018.
Paul IV, Pope. *Pastoral Constitution on the Church in the Modern World: Gaudium et Spes*. Boston: Pauline, 1965.
Paul VI, Pope. "Secularization and Evangelization Today in Europe." Council of European Episcopal Conferences on the Roman Catholic Church. Rome, 1985. Https://www.vatican.va/content/john-paul-ii/it/speeches/1985/october/documents/hf_jp-ii_spe_19851011_partecipanti-simposio.html.

Peck, Scott. *People of the Lie: The Hope for Healing Human Evil.* New York: Simon & Schuster, 1998.
Pembroke, Neil. *Moving Towards Spiritual Maturity: Psychological, Contemplative, and Moral Challenges in Christian Living.* New York: Haworth, 2007.
Petcu, Liviu. "The Doctrine of Epektasis: One of the Major Contributions of St Gregory of Nyssa to the History of Thinking." *Revista Portuguesa de Filosofia* 73 (2007) 335–95.
Peterson, Eugene H. *Practise Resurrection: A Conversation on Growing up Into Christ.* London: Hodder and Stoughton, 2009.
———. *Subversive Spirituality.* Grand Rapids: Eerdmans, 1997.
———. *Working the Angles: The Shape of Pastoral Integrity.* Grand Rapids: Eerdmans, 1987.
Pickerill, Eric. "The Secular Mystique: Mysticism and the Future of Faith in the West." MA thesis, Vrije University, Amsterdam. 2013.
Pinckaers, Servais. *The Spirituality of Martyrdom . . . To the Limits of Love.* Washington, DC: The Catholic University of America Press, 2016.
Plested, Marcus. "The Spiritual Senses, Monastic and Theological." Theology Faculty Research Publications (2017) 301–2. https://epublications.marquette.edu/theo_fac/758.
Ponticus, Evagrius. *The Prakticos and Chapters on Prayer.* Translated by John Bamberger. Trappist, KY: Cistercian, 1972.
Poorthuis, Martin, and Joshua Schwarz. *Saints and Role Models in Judaism and Christianity.* Jewish and Christian Perspectives 7. Lieden: Brill, 2004.
Pope, Alexander. "An Essay on Man." In *The Poems of Alexander Pope*, edited by John Butt, 501–47. Repr. London: Routledge, 1963.
Pretorius, Stephen P. "Understanding Spiritual Experience in Christian Spirituality." *Acta Theologica Supplementum* 11 (2008) 147–65.
Proctor, Marie-Therese, et al. "Exploring Christians' Explicit Attachment to God Representations: The Development of a Template for Assessing Attachment to God Experiences." *Journal of Psychology and Theology* 37 (2009) 245–64.
Pullan, Wendy. "'Intermingled Until the End of Time': Ambiguity as a Central Condition of Early Christian Pilgrimage." In *Pilgrimage in Graeco-Roman and Early Christian Antiquity*, edited by Jas Elsner and Jan Rutherford. Oxford: Oxford University Press, 2005.
Puls, Joan. *Every Bush is Burning: A Spirituality for Our Times.* Geneva: World Council of Churches RISK Series, 1985.
Puolimatka, Tapio. "Max Scheler and the Idea of a Well Rounded Education." *Educational Philosophy and Theory* 40 (2008) 362–82.
Putt, B. Keith. "'Too Deep for Words': The Conspiracy of a Divine 'Soliloquy.'" In *The Phenomenology of Prayer*, edited by Bruce Ellis Benson and Norman Wirzba, 142–53. New York: Fordham University Press, 2005.
Rahner, Karl. *The Christian of the Future.* New York: Herder and Herder, 1967.
———. *Foundations of Christian Faith: an Introduction to the Idea of Christianity.* New York: Crossroad, 1992.
———. *Theological Investigations, Volume 7.* New York: Herder and Herder, 1971.
Rambo, Lewis R. "Psychological Perspectives on Conversion." *Pacific Theological Review* 13 (1980) 21–26.
Reddy, Ajitha. "The Eugenic Origins of IQ Testing: Implications for Post-Atkins Litigation." *DePaul Law Review* 667 (2008) 667–77.

Reeves, Rodney. *Spirituality According to Paul: Imitating the Apostle of Christ*. Downers Grove, IL: InterVarsity, 2011.

Reichard, Joshua D. "Beyond Causation: A Contemporary Theology of Concursus." *American Journal of Theology & Philosophy* 34, no. 2 (2013) 117–34.

Reichard, Joshua D. "Toward a Pentecostal Theology of *Concursus*." *Journal of Pentecostal Theology* 22 (2013) 95–114.

Reinecker, Fritz. *A Linguistic Key to the Greek New Testament, Volume 2*. Translated by Cleon L. Rogers Jr. Grand Rapids: Zondervan, 1980.

Reno, R. R. *The Ordinary Transformed: Karl Rahner and the Christian Vision of Transcendence*. Grand Rapids: Eerdmans, 1995.

Ricoeur, Paul. *The Symbolism of Evil*. New York: Harper & Row, 1967.

Rilke, Rainer Maria. *Letters to a Young Poet*. Herter Norton. New York: WW Norton, 1934.

Rohr, Richard. *Falling Upward: A Spirituality for the Two Halves of Life*. San Francisco: Jossey-Bass, 2011.

Rolheiser, Ronald. "Saying 'Yes' to Santa Claus." May 1984. https://ronrolheiser.com/saying-yes-to-santa-claus/#.Yhr81ehBw2w.

———. *The Holy Longing: The Search for a Christian Spirituality*. New York: Doubleday, 1999.

———. *The Shattered Lantern: Rediscovering a Felt Presence of God*. New York: Crossroad, 2004.

Rosner, Brian S. *Known by God: A Theology of Personal Identity*. Grand Rapids: Zondervan, 2017.

Rupnik, Marko I. *In the Fire of the Burning Bush: An Initiation to the Spiritual Life*. Grand Rapids: Eerdmans, 2004.

Rush, Ormond. *The Eyes of Faith: The Sense of the Faithful and the Church's Reception of Revelation*. Washington: The Catholic University of America Press, 2009.

Russell, Norman. *Fellow Workers with God: Orthodox Thinking on Theosis*. Crestwood: St Vladimir's Seminary Press, 2009.

Salovey, Peter, and John Meyer. "Emotional Intelligence." *Imagination, Cognition and Personality* 9 (1990) 185–211.

Salter, Nadia. "Spirituality: An Interconnected Path to Healing." In *Spirituality, Education and Society: An Integrated Approach*, edited by Njoki Wane et al., 157–68. Toronto: Sense, 2011.

Sands, Justin. *Reasoning from Faith: Fundamental Theology in Merold Westphal's Philosophy of Religion*. Bloomington: Indiana University Press, 2018.

Scheler, Max. *On the Eternal in Man*. Hamden, Connecticut: Archon, 1972.

Schmemann, Alexander. *The Mystery of the Eighth Day*. Crestwood: St. Vladimir's Seminary Press, 1975.

Schneiders, Sandra. "Approaches to the Study of Christian Spirituality." In *The Blackwell Companion to Christian Spirituality*, edited by Arthur Holder, 15–34. Malden, MA: Blackwell, 2005.

———. "Spirituality as an Academic Discipline: Reflections from Experience." *Christian Spirituality Bulletin* 1 (1993) 10–15.

Scott-Baumann, Alison. *Ricoeur and the Hermeneutics of Suspicion*. London: Continuum, 2009.

Scougal, Henry. *The Life of God in the Soul of Man*. Wheaton: Crossway, 2022.

Scruton, Roger. *The Face of God*. The Gifford Lectures 2010. London: Continuum, 2012.

———. *An Intelligent Person's Guide to Modern Culture*. London: Duckworth, 1998.

Shannon, William. "Thomas Merton's Theology of Self." *Cistercian Studies* 22 (1987) 174.
Shaw, Lucy. "Living in the Gap: Exploring the Space Between Heaven and Earth." In *Things in Heaven and Earth: Exploring the Supernatural*, edited by Harold Fickett, 171–84. Brewster: Paraclete, 1998.
Sheldrake, Philip. *Befriending Our Desires*. Notre Dame: Ave Maria, 1994.
———. "Desire." In *The New SCM Dictionary of Christian Spirituality*, edited by Philip Sheldrake, 231–33. London: SCM, 2005.
Shults, LeRon, and Steven Sandage. *Transforming Spirituality: Integrating Theology and Psychology*. Grand Rapids: Baker Academic, 2006.
Smelick, Klaas, A., ed. *Etty: The Letters and Diaries of Etty Hillesum 1941–1943*. Grand Rapids: Eerdmans, 2002.
Smith, Huston. *The Soul of Christianity: Restoring the Great Tradition*. New York: HarperSanFransisco, 2005.
Smith, J. Warren. "Becoming Men, Not Stones: Epektasis in Gregory of Nyssa's Homilies on the Song of Songs." In *Gregory of Nyssa: In Canticum Canticorum: Analytical and Supporting Studies*, 340–59. Proceedings of the Thirteenth International Colloquium on Gregory of Nyssa (Rome, September 2014), edited by Guilio Maspero et al. Lieden: Brill, 2018.
———. "Gregory of Nyssa: Formed and Re-Formed in God's Image." In *T & T Clark Handbook of Theological Anthropology*, edited by Mary Hinsdale IHM and Steven Oakey, 147–56. London: Bloomsbury, 2021.
Smith, James K. A. *Desiring the Kingdom: Worship, Worldview and Cultural Formation*. Grand Rapids: Baker Academic, 2009.
———. *Imagining the Kingdom: How Worship Works*. Grand Rapids: Baker, 2013.
———. *How (Not) to Be Secular: Reading Charles Taylor*. Grand Rapids: Eerdmans, 2014.
———. *On the Road with St Augustine: a Real-World Spirituality for Restless Hearts*. Grand Rapids: Brazos, 2019.
———. *You Are What You Love: The Spiritual Power of Habit*. Grand Rapids: Brazos, 2016.
Smith, Julien C. *Paul and the Good Life: Transformation and Citizenship in the Commonwealth of God*. Waco, TX: Baylor University Press, 2020.
Snead, O. Carter. "The Anthropology of Expressive Individualism." *Church Life Journal*, December 2020. https://churchlifejournal.nd.edu/articles/the-anthropology-of-expressive-individualism/
Söelle, Dorothee. *The Silent Cry: Mysticism and Resistance*. Translated by Barabara and Martin Rutnscheidt. Minneapolis: Fortress, 2001.
Sookhdeo, Patrick. *Hated without a Reason*. Lancaster: Isaac, 2019.
Spader, Dan. *Walking as Jesus Walked: Making Disciples the Way Jesus Did*. Chicago: Moody, 2001.
Stamps, R. Lucas. "Atonement in Gethsemane: the Necessity for Dyothelitism for the Atonement." In *Locating the Atonement: Explorations in Constructive Dogmatics*, by Oliver Crisp and Fred Sanders, 142–68. Grand Rapids: Eerdmans, 2015.
Stonequist, Everett V. *The Marginal Man: a Study in Personality and Cultural Conflict*. New York: Russell and Russell, 1961.
Tacey, David. *The Postsecular Sacred: Jung, Soul and Meaning in an Age of Change*. London: Routledge, 2020.

———. "Spirituality, Religion and Youth in Secular Times." In *Spirituality for Youth-Work: New Vocabulary, Concepts and Practices*, edited by Phil Daughtry and Stuart Devenish, 3–15. Newcastle upon Tyne: Cambridge Scholars, 2016.

Taylor, Charles. *A Secular Age*. Cambridge: Belnap, 2007.

Teresa of Avila. *The Collected Works of St. Teresa of Avila* (Vol. 1). Kieran Kavanaugh and Otilio Rodriguez. Washington: ICS Publications, 1976.

———. "Soliloquies." In *Soliloquies of St Teresa of Avila*, 375–91. Collected Works. Washington, DC: ICS, 1976.

———. *Teresa of Avila, The Interior Castle*. The Classics of Western Spirituality. Mahwah: Paulist, 1979.

Thurman, Howard. *Meditations of the Heart*. Boston: Beacon, 2022.

Thurston, Bonnie, and Judith Ryan. *Philippians and Philemon*. Sacra Pagina Biblical Commentary. Collegeville, MN: Liturgical, 2005.

Thurston, Bonnie. "The New Testament in Christian Spirituality." In *The Blackwell Companion to Christian Spirituality*, edited by Arthur Holder, 55–72. Oxford: Blackwell, 2005.

Torrence, T. F. *Atonement: The Person and Work of Christ*. Downers Grove, IL: InterVarsity Academic, 2009,

Traherne, Thomas. "Desire." Cited by Philip Sheldrake, in *Befriending Our Desires*, Notre Dame: Ave Maria, 1994.

Trueman, Carl. *The Rise and Triumph of the Modern Self: Cultural Amnesia, Expressive Individualism and the Road to Sexual Revolution*. Wheaton, IL: Crossway, 2020.

Tyrrell, George. *Through Scylla and Charybdis, or the Old Theology and the New*. London: Longmans, 1907.

Underdown, Steven. *Living in the Eighth Day: The Christian Week and the Paschal Mystery*. Eugene, OR: Pickwick, 2018.

Underhill, Evelyn. *Mysticism: The Development of Humankind's Spiritual Consciousness*. Repr. London: Bracken, 1995.

———. *Practical Mysticism*. Repr. New York: Dodo, 2007.

———. *The Spiritual Life*. London: Hodder & Stoughton, 1937.

Volf, Miroslav. *The Church as the Image of the Trinity*. Grand Rapids: Eerdmans, 1998.

von Balthasar, Hans Urs. *Epilogue*. San Francisco: Ignatius, 2004.

———. *The Glory of the Lord: A Theological Aesthetics: Seeing the Form*. San Francisco: Ignatius, 1982.

Waaijman, Kees. *Spirituality: Forms, Foundations, Methods*. Leuven: Peeters, 2002.

Wach, Joachim. *The Comparative Study of Religion*. New York: Columbia University Press, 1958.

Wallace, Mark I. *The Second Naivete: Barth, Ricoeur, and the New Yale Theology*. Studies in American Biblical Hermeneutics. Macon: Mercer, 1995.

Webb, Val. *Like Catching Water in a Net: Human Attempts to Describe the Divine*. New York: Continuum, 2007.

Webber, Robert E. *Ancient-Future Worship: Proclaiming and Enacting God's Narrative*, Grand Rapids: Baker, 2008.

———. *The Divine Embrace: Recovering the Passionate Spiritual Life*. Grand Rapids: Baker, 2006.

Weil, Simone. *Waiting for God*. Translated by Emma Craufurd. New York: Harper & Row, 1992.

Wesley, John. *Sermon, What is Man?* In *The Works of John Wesley*, 7:167–74. Grand Rapids: Baker, 2007.

———. *The Witness of the Spirit*. In *The Works of John Wesley*, 5:124–34. Grand Rapids: Baker, 2007.

Westphal, Merold. *God, Guilt and Death: An Existential Phenomenology of Religion*. Bloomington: Indiana University Press, 1984.

Wilber, Ken. *Integral Spirituality: a Startling New Role for Religion in the Modern and Post-Modern World*. Boulder, CO: Integral, 2007.

Wilkes, Paul. *In Due Season: A Catholic Life*. San Francisco: Jossey-Bass, 2009.

Willard, Dallas. *The Disappearance of Moral Knowledge*, edited and completed by Steven L. Porter et al. New York: Routledge, 2018.

———. *The Great Omission: Rediscovering Jesus' Essential Teachings*. San Francisco: HarperOne, 2009.

———. *Living in Christ's Presence: Final Words on Heaven and the Kingdom of God*. Downers Grove, IL: InterVarsity, 2014.

Williams, Pip. *The Dictionary of Lost Words*. South Melbourne: Affirm, 2020.

Williams, Rowan. *Christian Spirituality*. Atlanta: John Knox, 1979.

———. *Holy Living: The Christian Tradition for Today*. London: Bloomsbury, 2017.

Winchester, Simon. *The Surgeon of Crowthorne: A Tale of Murder, Madness and the Oxford English Dictionary*. London: Penguin, 1999.

Wineapple, Brenda. *White Heat: The Friendship of Emily Dickinson and Thomas Wentworth Higginson*. New York: Alfred A. Knopf, 2008.

Wittgenstein, Ludwig. *Tractatus Logico-Philosopicus*. Translated D. F. Pears and B. F. McGuinness. London: Routledge, 2001.

Wong, Paul T. P. "Viktor Frankl's Meaning-Seeking Model and Positive Psychology." In *Meaning in Positive and Existential Psychology*, edited by Alexander Batthyany and Pninit Russo-Netzer, 149–84. New York: Springer, 2014.

Worthing, Mark. *The Sacred Life of Words: A Guide for Christian Writers*. Sydney: Morning Star, 2020.

Wright, Dana R. "A Tactical Child-Like Way of Being Human Together: Implications from James Loder's Thought for Post-Colonial Christian Witness." In *The Logic of the Spirit in Human Thought and Experience: Exploring the Vision of James E. Loder Jr.*, edited by Dana R. Wright and Keith J. White, 291–331. Eugene, OR: Pickwick, 2014.

Wyschogrod, Edith. *Saints and Post-Modernism: Revisioning Moral Philosophy*. Chicago: The University of Chicago Press, 1990.

Yaden David B., and Newberg, Andrew B. *The Varieties of Spiritual Experience: 21st-Century Research and Perspectives*. Oxford: Oxford University Press, 2022.

Young, Frances. *God's Presence: a Contemporary Recapitulation of Early Christianity*. Cambridge: Cambridge University Press, 2013.

Zappala, Crino R. "Well-Being: the Correlation between Self-Transcendence and Psychological and Subjective Well-Being." PhD diss., Institute of Transpersonal Psychology, Palo Alto, California, 2007.

Zohar, Danah. *Spiritual Intelligence: The Ultimate Intelligence*. London: Bloomsbury, 2000. Zohar, Danah, and Ian Marshall. *Spiritual Capital: Wealth We Can Live By*. San Francisco: Berrett-Koehler, 2004.

Index

a'Kempis, Thomas, 97, 107, 135–37
abandonment, 68–71, 98, 123
Abraham Maslow, 181–83, 217
acedia, 71–74
agency, 74–77, 92–94, 188
apophatic, 29
Athanasius, St., 208
attachment theory, 77–80, 114, 218
attunement, 34, 80–83, 95, 130
Augustine, St., 39–40, 51, 58, 100–102, 105–6, 190–93

Balthasar, Hans von, 76, 81–82, 83–86, 208, 216
Barth, Karl, 92, 145, 216
Batson, Daniel, 42
beauty, 83–86, 114, 128, 184, 216
believing soul, 45–47, 49, 57–58, 63, 69, 85, 152, 175–78, 193
Benedict's Rule, 126
Benner, David, 126, 182–83, 215–16
Blond, Philip, 56–57
Blumenstock, James, 163–64
Boersma, Hans, 116, 166, 204
Bonaventure, St., 202–3
Bonhoeffer, Dietrich, 122, 139, 192
Bordieu, Pierre, 130
Brown, Bren
Brueggemann, Walter, 131
Buechner, Frederick, 212

call and response, 23, 32, 50–53
Calvin, John, 56, 118, 148, 180, 203
Caputo, John, 11
Carmelite, 97–99
catechism, 86–88, 157
Chretien, Jean-Louis, 49–52
Christian forgetfulness, 8, 25, 73, 123
Christian mind-knowing, 86–91
Christianity, renewal of, xiii, 7, 9, 50
Christoformity, 135, 166
Christotherapy, 154, 173, 196
Chrysostom, John, 157
classical Christian spiritual tradition, 3, 17, 24–26, 53–55, 194
Clement, Olivier, 40 fn4, 189–90
Coakley, Sarah, 201
concursus, 91–94
contemplative, 73, 94–97, 99, 120, 176
conversion-new birth, 31, 43, 61, 91, 96, 103–4, 112, 139, 153–63
culture wars, 6, 8

Danielou, Jean, 61, 109, 116, 157
dark night, 97–100
de Magestro, 100–102, 192
deification, 208–9
desire, 12, 40, 44–45, 61–63, 105–8, 114–16, 130–31, 161–63, 173, 215
Dickinson, Emily, 55–56
discipleship, 82, 97, 135, 150–54, 170
divine embrace, 102–5, 118

237

INDEX

divine eros, 106, 189
divine mysteries, 4, 128
domestic monastery, 96
Dostoevsky, Fyodor, 85, 172
Dupre, Louis, 61, 134

Eastern Orthodox, 2-3, 88, 109, 208
Eckhart, Meister, 106
eighth day, 108-10
embodiment, 111-13, 121, 167
epektasis, 113-16, 189
Evagrius of Pontus, 71
Evangelical-Protestant spirituality, 103, 109, 113, 144, 166, 207
Evangelii Nuntiandi, 120
evangelization, 119, 121
evidence-based, 14. 119
experience, 7-8, 22, 58-59, 61-64, 83, 90, 116-19, 154, 158
experts in humanity, 119-22
expressive individualism, 128, 143

felt presence, 45, 62-64, 73, 148
Fowler, James, 176, 182
Francis, Pope, 75
Frankl, Viktor, 181
fullness, 76, 122-25

glorification, 57-58, 84, 209
God's workshop, 125-29
godfaring, 44, 147
Goleman, Daniel, 196
Gorman, Michael, 76, 118, 121, 167, 209
Gorringe, Timothy, 107

Habermas, Jurgen, 10
habitus, 129-31
Helminiak, Daniel, 47, 193
hermeneutics of hunger, 23
Hillesum, Etty, 183-84
homo spiritualis, 39-41, 108, 113, 193, 201
Hopkins, Gerard Manley, 83-84
how to believe, 34-35, 55
Humphrey, Edith, 17, 133-34, 150

Ignatius of Loyola, 70, 206
imperfection, 121, 237-141

interiority, 14, 54, 116, 165
Irenaeus, 167-69, 170-71

John of the Cross, St., 62, 97-99, 148
Jones, Alan, 96, 147, 196
Jung, Carl, 50 fn37, 145, 184-86

Kapic, Kelly, 80-81, 92
kataphatic, 29
kenosis, 209, 219
Kierkegaard, Søren, 146, 173
Kourie, Celia, 178
Kreider, Alan, 87, 154

Lewis, CS, 54, 86, 148
lex orandi, 141-44
liturgical clock, 110
liturgy, 87, 103, 109, 130, 132, 141, 143-44, 157, 166
Loder, James, 90, 144-47
logic of the spirit, 144-47
Lossky, Vladimir, 37, 41
Luhrmann, Tanya, 94-95
Luther, Martin, 74, 139

MacLachlan, William, 54
magister internus, 100-102
maladies of the soul, 73, 147-50
martyr moment, 150-55
McGinn, Bernard, 179
McKnight, Scot, 135, 165
Merton, Thomas, 61, 178, 192, 217-20
metanoia, 153-56
missio dei, 50, 57, 167
modern-day mystics, 59-62, 128
monastic, 71, 97-98, 125-29, 136
Monk-Kidd, Sue, 14, 38
Moser, Matthew, 82-83
Mulholland, Robert, 185-87
Myers-Briggs, 186
mystagogy, 156-59
mysticism, 59-61, 99, 200

Needleman, Jacob, 8
New Age, 6, 25, 55, 103
Nouwen, Henri, 65-67, 140
Nyssa, Gregory of, 44, 70, 109, 113, 116, 170, 188-89

Oliver, Mary, 171
ordo amoris, 59–61
Origen, 195, 202

palimpsest, 155
paroikos, 161–64
participation, 164–67
Pascal, Blaise, 36–37, 74, 77, 154, 159–60
pedagogy, 131
Pentecostal, 2–3, 92–93
Peterson, Eugene, 4, 16, 95, 149, 172, 213, 215
Pinckaers, Servais, 150, 152
post-modern age, 10
post-secular age, 9–14, 18, 20
post-secular sacred, 20
prayer, xiii, 9, 12, 16–18, 28, 58 fn63, 62–63, 72–73, 77, 97, 104, 110, 116, 136, 183–84, 190–92, 206
present-day seekers, 2

Rahner, Karl, 60–61, 204–7, 209
Rambo, Lewis, 43, 215
recapitulation, 167–70
reception, 47–50, 58, 119, 139
re-creation, 134, 209
redemption, 41, 49, 82, 88, 104, 108–9, 134, 155–56, 166, 168–69, 179, 200, 209–10
Reichard, Joshua, 92–93
religious awakening, 20
renewal, xii–xiii, 5, 7, 9, 50, 156, 204
Ricoeur, Paul, 23–24, 45–47, 174–76, 200, 216
Rilke, Rainer Maria, 15
Rolheiser, Ronald, 64, 96–97, 105, 177
Roman Catholic, 72, 88, 99, 113, 119, 172, 204, 206
Rosner, Brian, 79, 104

sacred encounter, 5, 20
sanctification, 4, 35, 40, 46, 78, 88, 94, 103, 110, 139, 157, 173, 200, 209–10
Santa Claus, 177
Scheler, Max, 46, 159–61
Schneiders, Sandra, 20, 177–80, 182
Scruton, Roger, 12, 85

second naivete, 174–77
secularization, 9–12, 119, 122–24
self-implicating, 1 77–80
self-transcendence, 119, 181–84
Seligman, Martin, 181
sensus fidei, 49
shadow, 66, 84, 152, 184–87
Sheldrake, Philip, 20, 106–7
sick soul, 46
Smith, Huston, 105–6
Smith, James KA, 105, 129–32, 133–34, 152, 214
sober drunkenness, 157, 187–90
Söelle, Dorothee, 19, 23
soliloquy, 190–93
soul, 45–47, 193–97
soul making, 96, 147 fn218, 196–97
spiritual directors/accompanists, 27, 80
spiritual education, 17, 30 35, 53–55, 102, 125, 145, 196
Spiritual Exercises, 70, 206
spiritual formation, 4, 40, 43, 55, 76, 86–87, 96–97, 107, 126–27, 157, 165, 167, 170–71, 185–86
spiritual intelligence-SQ, 197–200
spiritual senses, 200–204
spiritual theology, 2, 4, 204
supernatural existential, 204–7
surface culture, 14

Tacey, David, 13, 20 fn27, 50 fn37
Taylor, Charles, 11–12, 122–25
Teresa of Avila, 16, 58 fn63, 62, 99, 191
Tertullian, 151, 194–95
the beloved, 28, 64–67, 98–99, 188
the holy life, 76, 126, 172
theosis, 124, 167, 207–10
Therese of Lisieux, 70
Thurman, Howard, 153
Thurston, Bonnie, 22, 117
tragic spirituality, 210–13
transformation, 43, 47, 54, 63, 80, 90–91, 115, 146–47, 155, 158, 178, 182, 184, 199, 212–17
turn to the subject, 54, 116

Underhill, Evelyn, 17, 51–52, 59–60

Volf, Miroslav, 165
von Hugel, Frederick, 140

Waaijman, Kees, 157–58, 196
we are the work, 127
we seek him still, 44–45, 110
Webber, Robert, 102–4, 143, 166
Weil, Simone, 63, 126
Wesley, John, 41, 58
Westphal, Merold, 46–47, 91

Wilbur, Ken, 200
Willard, Dallas, 79–80, 95, 165
Williams, Rowan, 126, 128, 150, 179
Willimon William, 163, 174
worship, 84, 86–87, 94–97, 104, 108–10, 112, 119, 129–33, 141–44, 148–50, 157, 166, 187, 189, 201
Wyschogrod, Edith, 172

Young, Frances, 169

www.ingramcontent.com/pod-product-compliance
Lightning Source LLC
Chambersburg PA
CBHW050846230426
43667CB00012B/2163